GESTURES OF HEALING

GESTURES OF HEALING

Anxiety *&* the Modern Novel

John J. Clayton

THE UNIVERSITY OF

MASSACHUSETTS PRESS

AMHERST

For Sharon, whose gestures heal

Copyright © 1991 by
The University of Massachusetts Press
All rights reserved
Printed in the United States of America
LC 90–24889
ISBN 0–87023–739–X
Set in Linotron Sabon by Keystone Typesetting, Inc.
Printed and bound by Thomson-Shore

Library of Congress Cataloging-in-Publication Data

Clayton, John Jacob.
    Gestures of healing : anxiety and the modern novel / John J.
  Clayton.
        p.   cm.
    Includes bibliographical references (p.   ) and index.
    ISBN 0–87023–739–X (alk. paper).
      1. English fiction—20th century—History and criticism.
    2. American fiction—20th century—History and criticism.
    3. Psychoanalysis and literature. 4. Anxiety in literature.
    5. Modernism (Literature). 6. Family in literature. I. Title.
  PR888.P74C55   1991
    823'.91209—dc20   90–24889
British Library Cataloguing in Publication data are available.

CONTENTS

PART SIX. INDIVIDUAL STUDIES

M

ICHEL FOUCAULT has expressed, expressed wonderfully because precisely, the opposite of my own orientation.

According to Foucault in "What Is an Author?" writing has "freed itself from the dimension of expression." The "author" is, he says, dead, so dead that the news is old hat by now. Then he examines what an author *is* outside of our idealizations:

> These aspects of an individual which we designate as making him an author are only a projection, in more or less psychologizing terms, of the operations that we force texts to undergo, the connections that we make, the traits that we establish as pertinent, the continuities that we recognize, or the exclusions that we practice. (P. 110)

Foucault is, of course, neither right nor wrong; he has offered an analytical heuristic, a brilliant move designed to leave him with texts and without privileged authors. My own approach is so different that I can use his passage as a touchstone: if you find Foucault's orientation compatible with your own, you will probably be resistant to mine. Foucault has played a magician's trick to eliminate the human creatures who suffered and rejoiced and wrote out of this suffering and joy, adapting the language of our common experience. *But it's precisely those actual human beings who interest me.* I see their writing as expressions of pain and as complex gestures of healing to handle that pain. I am interested in what their writing did for them and what it does for me as a particular reader.

Why would anyone *want* to reduce the significance of the person writing?

Partly, it is to get rid of the magnified, reified, mythologized capital *A* author. But largely, I think, the postmodern critique of selfhood, of the privileged subject, is an instance of modern revulsion toward the self. Saul Bellow has spent a good deal of his intellectual life attacking modernist expressions of loathing toward the individual, a loathing that poses as philosophy. It is an old loathing. Musil, Ortega, Sartre, Beckett: long before a "postmodern" age, they saw selfhood as illusory, as hollow.

But the modernists' experience of loss of self was a condition filled with anxiety, even terror. Indeed, I begin my discussion with the "unthinkable anxiety" (D. W. Winnicott's phrase) of writers who experienced loss or fragmentation of self. This loss underlies the struggle within their fiction. For postmodernist critics, it becomes an easy intellectual position with political consequences. I delight in hearing self-satisfied theoreticians de- clare, with self-aggrandizing energy and moral arrogance, the end of selfhood.[1]

When someone looks at "texts" as if they were expressions of a cultural situation abstracted from their individual creators, like ads for Coca- Cola, I see their analysis as symptom disguised as philosophy. We are like a city half-wrecked by bombs. Can it be built up again? Certainly not in the old way—there is no going back. But—at all? Or do we bring in the bulldozers? There seems to be great apocalyptic joy in the prospect of laying it all flat. Modernists, too, expressed the illusory nature of the social self. Woolf yearned to break the boundaries of selfhood; Lawrence wanted to smash the old, dead self; Joyce disintegrated the self into voices, into styles. But they also experienced dread: loss of self, loss of center, was anguish as well as joy. What it was *not* was an easily held theoretical position.

I'm interested in modernism as more than a cultural movement; I think of it as *a condition of feeling shaped by particular kinds of childhood experi- ence during the unfolding of a particular historical moment.* As that condition became widespread, the arts responding to that condition be- came enshrined as modernist. Gestures of healing for a few artists became gestures of healing for an audience.

A couple of generations later, I was part of that audience. My own growing up, like theirs in certain ways, gave me affinities for their anxiety and for the strategies with which they handled their anxiety in fiction. In this book I want to deal with their pain, its source and the ways they handled it in their lives and in their art.

I begin with anxiety and the way it expresses itself in the work of modernist novelists. Then I try to understand the sources for modern anxiety, not, vaguely, in "the culture" but specifically in the childhood lives of the writers within their families and in relation to the larger community. In Part 3, I look at the ways in which the anxiety and instability of modernist writers got expressed in their lives and in the fantasies underlying their work. In Part 4, I examine ways in which the chaos of the writers' lives got defended against and expressed in their art; in Part 5, I ask how their fiction can be healing to the writers or to their audience. I end with three studies of individual writers: James, Woolf, and Lawrence. My orientation throughout is largely psychoanalytic, but I am not interested in measuring the experience in the fiction or the lives of these people against the yardstick of psychoanalytic theory. I feel that the writers were their own best self-describers. I am interested in psycho-analysis, especially in object-relations psychoanalysis, for clinical obser-vations and connections, and for theory when it gives me insight into particular patterns.

I am grateful to my wife, Sharon Dunn, to Professors James Cowan and David Willbern, and to the members of my Psychoanalytic Study Group, especially to Professor Lee Edwards, Dr. Edward Emery, Professor Wil-liam Kerrigan, Dr. Joel Rosen, and Professor Murray Schwartz, for advis-ing me, suggesting additions to the Bibliography, and reading parts of the manuscript along the way.

PART ONE

UNTHINKABLE ANXIETY

CHAPTER ONE

UNTHINKABLE ANXIETY

F OR A LONG TIME I have felt deep affinities to British and American fiction of high modernism—the canon of great novels by Henry James, Joseph Conrad, Ford Madox Ford, E. M. Forster, James Joyce, Virginia Woolf, D. H. Lawrence, F. Scott Fitzgerald, Ernest Hemingway, and William Faulkner. I began to read these novels because they felt true to my own life, to a life I felt was also somehow "ours." When I was in school, I was taught to read fiction as if it were lyric poetry, and poetry as if it were a linguistic pattern at the service of a coherent vision. But what interested me was—and still is—struggle: the way modernist fiction tries in complicated, self-contradictory ways to handle terror and pain.

One way to see *any* expressive art is as an attempt to end discords in its creator, to feed some hunger or cope with an experience that feels overwhelming, feels intensely dissonant—to express that experience and so gain control of it. Seen in this way, art isn't just a record of coping, it is the act of coping, a *gesture of healing*. This way of seeing is particularly fruitful, it seems to me, for early twentieth-century fiction.

As I shelve the clichés about modernist literature—shelve them not because they are false but because they aren't interesting to me—I grow increasingly aware of similarities among the human beings who made this literature. I'm not speaking, then, about similarities in technical experiment or similar philosophical affinities to, say, Bergson or Nietzsche. Rather, I see that modernist writers have a surprisingly similar way of being-in-the world, a surprisingly similar condition of anxiety. As I look at their *lives*, I am again surprised by similarities; surprised, because we're speaking of people as different as a grocer's son in the Midwest, an exiled aristocrat from Poland, the daughter of a prestigious man of letters. Yet, as

I shall try to show in the second chapter, both the psychodynamics of their childhood struggles and their pain in relation to the larger society had important common elements, and these elements underlie modernist fiction.[1]

It is now a century since the beginnings of high modernism, and, in a sense, we have all gone through the experience that generated modernism, in part an anxiety about *nothing,* the terror of nonbeing. Heidegger speaks of it as universal, the result of having fallen into everydayness and lost authentic being. But I see the experience as rooted in a particular historical moment. Modernism was created in certain pain-ridden, possibility-filled childhoods in the late nineteenth century. As Peter Loëwenberg writes, "Too much of history is still written as though men had no feelings, no childhood, and no bodily senses."[2]

Of course, childhood pain is not art. And art speaks in the vocabulary waiting for it, a vocabulary that is one aspect of the orientation to reality in all the arts and sciences. So I am not arguing that modernist fiction sprang forth from the psyches of the young Conrad, Lawrence, and Joyce unmediated by the arts, and especially the literature, and even more especially the fiction, of the period. But I am arguing that for each writer, the essential fable and the modes of its telling and retelling expressed and coped with psychic struggle.

Of course, enormous energy was liberated by that struggle, and without that energy, there would be no reason to study modernist fiction. I am aware of the explosive energies in modernism, its destructive-creative song of new life.[3] But in the course of this book I emphasize the struggle with inner demons or inner emptiness.

I see modernism, then, as shaped by common pain from a common source and from various attempts to cope with pain—*gestures of healing*—reparative acts that permit writers to feel whole and to make some link, other than alienation, with the world. These attempts are, I think, only gestures. They express longing for wholeness, they point to the place of wholeness even though they cannot make the artist whole. Or, if they can, it is only temporary: the pain has to be assuaged over and over, the broken places knitted again and again.

And yet the creation of the fiction is an act of great health and success!

The same paradox is true of Conrad, of Woolf, of all these novelists. Each of them has been crippled, and the crippling is expressed and given shape in the fiction, yet the act of shaping is an extraordinary expression of health and victory. Conrad writes, the artist descends within himself, and in that lonely region of stress and strife, if he be deserving and fortunate, he finds the terms of his appeal. (preface, *The Nigger of the "Narcissus"*)

Is the appeal answered? Yes, in the sense that the artist shapes that lonely region into a fictional landscape that permits the artist a glimpse of home—however painful home may be.

This gesture of descent and creation out of that descent, as if the artist were pulling a newborn self out of his or her own depths, is romantic and heroic—a gesture inherited from the nineteenth-century artist. It is more heroic in the twentieth century, indeed, because it is more solitary, this act of self-recreation. A postmodern artist or critic can't take such a gesture seriously—without irony, without quotation marks. I, on the other hand, am still seduced by moral seriousness, the painful struggle leading to creation, of the modernists. When I began to read, I felt they were coura-geous explorers who were enacting, in their struggles, *truth*. Allen Gins-berg once called Whitman a "lonely old courage-teacher," and that's it, precisely. For me, Conrad was a lonely old courage-teacher. So was Lawrence. In a different way, so was Virginia Woolf. If I could follow them into the world I was afraid to recognize, the world without support, perhaps I could find courage in myself.

To descend within the self, to explore the pain and create the fiction is not the same as to shape the modernist canon. Certain modern novels entered the canon largely for ideological reasons. They could be used to covertly defend the status quo, because they expressed distaste with the vulgar present yet permitted readers to keep their distance from political life, and because they valorized formal order and a pseudo-"tradition." BUT I believe, too, that works in the canon also expressed and struggled with anxieties that grew to be shared by most people in the post–World War I intelligentsia (see Chapter 9, "Healing the Culture"). I'm talking, then, about three periods, or, rather, three overlapping stages: the stage when the modern condition was created in the synapses of a handful of children; the stage when, within the framework of a particular cultural syntax, those children, grown, created a modernist fiction; and the stage when an increasing number of others felt what the modernists felt and defended themselves in similar ways, and modernism finally became en-shrined, institutionalized.

Anxiety is not a distinctly modern phenomenon, and surely there is more to modernist sensibility than anxiety. But I want to explore a particular form of anxiety that *is* modern and has largely shaped modernism. Its roots are in the seventeenth century, when the modern concept of the individual was created, the individual seen separated from rather than embedded in a community; the individual defined by isolation, not by relation. By the early twentieth century, writers were struggling with common anxieties. And I find that they express and mask these anxieties in similar ways—both in their work and in their lives.

Not the anxiety that derives from conflict between generations or between impulse and civilization; *not* the anxiety that follows from the stress of coping with war, colonial oppression, class oppression; *not* the anxiety that reflects the intensification of social change (though this certainly has relevance). What's similar in the anxiety of modernist writers is the experience of being a fragile or empty self in an empty world. I want to sketch a phenomenological description of this anxiety, trace its roots in family and society, and explore its implications for the lives of these writers and for their aesthetic choices. It is in response to this anxiety that their art becomes a gesture of healing.

Images of emptiness, hollowness, nothingness, *nada*, the void. The void isn't, for me, a metaphysical problem. It's a condition of psychological nonbeing. If the world ought to be a "holding environment,"[4] if as we grow we need to feel contained in the world as we were held by our mothers, these writers often experience the world as disconnected from themselves, unable to hold them, terrifyingly empty. The world is empty and the self, mirrored there, is empty, is unreal. Indeed, *these two experiences are finally one:* an experience of spiritual emptiness. Already in 1864 Cardinal Newman speaks of experiencing the world as "discarded from" the presence of God. He sees in the world no "reflection of its creator," and he compares this to looking into a mirror and not seeing his own face.[5]

This experience becomes central. Virginia Woolf's Rhoda in *The Waves* who, like her creator, ultimately kills herself, sees other people embedded in the world; as for herself: "I have no face" (*The Waves*, pp. 33, 203). Bernard, in a similar metaphor, says, "No echo comes when I speak" (p. 374). Rhoda uses words that themselves echo throughout modern literature: "I often fall down into nothingness" (p. 204). Woolf herself, in her *Diary*, speaks of the void around her: "No atmosphere round me. No words. . . . And this anxiety & nothingness surround me with a vacuum."[6] Near the end of her life, she, like her Bernard, speaks of the loss of an echo. "The writing 'I' has vanished. No audience. No echo. That's part of one's death" (*Diary*, 5:293). By 1940, "there's no public to echo back" (p. 304). "No echo comes back. I have no surroundings" (p. 299).

The world echoing and mirroring . . . *nothing*. The bubble-shaped cave at the summit of the Marabar Hills "mirrors its own darkness in every direction infinitely" (Forster, *Passage*, p. 125). "Nothing, nothing attaches to" the caves (p. 124). "Nothing is inside them" (p. 125). The echo of the caves destroys difference, identity, meaning; everything comes back "boum."

In a world experienced as a void, it is no accident that psychoanalysis began to change to fit new patients—not Victorian neurotics, conflict-ridden, repressing impulse, expressing their conflicts through classical defenses—but patients with broken selves, incomplete selves.[7] And I believe it is not only the *patients* who had changed. The lenses of these analysts had been ground by the makers of modernist art, by the sensibility of modernism. Not only had they read Sartre, for example, with his understanding of authentic and inauthentic being derived from Heidegger (this influence is particularly evident in R. D. Laing); not only had they read Joyce and Proust and Woolf: they had entered an age suffused with modernism. There is a clear link between post-Freudian analysts and modernist phenomenology and epistemology. It is no accident that their lenses are useful to me; they were ground at the same focal length that the writers themselves used to see the world.

I am willing to accept clinical descriptions from many sources, for example, Heinz Kohut, Melanie Klein, and Erik Erikson. But among theoretical approaches of the past twenty-five years the work of the British object-relations theorists seems particularly relevant to the condition of nonbeing I am describing. I don't read their work to find a theoretical model that I can apply to texts as some sort of a priori truth; I read it to sensitize myself more deeply to the particular pain and struggle in modernist work.

British object-relations theorists: I am speaking especially of W. R. D. Fairbairn, D. W. Winnicott, Harry Guntrip, Masud Khan, and R. D. Laing (an analysand and a popularizer of Winnicott's). For all their differences, each describes patients not fully *there:* "external relationships seem to have been emptied by a massive withdrawal of the real libidinal self" (Guntrip, p. 18). Each theorist explains feelings of emptiness and nothingness as inevitable by-products of evacuating the self from real contact that threatens its integrity—threatens it with collapse, fragmentation, or exploitation of authentic being. But then, the empty self experiences the world as empty and itself as false.

Kohutians, too, see patients not as conflict-ridden, but as damaged: they have experienced damage to their nuclear self, damage that leaves the individual fearing the destruction of self.[8] Kohut emphasizes patients whose selves are incomplete, fragmented, weak, patients "who despite the absence of neurotic conflict, are not protected against succumbing to the feeling of meaninglessness of their existence" (*Restoration*, pp. 241–42). They conceal this state with a false, grandiose self-sufficiency.

While Kohutians do not discuss their relation to British object-relations theorists, often the two groups sound as if they are describing, in slightly different language, the same patients. Fairbairn and Guntrip speak of *schizoid* characters. Kohut specifically declares schizoids unanalyzable (p. 192), and yet his description of patients with treatable "narcissistic disorders" sounds very much like Guntrip's description of "schizoids": "The nuclear self," Kohut writes about a typical patient, "was . . . not only fragmented and weak, it was out of touch with the functioning surface of the personality; it had gone into hiding" (p. 206).

But that is a working definition of schizoid pathology. *Schizoid* means that there exists a split in the psyche of patients; that is, the ego is split, split in such a way that the most alive part of the self is hidden. And that is the point of the split, to hide. They meet the world with a part of themselves, a presentation self, a persona, a "central ego" in Guntrip's and Fairbairn's language. But it isn't simply that we "prepare a face to meet the faces that [we] meet." It's not simply a reasonable tactic, chosen because of course there's no way to live in the world with one's full being operating all the time. Rather, deeply schizoid individuals have lost contact with the parts that exist beneath the ego. They bring to the world—to use Winnicott's language—a "false self," while those parts which are full of feelings, which are rich in the experience of being—these parts are not available.[9] And so it is as if they touch the world with thick gloves.[10] But the world has been so drained of life—since the self with which they contact the world has been drained of life—that (in Guntrip's words) "the world is a frightening emptiness" (p. 68). For Guntrip, for Fairbairn, a sense of futility is "the specific schizoid affect" (Guntrip, p. 27). They are unable to be *fed*.[11] They hunger because they feed a false self. So the self is voracious—like Kurtz, who is all mouth—but unsatisfiable, since the self being satisfied is a false self. An unreal self in an unreal world.

I began by speaking about seeing one's own face—or *not* seeing one's own face—in a mirror. I have been made particularly sensitive to mirroring from reading the work of contemporary psychoanalysis. In both Lacan and Winnicott, for example, the world, in the person of the mother, mirrors the child to herself—in a sense, creates the self. In Lacan, it is inevitably a false self, but in Winnicott, it is not. The child sees herself in the mother's eyes, and if the mother is truly responding to the baby, not forcing the baby to respond to the mother, then the world and the self are both enriched. One of Winnicott's patients, reciting "mirror, mirror on the wall," said, "Wouldn't it be awful if the child looked into the mirror and saw nothing!"[12] In Woolf's "The Lady in the Looking-Glass: A Reflection," Isabel looked in the mirror: "Here was the woman herself. She stood naked in that pitiless light. And there was nothing. Isabella was perfectly empty" (*CSF*, p. 219).

Of course, to seek for yourself in a mirror is self-defeating. All you will find is the seeker, seeking. Louis Sass, in a brilliant essay in *Representations*, compares modernist self-reflexivity to schizophrenia.[13] He does not see, as the source of schizophrenia, regression to primal process thought, to untrammeled id. He sees in schizophrenia not too little consciousness of self but too much: "Acute *self*-consciousness has the effect actually of *effacing* the self" (p. 8). Loss of self, he argues, "may develop *not* from a weakening of the observing ego or a lowering of the level of consciousness but, to the contrary, from a hypertrophy of attentive, self-reflexive awareness" (p. 10). He explains that when one looks hard at one's own experiencing, selfhood is destroyed. It is "a dizzying process in which an intent observing ego undermines the sense of self in the very act of searching for it" (p. 23).

I find Sass very useful in analyzing the modernist sense of the emptiness of self and world. By the late nineteenth century, the noumenal world felt emptied of life; it seemed unreal. But an unreal world makes the self unreal as well. An old Zen saying: "Without a moon, the water does not shine." This is the world experienced as *nothing*, giving back a self experienced as nothing, too. And the more that self gets examined, the less real it feels. In the extreme case, world and self disappear.

An essay by Richard Poirier, "Writing Off the Self," contrasts European visions of the loss of self with visions of American origin, particularly by Emerson and Stevens. His discussion of a world without self in Stevens is wonderful. Speaking of Stevens's "The Death of a Soldier," Poirier writes about "the power of restraint on any human urge to *figure* in the scene. Stevens has phased the poem into a mood wherein the human will, instead of registering its supposedly inherent resistance to self-dispersion, simply relaxes into it" (p. 237). I also find an affirmative vision of world without self in Virginia Woolf's writing. As I will show in my chapter on Woolf, she longs for a condition of selflessness, for loss of boundaries, though it is a longing mixed with anxiety. For Lawrence, it is only by breaking the integuments of self that new life can be found. To Lawrence, as to Winnicott, there is a false self which we fabricate as armor, but which then imprisons us. Underneath is not nothing, not nightmare, but authentic being. In most modernist work, however, the experience of loss of self leads not to Being, but to emotional chaos. A world that cannot give the person back to himself, back to herself. That is the world of the modern novel. Gerald, in *Women in Love,*

> went to the mirror and looked long and closely at his own face, at his own eyes, seeking for something.

Instead, he finds nothing.

> It was not real, it was a mask. He dared not touch it, for fear it should prove to be only a composition mask. His eyes were blue and keen as ever, and as firm in their sockets. Yet he was not sure that they were not *blue false bubbles* that would burst in a moment and leave clear annihilation. He could see the darkness in them, as if they were only *bubbles of darkness*. He was afraid that one day he would break down and be a purely *meaningless babble* lapping around a darkness. (Pp. 224–25, italics mine)

How close this is to Forster's use of the cave, "bubble-shaped," mirroring darkness, echoes becoming babble!

The nights in the "Time Passes" section of *To the Lighthouse* are "full of wind and destruction"; and "should any sleeper fancying that he might find on the beach an answer to his doubts, a sharer of his solitude . . . go down by himself to walk on the sand, no image with semblance of serving and divine promptitude comes readily to hand bringing the night to order and making the world *reflect* the compass of the soul" (italics mine). Mr. Ramsey stretches out his arms, but Mrs. Ramsey has died, and his arms remain empty (pp. 193–94). Later, Lily Briscoe calls and does receive a kind of answer, the "invisible presence" of Mrs. Ramsey.[14] A great deal of the work of *To the Lighthouse* is to get us to experience as present the absent mother, to experience centeredness, mothering, in an empty world. And we do—at least, *I* do. But I experience still more the longing for Mrs. Ramsey, the longing for answer. The longing (and rejecting) Lily Briscoe, the longing, unsatisfied Mr. Ramsey. The novel is haunted by such long-ing; it is haunted by the absent mother. It is a longing not of a single character nor of a set of characters. It is the *novel*—its voice, its figurative language—that longs. It is the reader who longs.

The call that is not answered, the questioner left in emptiness, holding out his hands: in the Marabar caves each call returns as terrifying echo, cancelling distinction, value, meaning. However, there is in *A Passage to India* another call, that of Professor Godbole singing to Krishna. Krishna refuses to come. "But he comes in some other song, I hope?" Mrs. Moore asks. "Oh, no, he refuses to come," Godbole repeats. The passage ends in a moment of silence—but a silence strangely beautiful: "No ripple dis-turbed the water, no leaf stirred" (p. 80). So there is an ambiguity about Krishna's refusal to answer the call. The nonanswer may be terrible, may be beautiful. Westerners experience the absence as terrifying; Hindus in the novel do not. Godbole says "absence implies presence, absence is not nonexistence, and we are therefore entitled to repeat, 'Come, come, come, come'" (p. 20). The novel itself longs to experience life as do the Hindus—but it doesn't lie. Over and over it reaches for the transcendent, toward the sky arching above the earth—but "outside the arch there seemed always an arch, beyond the remotest echo a silence" (p. 52). The way the "inci-dent" in the cave is told, the reader is put into the role of questioner, demanding an answer. Answer is always denied but the longing for an-swer is not negated.

Cardinal Newman has faith in spite of a world that seems empty of God; he is ultimately *held*. Among the creators of the modernist novel, the struggle to fill that emptiness is much more terrible. It is as if we were in the universe of Lear on the heath, beyond all contained, bounded spaces, the self disintegrating in the emptiness.[15] But in *King Lear*, a natural order—a condition in which the human being is located and held—is disturbed and at the end is restored. In the case of modernist writers, there is no natural order to be restored; it is as if now the natural order is that of the heath. *It is not really metaphysical certitude that is at stake—it is wholeness, fullness of being.* For emptiness *outside* reflects/is reflected by emptiness *inside*. In fact, *outside* and *inside* are inadequate metaphors for a single experience. In *Heart of Darkness*, the hollowness in the heart of Kurtz is the hollowness of his environment, in particular, his linguistic environment. It is a world in which meanings are exposed as "lies" or hypocritical rationalizations: tribespeople become "enemies" or "crimi-nals," noble ideals turn out to be legitimizations for rapacity. We are introduced to Kurtz as a "voice," as "words." But in the absence of social authority—"neighbors ready to cheer you or to fall on you"—the voice, the words, the self, prove "empty" (p. 50).

There are in modernism a hundred variants on a single metaphorical relation: a surface appears solid but is false, and underneath is nothing. Or, more precisely, "nothing" describes the experience of recognizing the falsity of the surface. The manager of the central station is a "papier-mâché Mephistopheles," a hollow man. "We are the hollow men / the stuffed men." I am speaking of the self, I am speaking of the fabric of society. Resting on nothing, one is nothing pretending to be something.

Nothing as (desperate) play on words. The caves: "Nothing, nothing attaches to them." "Nothing is inside them." Or, as in Hemingway,

"He was in despair."
"What about?"
"Nothing."

In "A Clean, Well-Lighted Place," the locus classicus of nothingness, this "nothing," translates into "*nada*," god of the waiter's antiprayers:

What did he fear? It was not fear or dread. It was a nothing that he knew too well. It was all a nothing and a man was nothing too. It was only that and light was all it needed and a certain cleanness and order. Some lived in it and never felt it but he knew it was all nada y pues nada y nada y pues nada. Our nada who art in nada, nada be thy name thy kingdom nada thy will be nada in nada as it is in nada. Give us this nada our daily nada and nada us our nada as we nada our nadas and nada us not into nada but deliver us from nada; pues nada. Hail nothing full of nothing, nothing is with thee.

A barman asks him, "What's yours." He replies, "Nada" (pp. 382–83). Exactly. Nothing is his, in the sense that he is not connected to anything. What's left, what's "his," is . . . *nothing*. The false surface—traditional prayers to a comforting deity—collapses into mournful burlesque.

Again and again, the emphasis on the falsity of surfaces.

Everyone has cited the passage from *A Farewell to Arms* in which Frederic Henry is "embarrassed by the words sacred, glorious, and sacrifice and the expression in vain. . . . and I had seen nothing sacred, and the things that were glorious had no glory and the sacrifices were like the stockyards at Chicago if nothing was done with the meat except to bury it" (pp. 184–85). It isn't that the narrator has lost his values. Indeed, the stockyard passage is spoken by a narrator whose values are not damaged.

He is disillusioned and cynical, but the cynicism implies longing for a different sort of world, one in which things *were* sacred and glorious. What's left is false surface, false language, the language of Mr. Kurtz, who, before he discovered "the horror," believed "each station should be like a beacon on the road towards better things, a centre for trade, of course, but also for humanizing, improving, instructing" (*Heart of Darkness*, p. 33). Words don't work anymore. "Words go straight up in a thin line, quick and harmless," Addie Bundren says in *As I Lay Dying*, "and how terribly doing goes along the earth, clinging to it, so that after a while the two lines are too far apart for the same person to straddle from one to the other" (p. 160).

It is, of course, not in literature alone that this condition is to be found. At the cusp of the twentieth century, the ego, all structures of thought, and civilization itself are seen increasingly as false surface, defensive surface. The lens itself is examined. In Freud, the ego is a compromise between reality and dark powers. Ideals are seen not as discoverable in the world but internalized from parents as a way of alleviating guilt. Ideas are generally rationalizations or symbolic translations of unconscious struggle. In Marxist epistemology, ideas and values express the interests of a particular class and cannot be considered as universal. The development of the sociology of knowledge is a symptom of the same suspicion. Now ideas have to be regarded as expressions of the holders of the ideas, their class or their social group. One can no longer speak about reality; the question arises: whose reality? Why is this the version of reality perceived? Nietzsche offers a new test of truth—is an idea life-affirming? And he offers in mythological form the loss of externally derived values. We have killed God; we must realize this and become gods ourselves.

We become concerned with the knower, the real-izer: the maker of reality. History moves toward historiography. Impressionist painting is of the experience of light, of a *seen* rather than a *scene*. The novel becomes inordinately concerned with point of view—the particular window(s) through which the world is experienced. This is not, as some of us were once taught, a simple advance in technical sophistication. It indicates the problematic nature of the known world.[16] Paul Armstrong writes of James, Conrad, and Ford, "These three literary impressionists take the novel beyond representation by pursuing its epistemological principles so radically that they make them thematic" (*Challenge*, p. 16).[17] What they represented was the act of knowing and representing. The given world is given *by someone;* the artist is forced to examine the gift, to focus on the giver. Every field of knowledge, then, is forced to look at its own looking. In its extreme form, we have Sass's model of schizophrenia.

Many novels become a kind of detective story. The reader has to ferret out truth under a suspect surface—the story a narrator tells. Perhaps John Dowell in *The Good Soldier* is mad, perhaps he is sane; some critics argue that he is not supposed to be trusted, while others point out his similarity to Ford himself.[18] But the significant point is this: the *question* of his reliability is forced on us. The novel forces us to be suspicious. *The Good Soldier* is one of the great novels about the false surface of civilization and the breaking down of that false surface.

When the novel was first published in 1915, Theodore Dreiser reviewed it for *The New Republic.* He feels irritated "to the point of . . . laying down the book" and suggests to Ford "that he begin at the beginning" and that "once begun, it should go forward in a more or less direct line."[19] Dreiser is not a fool; he is simply a premodernist frustrated by modernist epistemology. He isn't content to be a reader-detective.

Those of us brought up on modernist texts are delighted to be allowed inside the drama of concealment and uncovering. It is a drama that reaches its climax in an apparently anticlimactic ending. Dowell tells us, casually, "It suddenly occurs to me that I have forgotten to say how Edward met his death." It is a brilliant moment. The final revelation, it still maintains the surface. Edward, about to kill himself, says no more than "so long, old man. I must have a bit of a rest, you know." Dowell "didn't know what to say." He denies responsibility, tells us how he "trotted off with the telegram to Leonora" (pp. 255–56). The reader wants to reach into the page and grab Dowell, confront him with his denial, his concealment—to himself as well as to us—of the complex meanings of what Edward's suicide must have meant to him. Sure, I want to say, sure, you simply forgot to tell us. And of course it's natural that, knowing your friend is about to kill himself, you wouldn't try to stop him, you'd just trot off like an obedient pony. And of course—now I am really insisting— of course you didn't know at this moment that Edward had been your wife's lover. Nonsense! But unlike Dreiser, I am caught up in the lovely subterfuge, caught up in watching Dowell's process of fictionalizing his life, refictionalizing it, to stay safe.

And I accept the ambiguities. How much does Dowell know when he accepts the suicide of his friend? His trotting off with the telegram to

Leonora seems overdetermined. The novel, like so many modernist texts, refuses closure. If, on the one hand, I have to be a detective, on the other I have to accept reality without demanding a simple solution or a single reading. A modernist text like *The Good Soldier* insists on a world in which there are only multiple interpretations, none final. Yet I am also aware—in fact, I insist on it—that this epistemology of *Que sais-je?* is itself the narrator's defense, protecting the surface, the status quo.

Modernist writers, feeling themselves in a world that is not a given but rather is shaped by the artist out of dross and confusion, *defamiliarize* the reader, immerse the reader in uncertainty, in bewilderment. Paul Armstrong, in *The Phenomenology of Henry James,* shows that James, Ford, and Conrad "all assign the greatest thematic and aesthetic importance to the experience of bewilderment" (p. 209). That is exactly right. Bewilderment implies a world whose surface gives multiple meanings, contradictory signs that need decoding. And so the reader becomes a detective. Of the writers in this study, only D. H. Lawrence is different. Apprehending a world ultimately there on its own, needing simply to be touched in silence, he gives us the mystery that waits in the darkness beneath the surface; he needs us to enter not into bewilderment but into *wonder.*

Ford's *The Good Soldier* describes a world hysterically intent on *staying at the surface.* Its narrator, John Dowell, admitting that the ways of "good people" are "disagreeable," says, "You meet a man or a woman and, from tiny and intimate sounds, from the slightest of movements, you know at once whether you are concerned with good people or with those who won't do. You know, that is to say, whether they will go rigidly through with the whole programme from the underdone beef to the Anglicanism." True that "with all the taking for granted, you never really get an inch deeper" (p. 37), but Dowell accepts the condition of this life-in-death. Not *accepts, requires:* he and everyone in the novel lie to protect the false surface, to protect, to "nurse" one another. Dowell needs his friend's wife to lie to him about the relationship of his wife to her husband. She looks him "straight in the eyes; and for a moment I had the feeling that those two blue discs were . . . like a wall of blue that shut me off from the rest of the world" (p. 45). They need a premodernist world; they need to stay premodernist readers.

Protection by concealment. The price of settling for the false, surface life is living like Prufrock or the hollow men. And the price of breaking the surface? Terror of facing the truth, of course, but ultimately terror of inner chaos and self exposure. "We are all so afraid, we are all so alone, we all need from the outside the assurance of our own worthiness to exist" (p. 115). As drama, the novel takes the form of a series of revelations, breaking through the false surface. If the characters try to keep the hollow surface of reality unbroken, the reader takes on the role of suspecting and breaking down civilized surfaces, becomes a modernist reader-detective.

We are in the age of the Freudian case history. Speaking of Freud's study of the Wolf-Man, Frederick Karl says, "Freud's sense of his mission here, to find coherence in what appeared to be incoherent materials, placed him within the Modern avant-garde" (*Modern and Modernism*, p. 173). Freud is certainly a modernist reader in his undermining of surfaces and in his understanding of the complex overdetermination of all events.

I am indebted to Shoshona Felman for making me aware of my role as reader-detective. As she points out in "Turning the Screw of Interpretation," the insistent critical question of the reliability of the governess in *The Turn of the Screw* has been built into the text itself.[20] Ghost story? Study of madness? "The story won't tell," as James's second frame narrator tells us. Narrators within narrators, emphasizing narrativity. It becomes impossible to use the word "real" without quotation marks, without irony, without the need to question it. *A Portrait of the Artist as a Young Man* becomes a portrait *by* the artist of the process of breaking a given world, making his own. It is a modeling of the necessity for all human beings to shape the meaning of their realities, the meaning under a false surface.

In literary criticism, too, I am faced with my own shaping of reality as soon as I begin to write.

My 'I', then, is *my eye*. There is no transparent lens. I am forced to look at my unique looking, at the ways I create what I am seeing. I am forced to ask who is speaking in this book—and not to reply with easy answers: an American, an academic man of letters, a Jew, a reader in a postmodern age examining modernism, a white male in a culture that has gone through the experience of feminism. Those partial identities have surely helped shape the contours of my eye/my *I*. But so, too, has my place in the particular family I came from: a mother who came to this country as a child from Bessarabia, Yiddish and Russian her native languages, to turn herself into an American and, by age twenty-five, a successful businesswoman; a father—the son of a cigar-roller from Odessa—who was handsome and warmhearted but ignorant, frightened, and bullheaded. She married him and expected to become a good traditional Jewish wife, staying at home, living through his success. But my father was a failure. He yelled, bullied, despised himself. She lived through me instead. I lay myself open to the charge of distorting the texts and writers I am trying to interpret. Am I a trustworthy witness? Or am I reading through a distorted lens ground in my own childhood? There are two answers to this: The first is that there is no alternative—no clear, neutral lens; what modernism as well as psychoanalysis teaches is that all understanding is *somebody's* understanding. The only difference is that I am putting my cards on the table. I can attempt to quiet myself, to exhibit "even, hovering attention" as Freud demands—not, as he thought, to remove myself from the encounter but to remove my busy, everyday, superficial self. I can try to be open to the text or person, to establish empathy in my reading rather than use the text as projective screen.[21] But I come to the text as the particular person I have become. Second, while my particular lens cannot produce an objective vision of a writer or a text, yet because of its particular focal length it may have particular power. Kafka's reading of society was no less insightful for his neurotic anxiety. Indeed, his conflicts gave him schema that allowed him to interpret his own times and prophesy ours.

In my own case, the pattern of controlling, narcissistic, marvelous mother and unsuccessful, shattered father gives me, I believe, peculiar sensitivity to modern novelists who came from similar families. And then, too, I know the anxiety I'm speaking of, though I've experienced it only at moments and surely with less intensity than have these writers. Still, I am attuned. But I am attuned only to *particular aspects* of their work.

This *I*—this limited, individual I—makes me uneasy. I clear my throat as if to speak with a "purer" voice. I am aware of the limitations as well as the sensitivities of my *I*. Of course, I am not purely my limited *I* either; at the same time that I am the child of my parents, the writer, the American man, I am *not,* for I am someone who understands my own limitations. I understand that I am not speaking ex cathedra. There is no chair in some high place from which I can speak, speak as *we* or as an I who speaks for us all, normatively. I speak, then, filled with epistemological doubt. My "I" is an aspect of the condition I am examining.

I don't see epistemological doubt as the root of modernism, but I do see it as the central expression of modernism and its associated affect as anxiety, even terror. To experience the falsity or arbitrariness of surface, to experience beneath the surface the absence of any necessary system of thought, any grid, is to experience either Nirvana or nada. In Sartre, in Beckett, in modernist literature generally, silence, the unnamed, the unnameable—the chestnut tree that is not a tree of that genus but *this thing itself*—creates terror more than freedom, though it creates both. Terror of having no ground under one's feet, of being nowhere.[22]

This feeling, this condition, is everywhere in Conrad. In his first novel, *Almayer's Folly,* the failed idealist, unable to get away from his life, thinks, "But how? If he attempted to move he would step off into nothing, and perish in the crashing fall of that universe of which he was the only support!" (p. 117). What a perfect expression of the terror. I think about Lord Jim after he jumps from the ship, cut off inside the silence: "A silence of the sea, of the sky, merged into one indefinite immensity" (p. 83). Boundaries dissolved, self dissolved.

Marlow, speaking of the steamboat lost in the mist, says, "Were we to let go our hold of the bottom, we would be absolutely in the air—in space" (*Heart of Darkness,* p. 43). A deeper expression of the experience is the disorienting fever that kills Kurtz and almost kills Marlow. It is regression to infantile chaos. According to recent research, chaos—loss of boundaries, disorientation—may not, in fact, be the experience of infants.[23] But certainly the novel, with its description of fevered crawling through jungle and incoherent speech, asks us to see psychic disintegration as regression.

In *Nostromo,* Decoud is lost in a mist on a tiny island in the middle of the Gulfo Placido. In symbolic form, he is in the midst of the same torpor, or lassitude, that Conrad himself fell into. Conrad *felt* alone; Decoud *is* utterly alone and, as it were, in a state of sensory deprivation. A dilettante, without personal direction, without values, Decoud finds himself in a place that precisely expresses his phenomenological condition. Filling his pockets with silver bars, he drowns himself.

This absolute loss of orientation can be seen as calling up what D. W. Winnicott calls "unthinkable anxiety," an "acute confusional state that belongs to disintegration of nascent ego structure" (*Playing and Reality,* p. 32). It is an experience of absolute abandonment—originally, abandonment by the mother—an experience of madness, a "*break-up* of . . . *a personal continuity of existence.*"[24] Kohut, too, describes "disintegration anxiety" as the "deepest anxiety man can experience."[25] Whether "regression" or not, this is ultimate disconnection from the world as breast, as place of life. It is not social alienation that is at stake, nor even confusion over values. It is *being-in-the-world.* No wonder that Conrad viewed his writing as an expression of "solidarity," of "fellowship with all creation," awakening "in the hearts of the beholders that feeling of unavoidable solidarity . . . which binds men to each other and all mankind to the visible world."[26] I am suggesting that Conrad's art is an attempt to restore his primal connection with the world, that a primary anxiety out of which he and other modernists write is disconnection from the living world and disintegration of ego structure. Suicide, which Conrad attempted as a young man and which ends the lives of so many of his characters, is partly a way of restoring connectedness with the world and a way of being whole.

As I have already shown, one of the most precise writers of nothingness is Hemingway. When *In Our Time* was first published (1925) and Hemingway unknown, D. H. Lawrence wrote a brilliant brief review. He describes Nick as "through with everything. It is a state of *conscious,* accepted indifference to everything. . . . Avoid one thing only: getting connected up. Don't get connected up. . . . This is a negative goal, and Mr. Hemingway is really good, because he's perfectly straight about it. . . . He wants just to . . . maintain a healthy state of nothingness inside himself, and an attitude of negation to everything outside himself."[27] Lawrence is wonderfully insightful about the state of nothingness and negation, but he ignores the *anxiety,* the terrible, unspoken disquiet under the stories and vignettes. It's what we don't think about, what we refuse to think about— the swamp in "Big Two-Hearted River" that Nick avoids fishing, for example—that we feel so intensely. In "Now I Lay Me," the traumatized narrator is afraid to go to sleep, "because I had been living for a long time with the knowledge that if I ever shut my eyes in the dark and let myself go, my soul would go out of my body." He protects himself with the concerns and the prayers of childhood.

According to Harry Guntrip, fear of sleeping may be fear of an "irrecoverable surrender to regression."[28] But such regression is not "in the service of the ego," because there is nothing to *hold* the regressed psyche. A look at the narrator's childhood in "Now I Lay Me" shows why. Childhood is experienced as powerlessness in the face of a tyrant mother, with no support from the father, who seems weak, crippled. The boy's grandfather represents a lost world; when the grandfather dies, they move from his house into one designed by the mother. The narrator's father is not able to stop his wife from destroying the Indian arrowheads—images of male identity and power—that he has collected: "Our Father" offers no protection. Marriage is castration. So it is terribly ironic that this traumatized soldier who can't sleep is given an orderly who is sure that his troubles will be over when he marries. The story knows better. The reader has seen that marriage destroys a man. The narrator wants to go back to childhood, but a childhood away from the world of women. Regression, however, is dangerous. Looking into the broken self, he fears his soul slipping out.

Nick's relationship to his grandfather, to the lost world his grandfather represents, is strangely similar to relationships to the grandfather in Faulkner, Fitzgerald, Conrad, and Ford.[29] Again and again the grandfather's world, in some way aristocratic, represents established truths, a solid world. The writer clings to that disappeared world of an imagined, a mythologized, grandfather, who asserts timeless values.

The model is perhaps most true of Faulkner. Quentin's suicide in *The Sound and the Fury*, for instance, has to be seen in relation to precisely the loss of timeless values: loss of the grandfather's world.

The central agony that Quentin has to endure is not sexual guilt, nor even the loss of Caddy. The climactic scene in the Quentin section is the memory of his conversation with his cynical father. Quentin threatens suicide. His father, who, unlike the grandfather, represents the absence of absolute values, neither agrees nor disagrees that such an act can be courageous, for "every man is the arbiter of his own virtues." Imagine a father playing philosopher when his son threatens suicide! Then he explains Quentin's motive for having claimed to have committed incest with Caddy: Quentin was trying to turn ordinary human folly into a damnable act, an act that could *matter*. But nothing matters finally. Quentin summarizes what his father taught: "that all men are just accumulations dolls stuffed with sawdust swept up from the trash heap where all previous dolls had been thrown away the sawdust flowing from what wound in what side that not for me died not." It is a passage that echoes Eliot's stuffed men and Marlow's vision of the manager as "papier-mâché Mephistopheles." And it echoes Hemingway: "Our nada which art in nada"— in negation, the reminder of a lost spiritual affirmation.

Finally, his father tells Quentin that he will commit suicide only when he realizes "that even she was not quite worth despair." And again and again Quentin echoes in shock his father's casual assertion that these feelings are *temporary*. Temporary! If they are temporary, if they belong to time, then they have no ultimate value. By the day of his suicide, Quentin is trapped or fears being trapped in his father's thought, trapped within a world in which things stop mattering, in which nothing is eternal. Then isn't his suicide, still more than the breaking off of his watch hands, the expression of a longing for the safe, the permanent, the eternal? Quentin sees death itself as the eternal that has been lost: "I used to think of death as a man something like Grandfather" he says and imagines his grandfather and Colonel Sartoris on a high place. "Grandfather wore his uniform and we could hear the murmur of their voices from beyond the cedars they were always talking and Grandfather was always right" (*Sound and the Fury,* pp. 218–20).

I've suggested that nothingness and disorientation are the primary agonies for Quentin. And yet they are—precisely—*chosen* to keep the self safe from engulfment. The honeysuckle—life in the senses, erotic life—terrifies, overwhelms Quentin. He retreats into an irrational rationality, into the spiral of self-consciousness. He lives life on the surface, but the emptiness, which he has created out of fear, is itself equally fearful. He grasps at false protective structures—the timeless world of his mythicized grandfather. His suicide is into that world and into peace. It reflects escape from the "unthinkable anxiety" that Winnicott describes. Like Decoud's suicide, like Septimus's, this, too, is suicide as attempt to restore a primal connection with the world. And in his Nobel Prize speech, Faulkner, like Conrad in his preface to *The Nigger of the "Narcissus"* and many of his other writings, describes the role of the artist as restorer of lost connections by reminding man that "he is immortal," by connecting him to the "courage and honor and hope and pride and compassion and pity and sacrifice which have been the glory of his past." The speech—its ponderous, elegant syntax and diction as much as its credo—connects the speaker himself to the world of the grandfather, to meaningful life.

To live in the grandfather's world—as Hightower, Emily, and so many of Faulkner's characters try to do—is obviously impossible. Faulkner knows that very well. But it is longed for, since to live in the empty world—the world experienced as empty—is terrifying. Ultimately, to live in the empty world is to risk nonbeing, to risk that one's self will collapse. There is a relevant theater exercise in which actors are told to walk as if they are being held by a thick atmosphere. They can hardly fall, they are so completely supported. They can rest against it, the way you can rest against a strong, steady wind. Actors feel the ease. Then they are told that the atmosphere has vanished; they are in a vacuum and have to support themselves. Now, every act is effort. They have to keep themselves from falling, from falling down, from falling apart. That is like the terror underlying modernist fiction. Lawrence gets at the experience powerfully in a series of poems in *Last Poems:*

It is a fearful thing to fall into the hands of the living God.
But it is a much more fearful thing to fall out of them.

(*Complete Poems* 2:699)

The British psychoanalyst Marion Milner finds here the title for her book about the lost soul, Susan, *The Hands of the Living God*. For Milner, the hands of God express "the background awareness of one's own body, that which one both holds and is held by, after infancy." This awareness, Milner says, "must have been largely indistinguishable from the awareness of one's mother's body doing the holding; so it was not surprising, surely, that . . . Susan was left feeling herself as a disembodied spirit" (p. 53). Lawrence, too, associates the hands of God with the condition of being held in infancy, saying "the hands of the living God . . . *cradle* so much of a man" ("Abysmal Immortality," italics mine). But, Lawrence says, when a person has fallen,[30] he falls "down the godless plunge of the abyss." The condition of modernist anxiety is the inner chaos of being unheld, of falling, the terror of unthinkable anxiety.

It is inner chaos—or, at best, a half-life, a life cut off from whole being, or connected being-in-the-world. It is a life many of us have lived at times; I believe that this is why we are able to resonate to this fiction. And modern novelists—am I suggesting they defended themselves by splitting, meeting the world with a false self? Am I saying that they were "schizoid"? I'm suggesting, rather, that they had schizoid tendencies that enabled them to apprehend extreme schizoid states and project them into fictional characters and powerful expressions of feeling. I would suggest, too, that increasingly after World War I, an audience was coming into adulthood with similar anxieties and defenses. In a sense, the defenses of a whole class within a particular culture were schizoid—and still are. For these people, largely upper-middle-class, experiencing the world without firm structures, a floundering self in a floundering world, a motherless and fatherless world, modern novelists seemed to echo their unease, focus it, universalize it, and even provide strategies to contain it.

PART TWO

NO GROUND TO STAND ON

I N T H E F I R S T C H A P T E R I described a particular form of anxiety shared by modernist writers. Now I want to look at the childhood patterns that shaped their anxiety, both in the family and in relation to the larger society.

Most descriptions of literary movements ignore the individual human beings who shaped them—who lived certain lives and responded in their writing to certain pressures. I want to know how British and American fiction of high modernism was engendered. It's not enough to say that modernism responded to social conditions or intellectual currents. I need to know how the particular lives of James, Conrad, Ford, Forster, Joyce, Woolf, Lawrence, Fitzgerald, Hemingway, Faulkner, all seemingly so different, produced writers who shared common anxieties and defenses and became canonized as *the* modern novelists.

I'm sure about this: Nietzsche, for instance, didn't do it. While his insights into the loss of values and the new, fearful freedom of the self are relevant, suggestive, analogous, Nietzsche didn't shape the vision of the shapers of modern fiction. Writers may be influenced by philosophers, but the essential gestures within fiction or poetry of any power derive from deeper and earlier sources. Lawrence read Nietzsche and responded to his ideas on the self, on aristocracy, on the irrational, and on the relation of truth to human experience.[1] But his use of Nietzsche is largely a way of justifying his life, of finding a language to reconcile the poles of his nature, and of coping with weakness. The recurrent struggle in his fiction was formed, I would argue, during the childhood wars in his family. *He suffered the dreaming of his parents.* Conrad's terrors and fantasies, his life choices, and even the direction he would take when he became an

artist, are latent in him before he leaves, at age seventeen, for Marseilles—
long before he'd read Schopenhauer. Writers find the philosophers and
artists who give expression to what they are already struggling with in
their lives.

We don't simply dream the dreams of a culture or a subculture; we are
also the dreamers of the particular dreams of our particular parents. Their
ghosts prompt our lines. Conrad is interpreting the world through the
schemas planted in him as a child of failed, dying revolutionaries, broken
idealists. Hemingway is enacting the struggle that was not openly enacted
between his father and mother. In a sense, that struggle does take place
thirty years later—in the son's fiction.

In the same way that it is a distortion to speak of modernist fiction as
expressive of a general cultural tendency, it is also a distortion to speak of
it in broad sociohistorical terms, expressing a "late colonial stage of modern capitalism." Sentences which begin "Market capitalism demanded
from culture" should be put quietly to sleep. E. M. Forster, a timid,
bullied, sensitive, mother-haunted child in Tonbridge, was not, even unconsciously, the servant of a socioeconomic order that "required" a certain kind of fiction.[2] Too often, theorists offer very shaky assumptions
about relations between consciousness and society. Eli Zaretsky writes,
"In opposition to this harsh world that no individual could hope to affect,
the modern world of subjectivity was created" (*Capitalism*, p. 41). When
had writers ever been better able to affect the world? Was the late nineteenth century any less open to individual initiative, than, say, the eighteenth? Was it any harsher for the shapers of modern literary consciousness? Should we call Henry James's life especially harsh? God knows, it
was terribly difficult to grow up intact in the James family, but a harsh and
inexorable environment wasn't the problem. Chaos was the problem.
Certainly, that chaos is expressive of chaos developing in the larger society, but precisely *how*? And how, in turn, is it expressed in James's
fiction?

Nor is it enough to speak of the influence of literary movements. Many
critics, Charles Newman and Frederick Karl among the most recent, show
that modernist consciousness is already implicit in the work of Baudelaire
and Flaubert.[3] Certainly these early modernists became models for writers
of modernist fiction. But why was Flaubert chosen as a model? Why did
James turn to Flaubert, Conrad to James?

How, then, does a writer respond to a particular society at a particular
time? You can't reify gigantic socioeconomic forces (market capitalism,

imperialism, industrialism, infusion of the bourgeoisie into electoral politics) and give them agency. You've got to get back to the struggle of the individual writer to live, to shape his or her self, to respond with art to frustration and terror and grief and rage and humiliation.

It is not, of course, simply life in the isolated family of origin we have to examine. The child in the family exists in relation to a number of larger communities—social, ethnic, geographical, cultural. We need to know what it was like for the child to grow up in relation to these communities, too. And then, the family itself is not a static institution with constant effects. It changes in relation to the larger society; it changed greatly in the nineteenth century in both Britain and the United States. And, depending on the place of family within society, it has different effects on the developing self. We need to ask: What is the meaning of family in Britain and the United States in the late nineteenth century? What is the relation of the families of modernist novelists to ambient communities? What is the writer's relation to both family and community? What conditions in family and community produced the soil for the growth of modernism? Or let me turn the question around: *How did the psychic struggle of these novelists in particular families at a particular historical moment give them the soil for the growth of a sensibility attuned to the problems and contradictions in the larger society?* It seems to me a kind of cultural natural selection took place; these writers, with a common sensibility rooted in their early lives, were the ones moved to speak in a voice we call *modernist*.

There seems to be a problem: the writers in this study were born over a half-century span—from James, born in 1843, to Hemingway, born in 1899. Conrad's *Heart of Darkness* was published serially the year Hemingway was born. If individual consciousness is enmeshed in a historical moment, how can I speak about the similar childhoods of writers born so many years apart?

The problem is really one of an analysis that expects to see a causal relationship between changes in production and social organization and changes in consciousness. The point is there is no such thing as a single "historical moment." Different families reach a historical moment, become the moment, at different times. Over more than a half-century, an increasing number of families lived lives, influenced by changes in technology and social conditions, that became the soil for the growth of modernism. And even that is putting it too rigidly. It's better to think of individuals and families as geological formations of many strata: cut away a crosssection and you will find layers from many epochs. Various cultural periods live in each of us. Still, Henry James was, one might say, a pioneer of living the kind of childhood out of which modernism bloomed. That is, while the family in which he grew up was deeply embedded in mid-century cultural life, it was also a living experiment in modernist chaos, and this very contradiction shaped his art. Conrad grew up as a child of a feudal aristocratic family, and yet the conditions of his childhood, including exile from his aristocratic roots, made his upbringing similar to that of William Faulkner, born forty years later.

In the following two chapters, I will explore the soil for modernism in writers' families of origin as well as in the larger society of which these families were a part.

CHAPTER TWO

FAMILY GHOSTS

M ANY OBSERVERS HAVE described relevant changes in the bourgeois family. They see the family increasingly cut off from work life, "a tent pitch'd in a world not right," as Coventry Patmore put it in "The Angel in the House."[1] Two contradictory processes occur. On the one hand, pressure on the family intensifies; it becomes all-important, "an enclave protected from industrial society."[2] The family is mythologized into "a haven in a heartless world."[3] The wife is a "guardian angel" turned to in defense against "the weakness consequent upon a baffled search for truth" (Houghton, p. 388). On the other hand, the family is seen as coming apart. Steven Mintz speaks of the "enormous burden of expectations placed on children within certain Victorian homes, and a resulting sense of intense personal responsibility and potential weakness."[4] Stephen Kern writes about the "excessive intimacy and interdependence that the family imposed upon its members."[5] Not such a haven, then. Certainly in the United States but also in Britain, more and more families relocate and scatter; relations between family and community are more likely to follow urban models, in which your community is not coextensive with *the* community, not even within your own class. The family is increasingly isolated, increasingly intense, increasingly all there is for support. But at the same time, observers see the family losing its power. Lasch says simply, "The family has been slowly coming apart for more than a hundred years" (p. xiv).

The contradiction is only apparent. While there is increasing reliance on family, its source of strength, critics argue, has collapsed. That is, in the context of a "general challenge to authority" (Zaretsky, p. 36), the family, cut off from public life, work life, loses its own authority as well. Max Horkheimer calls the family the "germ cell" of bourgeois culture.[6] He speaks of the traditional father-child relationship, in which "the child respects in his father's strength a moral relationship," as providing the child's "first training for the bourgeois authority relationship" (p. 101). This *patriarchal* authority diminishes. The father begins to lose his traditional place as family lawgiver, even as representative of God. Alexander Mitscherlich, too, argues that this father has disappeared and discusses the meaning of this disappearance.

> The patriarchal structural components of our society are closely associated with magical thought. It assumes the omnipotence-impotence relation between father and son, God and man, ruler and ruled, to be the natural principle of social organization. Historical development, however, has been marked by a strengthening of the conscious critical capacities, which have relativized the . . . relationship. This makes filial dependence and paternal authority no longer seem necessary and permanent but concessions subject to revision.[7]

This change, Mitscherlich argues, results in "alienation and its psychical concomitants, anxiety and aggressivity" (p. 141).

Mintz sees what was happening in more subtle terms. He agrees that the father's authority was gradually undercut.[8] He argues, however, that in the nineteenth century, the father remained "the embodiment of moral and intellectual authority" (p. 50). In response to a changing society, families had to provide for social stability by instilling self-government. Simple obedience was no longer the appropriate model for relations between generations. "Children had to be trained in independence—to develop a capacity for self-reliance, self-assessment, and self-direction" (ibid., p. 31). However, this plan has an obvious built-in contradiction. It became increasingly difficult to maintain the balance between independence and authority. According to Jan Dizard and Howard Gadlin, "the parent, valuing self-direction and nonconformity over obedience to external authority, must assume a stance that undermines his or her own authority. Ultimately the parent can demand neither obedience nor attachment" (*The Minimal Family,* p. 81). Finally, the traditional, father-led family dissolved.

In *Domestic Revolutions*, Steven Mintz and Susan Kellogg describe the intense metamorphosis into the "democratic family." While the book is mostly about changes in America, in Britain *and* America, "within marriage the older ideals of patriarchal authority and strict wifely obedience were replaced by new ideals of 'mutual esteem, mutual friendship, mutual confidence'" (p. 46). The moral authority of the new family centers on the mother, not on the father. Lears speaks of women as "repositories of moral and cultural authority" (p. 16). We read this, too, in Ann Douglas's *Feminization of American Culture;* Douglas defines the alliance between the nineteenth-century minister and the middle-class woman. Mintz and Kellogg, too, argue that rather than the father as spiritual guide in the family, "there was a growing consensus that only women, through their uplifting influence over the home and children, could be a source of moral values" (p. 55). As John Demos puts it in *Past, Present, and Personal,* "As mother's importance waxed, father's inexorably waned" (p. 50).

Demos, Mintz and Kellogg, Lasch, and others describe the "wrenching apart of work and home-life," which Demos calls "one of the great themes in social history. And for fathers, in particular," he says, "the consequences can hardly be overestimated" (Demos, p. 51). Increasingly in the nineteenth century, as the father enters a sphere separate from the rest of his family, two things happen. First, his dominant place in the home, his position of spiritual center, is by necessity taken over by his wife, the ongoing, daily parent; he is the absent, distant deity, and, like the Victorian God, increasingly less real; he may not be less powerful in imagination but he is less visible, less engaged. Second, he is under greater pressure to be the heroic provider of the family. But who in modern social organizations is made to feel a hero? Perhaps this need, this longing and frustration, along with the loss of a transcendent position, underlie the call for the hero by nineteenth-century figures like Carlyle and Nietzsche. Indeed, Walter Houghton tells us, "The truce from cares which the Victorians found in contemplating the hero is a truce from the cares of living in a world where one feels an acute sense of weakness, whether engendered by indecision and enervating analysis . . . or by the cramping pressure of 'fate and circumstance.' The reaction is psychological and nostalgic" (p. 340).

I am certainly not making a plea for the return of the patriarchal family. I am arguing that in its transformation, which is an inevitable aspect of a larger social revolution, traditional grounds of support have been lost. The invisible envelope that people walked around inside of became visible; then torn; then discarded. It is largely the lack of this support that, in extreme form, has shaped modernist anxiety and the responses to that anxiety in modernist art.

Freud, more than anyone, made the family visible. But the family relationships that he made visible were ones that had already become problematic; they were evidence of friction in the machine. And they were fast disappearing. Oddly, though he is writing at the turn of the century, he is not describing very well the families of most modernist novelists.

Freud's mythological picture of The Family: there is a powerful, tyrant father; a (castrated) loving mother; a war between (male) child and father. Neuroses are the wounds of battle. Defenses, always imperfect, ultimately assuage castration anxiety and oedipal guilt. It is a Victorian model—of a patriarchal household in the midst of a society undergoing intense generational change, so that conflict between father and son is exacerbated.[9] I can find few writers in the canon of modernism brought up in such a family. Certainly Kafka—but then, Kafka gives us the experience of helplessness in the presence of arbitrary power, not the anxiety of emptiness. Indeed, Teutonic families and childrearing practices have been shown to be more rigidly authoritarian and patriarchal than those of Anglo-American origin.[10] The writers who make up the British and American modernist canon—James, Conrad, Ford, Lawrence, Woolf, Joyce, Forster, Hemingway, Fitzgerald, Faulkner—come from a family surprisingly different from that examined by Freud. It is the mother who is the crucial, controlling, organizing figure. But while she imposes control, she is, at least initially, emotionally withdrawn. This combination of impingement on the child and emotional withdrawal is a pattern found to some extent in the childhoods of James, Forster, Woolf, Lawrence, Fitzgerald, Hemingway, Faulkner. The father is in most cases shattered—a failure in his own eyes and in the eyes of his family (though not necessarily in the eyes of the world)—and he is personally weak. When he is not a failure, he is absent. In compensation, there is, generally, a family mythology of past greatness, often centering around a grandfather. In each family—and this is the chief point—I see a condition of instability.

I want to argue that this family background offered neither the necessary mothering nor the necessary fathering for the developing self. At an earlier time, when the enveloping community was itself coherent, with a solid belief system, the problems in one nuclear family would not have been so overwhelming. Early modernist British and American novelists, who were, as I shall show, all exiles except for Woolf (if, indeed, even she is an exception), grew up without a supportive surrounding community, and so the failures in the family were determinative. I believe that the resulting structural weakness of the writers' selves created the conditions for their anxieties. They grew into adulthood with a fluid personality structure both exciting and dangerous; in order to cope, they made themselves up, and they shaped an art in which they teetered on a high wire between expression and psychic disintegration.

I'm not arguing that these conditions exist only for novelists or only for *early* modernist writers. T. S. Eliot, for instance, comes from a background describable precisely in all these terms.[11] And later modernist writers too: Bruce Bawer's *The Middle Generation,* exploring the lives and work of Delmore Schwartz, John Berryman, Randall Jarrell, and Robert Lowell, sees each as coming from similar family backgrounds.[12] The pattern holds, too, for many more recent writers of fiction, John Cheever among them. Indeed, I am also suggesting that the lives of modernist writers, *a*typical at the turn of the century, became closer to the norm as the century progressed.[13]

These shared family patterns contain too high a degree of similarity to lay them at the door of coincidence. Am I forcing these families into a procrustean bed? I don't think so. The bed was provided by the writers' families in the context of a collapsing community and, in each case, particular conditions of dislocation.

I have noted the breakup of the patriarchal family. I am not suggesting that the patriarchal family is necessary to produce a child whose self is strong and whole, a child who feels held and doesn't hunger for merger. Patriarchal relations were at least as crippling as modern ones. What is necessary is parenting that neither abandons nor impinges on the child. But the collapse of the patriarchal family, when it was the normative family, was a powerful impetus to modernism.

Controlling mother, weak father who has fallen: This description is a kind of cultural metaphor for altered relations in the modern nuclear family; it is also a description of the actual families of British and American early modernist novelists. All of these novelists of high modernism do not precisely match all parts of the pattern. But the outlines are strangely consistent. And I see the pattern reenacted in their adult lives and in their work. I believe this pattern is the source of the particular anxiety that permeates modernist work and the particular defenses against it.

It is Mary James who controlled the James household. Jean Strouse writes, "Like her mother, her mother-in-law, and countless other women throughout history, Mary James governed her family by means of self-sacrifice. And her husband and children idealized this practice" (p. 26). Henry Sr., on the other hand, son of a wealthy, tyrannical merchant, appeared delicate, shaken, crippled. He was a black sheep. While from the outside he may be regarded as a serious intellectual, a minor philosopher, with a set of admiring friends that included Emerson and Thackeray, he never experienced himself as complete. Like all his children, he had break-downs and felt himself to be a failure, a man without a profession, a wanderer—certainly not the stereotypical Victorian master of the house-hold. Strouse quotes Lila Cabot, who recalled "the James house ruled by Mrs. James where HJ's father used to limp in and out and never seemed really to 'belong' " (p. 44).

In *A Prison of Expectations,* Steven Mintz suggests that it was typical for children growing up in Victorian families to be

> preoccupied during their young adulthoods with . . . questions of religious belief. [They] felt wracked by doubt and weary of uncertainty and religious controversy. All regarded their families' religion as cold, stern, and lifeless and craved a religion that was more life affirming. All craved sanctification that would free them from egotism and guilt. All sought a faith that would be consistent with the evidences of their own feelings. (P. 57)

Henry James, Sr., grew up amid just such a struggle with his authoritarian, Calvinist father. But the result of that struggle was not typical. Mintz argues that in Victorian Britain and America, "the religious conflict . . . provided the child with a vehicle through which to assert a degree of autonomy and independence while struggling to maintain family bonds." In other words, religious conflict was a coded expression of a deeper conflict of self-assertion versus subordination to authority. And rather than "breaking the bonds of family,"

> filial revolt provided a ritualistic way for a child to demonstrate a capacity for self-government while reaffirming loyalty to certain fundamental family val-ues. . . . The pattern of family conflict can be viewed as an instrument for maintaining cultural continuity, while permitting important modifications and adaptations. (P. 88)

Not in the case of Henry James, Sr. His father was too rigid and tyranni-cal, the intensity of conflict too high, to permit Henry James, Sr., to be-come independent while maintaining continuity. He was left half-broken, stranded, desperate. If, in spite of the struggle between father and son, Robert Louis Stevenson—one of Mintz's examples—"developed a con-ception of the father's role that was virtually identical to his parents,' " Henry James, Sr., did not. He became a confused and ineffectual father.

Henry James, Jr., grew up, then, in a family with a loving but broken father and a mother whose power was, if benevolent, also definitive and threatening. Like all the James children, he lacked support for his developing self.[14]

Joseph Conrad's father was a hero—but a shattered hero. If Henry James
lacked in his relationships to his mother and father the basis for a stable
self, look at Conrad! When Conrad was four, his aristocratic father, who
tried to organize an insurrectionary committee in Warsaw, was arrested as
an agitator and, with his wife, was sentenced to penal exile. During his
early years, Conrad was separated from his mother, especially, of course,
after his parents were arrested. Then, together in exile, they lived on
dreams, lived in misery, facing cold, hunger, and disease; Conrad, always
sickly, came near to dying, and both mother and father developed the
tuberculosis that killed them.

Conrad grew up with no friends, no one his own age to play with.
While his mother was dying and even more after she was dead, he lived in
the shadow of the gloom of his father, Apollo, who alternated between
energy and idealistic fervor on the one hand and lethargy and utter
despondency on the other. "I shield him," Apollo writes, "from the atmosphere of this place, and he grows up as though in a monastic cell" (Karl,
Conrad, p. 69). Like Woolf's father, Leslie Stephen, but with far more
reason, Apollo bewept himself as a tragic victim; he modeled for his son a
despairing idealism.

Conrad's mother, Ewa, was not, as far as we know, a controlling figure;
but, especially after her death, she was the radiant spiritual center of the
family. From adolescence, she was emotionally unstable—and emotionally unavailable for much of Conrad's early years; then she was mourned,
like Virginia Stephen's mother, Julia, as the sacred image of loving perfection. Apollo, guilty for having led her to her death, made her a saint, and
Ewa's brother Tadeusz, who took over Conrad's upbringing after Apollo's
death, kept alive her sacredness. Conrad, then, grew up seeing through the
eyes of a romantic, an idealist for whom the world was a theater of defeat
and heartbreak. At the same time, he must have been secretly enraged at
this gloomy, life-denying quixotic father who killed his mother. His first
novel, *Almayer's Folly*, which haunted him, which, half finished, he carried with him from place to place for years, is largely a portrait of a self-
deluding dreamer. Throughout his work Conrad was troubled and fascinated by the destructive idealist. As late as *Victory* (1915) we can see his
anger in the portrait of Heyst's philosopher-father. It was an anger exacerbated after Conrad's father's death by the criticism of his uncle, Tadeusz

Bobrowski, his mother's brother, who blamed Apollo and idealism for his sister's death. Conrad grew up needing a father's support and missing his mother; he was hungry to regress to a world in which he could be *held*, nurtured. Hungry for nurturance, yet he knew from both his tragic father and his realistic uncle that this world nurtured no one.

Ford fits my family model least obviously. His father, while he seems to have been disappointed, was not the failure that, for example, Edward Fitzgerald was; though not well off, Francis Hueffer was no bankrupt like Joyce. He was reclusive and, according to W. M. Rossetti, had "a certain tinge of hypochondria in his outlook on life."[15] But he was an influential music critic, who wrote about Provençal music and helped introduce Wagner into England. And yet as much as any of the other modernist writers, Ford lacked a father to support his development of a self. Ford barely knew his father. Essentially, he was not fathered except to be criticized. He felt his father's contempt and indifference, but not, like Kafka, his father's wrathful judgment. As an adult he remembered again and again his father speaking of him as "the patient but extremely stupid donkey" (*Memories and Impressions*, p. 46).

Ford Hermann Hueffer became Ford Madox Ford partly as a substitution of fathers; he was giving up his German father (Franz Hüffer, who had anglicized his name to Francis Hueffer) for his English grandfather, Ford Madox Brown. Brown, an important artist, had lost his beloved son Oliver when Fordie was an infant; and so, especially after Francis Hueffer's death when Fordie was sixteen, he became a substitute son to his grandfather. His iconoclastic, passionate, irascible, generous grandfather was the first of a number of substitute fathers for Ford. Conrad, sixteen years older, was another; Arthur Marwood, the perfect aristocratic Englishman, was a third.

Ford's mother also differs from my model. Very little has been written about her. I have no evidence that she was the controlling center that Mary James was. Ford and his mother, like most of these writers with their mothers, remained close. We know she was, even when Ford was difficult, always supportive, always self-sacrificing. The other mothers in this study favored their novelist sons over their other children; Ford's mother favored his brother. Ford, then, was not the oedipal victor that Faulkner and Lawrence were. Like all the other writers, however, he is a child growing up with a fragmented, unsupported sense of self.

During D. H. Lawrence's childhood, his father was mythologized as a crude, raging, drunken bully, his mother as a sensitive, artistic, loving nourisher. Later, the mythology was rewritten: Lawrence began to see his mother as controlling and life-denying and his father as essentially life-affirming, a man destroyed by his wife. But in both versions, it is Lydia Lawrence who is the powerful center of the family; Arthur Lawrence is very much on the periphery, glowering at his defeat. D. H. Lawrence was, especially after the death of his older brother, William Ernest, oedipal victor—but a victor in danger of being engulfed and destroyed by his prize. As in the case of Faulkner, it was the artist's *mother* who supported the development of his artistic self; alienated from his father, Lawrence developed a strong cross-identification with his mother. Yet, at the same time, he felt murderous hatred for her. As Peter Blos (following Mahler) shows, it is important for a child to make a bond with a father to help him "resist regressive pull to a reengulfing, symbiotic mother" (p. 19). Dorothy Dinnerstein argues, in *The Mermaid and the Minotaur,* that "*the essential fact about parental authority, the fact that makes both sexes accept it as a model for the ruling of the world, is that it is . . . a sanctuary from maternal authority*" (p. 176). The accusations of Lawrence against his mother are read most usefully as a rage against his own longings to be regressively engulfed by his mother. A sensitive, physically small and weak child, Lawrence was considered effeminate by some. Lacking a father he could identify with, and impinged on by a powerful mother, he had to struggle to make a man of himself.

It became necessary during the 1960s, 1970s and early 1980s to emphasize the impact of the pre-oedipal mother, neglected, perhaps feared, by Freud. In turn, relationship with the pre-oedipal mother came to be seen not just as the fundamental one which it is but as the only significant relationship for the development of a child. That imbalance seems to be righting itself. Certainly, the anxiety and instability in the lives of the novelists of this study are related to the failure of fathers. Anna Freud once wrote, "The infant's emotional relationship to its father begins later in life than that of its mother, but certainly from the second year onward it is an integral part of its emotional life and a necessary ingredient in the complex forces which work towards the formation of its character and its personality." She went so far as to say that while a child will accept mother substitutes, "there is . . . no father substitute who can fill the place which is left empty by the child's own father."[16]

Peter Blos gives the clearest account I know of the importance of a father for a growing child. He speaks of the need for the father's blessing, citing the story of Jacob and the angel. Blos is interested not so much in the triadic, oedipal-stage father as in the dyadic bond between child (specifically, the son) and father. He emphasizes the importance of attachment to the father at a time before experience of the father is instinctively conflicted (p. 16). At first, Blos says, "the little boy in his effort to distance himself from the symbiotic mother turns to the father, replicating initially a dependency and closeness which he tries to transcend by the change of object" (p. 13). But beyond this flight from engulfment by a change of objects, the father provides the son with a figure to idealize, an ego ideal to serve as the basis for the child's identity (p. 38). Blos believes that gender identity, too, is fostered by the father's presence as well as by the mother's love of and affirmation of her husband's maleness (p. 16).

It is the absence of fathers whom the child can use as refuge from engulfment, as ego ideal, as shaper of sexual and personal identity, that we see in these novelists.

Nearly all the fathers were weak or broken. Nearly every one of them— James, Conrad, Hueffer (from an aristocratic family), Forster, Joyce, Stephen, Fitzgerald, Hemingway, Faulkner—is resonant with lost family power or glory. They are felt and feel themselves to be professional failures, financial failures. Often they are alcoholics or heavy drinkers: Joyce, Lawrence, Faulkner, Hemingway. Most are cowed by their powerful wives, to whom they surrender power in the family, retreating into a world of male camaraderie or isolation.

In the the fiction, too, fathers are failures. In *Beyond Egotism*, Robert Kiely writes:

> What distinguishes the family mythology of the early twentieth century from that of the high Victorian period is that the arbitrary character of paternal rule remains, but not the power. Different as Simon Dedalus, Walter Morel, and Mr. Ramsey may be from one another, their authority is a hollow structure, a mechanical pretense of solemn purpose propped up with boasting and bullying that imperfectly conceal a pathetic dependence. Apparently, the repeated religious, political, and social challenges of the nineteenth century had left the patriarchal figure, rather like that of Edward VII or George V, rulers without substance. (P. 50)

The weakness and failure of these men had models in the lives of these writers. Joyce saw his father as failure and as talker; in Stephen's words, he was "a good fellow, something in a distillery, a taxgatherer, a bankrupt and at present a praiser of his own past" (*Portrait*, p. 241). Stanislaus, James's closest brother, writes bitterly about his father:

> He had failed in all the careers that had seemed open so promisingly before him—as a doctor, as an actor, as a singer, as a commercial secretary, and lastly as a political secretary. He belonged to that class of men regarding whom it is impossible to postulate any social system of which they could be active members. They are saboteurs of life though they have the name of *viveurs*. (*My Brother's Keeper*, p. 29)

Joyce was closer to his father than was Stanislaus; closer, too, than was his autobiographical hero Stephen to Simon Dedalus. But like Stephen, he expended a great deal of his imagination on separating himself from his father, on refathering himself. Joyce's mother was not, like Lawrence's, self-righteous, possessive, powerful, controlling. She was not, like Woolf's or Forster's, withdrawn, emotionally depriving. She was simply the stable center, the moral center of the household, the model for Woman, for Nora Joyce, for Molly, for Ireland, for the life force, in Joyce's work. According to Stanislaus, she was terrified of her husband, cowed by him, but she was in no other way weak. She was the center Joyce had to feed from and, in guilt and self-assertion, to flee.

Virginia Woolf is the only woman I am considering in this discussion of British and American modernist novelists. I would expect to find effects from early childhood different from those experienced by male writers. I am surprised to find that her psychic patterns—her longings, her anxieties, her defenses—have as much in common with male writers as they do. She has so much in common with the men! She is surprisingly close to D. H. Lawrence in her desire for merger with her mother and her need to escape the insensitivity of her father; close, too, in her fear of engulfment. The power of the imagos of mother and father seem to override questions of gender.

Julia Stephen was "central":

> of course she was central. I suspect the word "central" gets closest to the general feeling I had of living so completely in her atmosphere that one never gets far enough away from her to see her as a person. . . . She was the whole thing. (*Moments of Being*, p. 83)

She was central, she was commanding, and yet she was distant, emotionally absent. She was more loving to and supportive of the boys in the family, but she was also often remote, sacrificing herself to her husband and to the poor, but not available to her children. DeSalvo points out how little she was able to protect her daughter from the sexual assaults of Gerald and how little strength she had left over after meeting the demands of Leslie Stephen. The Kohutians Ernest and Ina Wolf see her as narcissistically injured, needy, unable to offer nurturance.[17] Perhaps; or perhaps she was simply used up. In either case, she shaped in Virginia an unusual hunger for a mother but left the hunger more than usually unappeased. And then she died. And Viriginia Stephen was forced to bury her own ambivalence and, under pain of terrible guilt, distort her mother into an image of sacred perfection. Julia Stephen died leaving Virginia to the sexual demands of George as well as Gerald and to the emotional demands of her father. And yet, Virginia remembered her with deep love, "beautiful, emphatic, with her familiar phrase and her laugh . . . lighting our random lives as with a burning torch, infinitely noble and delightful to her children."[18]

Louise DeSalvo unfairly distorts Leslie Stephen into a Victorian monster, forcing sexual demands on his stepdaughter Stella, tyrannizing Virginia and Vanessa. There is no evidence at all—merely surmise at the service of a tortured interpretation—that Leslie Stephen was sexually active with Stella.[19] But that he was a tyrant is clear. He ordered, raged, demanded attention and service. And yet, he was a pitiful, impotent tyrant, making demands not on the basis of his strength but on the basis of his pathetic state as widower, on the basis of his need, his loneliness, his frailty. Moreover, he was not *only* a tyrant. He supported Virginia's interest in writing, her hunger for reading; he gave her access to his library and to his conversation. If Edith Wharton was a writer with a strong cross-identification with her father, so, too, was Woolf, though with greater ambivalence. Part of Woolf's problem, then, like that of Faulkner, James, and most of the other writers I am considering, is the intense presence of a central but emotionally distant mother and the lack of a father who can give her solid ground beneath her feet.

In "The Faithless Mother," Peter Hultberg emphasizes the abandonment and betrayal by mother figures in the work of E. M. Forster. Using Kohutian language, Hultberg writes, "Forster suffered deprivation in both areas of the bipolar self, in the area of the grandiose self because of inadequate mirroring on the part of the mother, and in the area of the idealized selfobject because of the lack of a father . . . whom he could idealize unconditionally" (p. 236–37). In ordinary language, while Forster was loved, he was not given simple empathic tenderness by his mother, who used him to fill her own needs, and he had no father to look up to, to support him and help him shape himself. While Hultberg unfairly carica-tures Mrs. Wilcox and Mrs. Moore as narcissistically deprived women who betray and abandon others, he is essentially right: Forster grew up with a mother and a great-aunt who, calling him "The Important One," demanded (as did Lawrence's mother) that the boy be *their* importance. His mother, herself abandoned, was emotionally withdrawn. She gave affection, but only in exchange for perfection. Like Lawrence's mother, she was possessive but cool and brisk (Furbank, p. 22). During Forster's first year, his father was dying and his mother was absorbed in nursing and worrying about Edward; after Edward's death, Forster's mother left him on and off for a year and a half to search, purportedly, for a place to live. Each time, on her return, he would run to her, according to his great aunt Monie, "in a sort of ecstacy as tho' they had been separated for years . . . half stifling her with kisses as she carried him off" (p. 14). Forster was the child of a depressed, absent mother. He had to work hard to bring about the gleam in her eyes (Hultberg, pp. 236–37). Unlike Hemingway's mother, she stayed close to her son throughout her long life; like Heming-way's mother, she was cool, possessive, and yet, at the same time, engulf-ing. Forster was unable to separate from either his possessive mother or his doting great-aunt.

Like Faulkner, like Lawrence, an "unmanly" boy—physically small and unathletic like them—Forster was teased brutally by other boys; he retreated to his mother, who swathed him in coats and mufflers. Unlike Faulkner and Lawrence, he had no male alternative in a world of imping-ing women. His biographer, P. N. Furbank, says that very early Forster began a "love-affair" with his mother (p. 21). It made him happy and sensitized him but cut him off from other children (except boys like the gardener's child, working-class boys, whom he grew to love). After Fors-ter graduated from Cambridge, it was his mother with whom he traveled to Italy. Think of Joyce, who rebelled, refathered himself, fled to Paris and later, unmarried to her, with Nora to Italy. Think of Faulkner, who joined the RAF and returned to Oxford, Mississippi, as a self-imagined hero. Forster never openly rebelled; when he wasn't out of England, he lived with his mother,[20] while slowly he brewed a rich *inner* life, an imaginative life that rebelled against convention, that emphasized eros, feelings, im-pulse, and the world beyond our knowledge and control.

Where Angels Fear to Tread, Forster's first novel, expresses clear analogies to his own childhood situation.[21] A young woman of inferior family has married into a "good" family; after her husband dies, rather than be ruled by his family, she travels, leaving her child, who is brought up by her dead husband's mother, Mrs. Harriton. Unlike Forster's own mother, the young woman is stupid; she marries again, an Italian she scarcely knows. Dying in childbirth, she leaves a little boy, and it is this child that interests me. Mrs. Harriton, sure that the baby's father is a scoundrel, sends a brother and a sister to reclaim the child. The brother, Philip, acknowledges his failure and grows close to the baby's father, an earthy, passionate, honest man. The sister, representative of Mrs. Harriton in England, steals the baby—and inadvertently kills him. The baby dies in the mud after a carriage overturns. But symbolically he has already been smothered. Even before the accident, the baby lies held by the half-crazy sister in a frozen, unnatural position, crying noiselessly. Earlier in the novel, the baby's healthy crying is commented on by his Italian father. This silent crying is an image of British repressiveness, a smothering of expressivity and natural life. It is the mother-surrogate who does the smothering. When the baby dies, his father, who loves him, hurts Philip terribly, but Philip ends by loving the Italian.

It is as if Forster is generating a solution for his own smothering—to turn to a bond (however injuring) with the lower-class, passionate, unrepressed male. Indeed, in his early fabulist tale of departing bourgeois competitive life for "The Other Side of the Hedge," the narrator finds paradise in companionship with working people. The inhabitants of this paradise wear workingmen's caps. At the end he takes a can of beer from a man with a scythe. The man is his lost brother. It is as if Forster is imagining being fed, being nurtured, by a male, a male of the working class.

In novel after novel, Forster imagines a tender brotherhood with a passionate, often crude male beneath himself in class. In *The Longest Journey,* it is a literal (illegitimate) brother, Stephen, whom the protagonist Rickie needs to learn to love and join with if he is to be "saved." In *A Room with a View* and *Howards End,* it is a young woman who needs to cross class lines to meet the Other; in *A Passage to India,* the other is a doctor but an *Indian*—again, in imperial India, beneath Fielding in class. In each novel, the passionate other is damaged by the upper-class protagonist and, in turn, damages the protagonist. To cross boundaries is dangerous, destructive—but saving.

Of course, in Forster as at times in Lawrence, the fantasy is homoerotic.

Forster and Lawrence both create passionate, dark, working-class males and imagine union with them. But I would argue that the homoeroticism is itself largely a solution to the problem of being engulfed and smothered by a mother who is at the same time emotionally cool and of being deprived of a father with whom the child can identify, a ground for the development of a self.

It was Mollie McQuillan Fitzgerald's family, not Edward's, that was well respected in St. Paul, Minnesota. "In a neighborhood of imposing houses known by their owners' names," Bruccoli writes, "Scott was keenly aware of his father's failure" (p. 24). It was his mother's family's money that sent Scott to school. Centering her ambitions on son instead of on failed husband, like Lydia Lawrence she gave her son a sense of his specialness. But if his aristocratic pretensions derived from the contrast between his mother's sense of him and his father's actual status, they were nourished, too, by his father's images of past family glory. Through his father's stories, Fitzgerald looked back on his Southern ancestors, distantly connected to Francis Scott Key, as charmed, glorious, aristocratic.

This glory intensifed his father's present failure. Scott never forgot the day that Edward Fitzgerald lost his job as a salesman: "That morning he had gone out a comparatively young man, a man full of strength, full of confidence. He came home that evening, an old man, a completely broken man. He had lost his essential drive, his immaculateness of purpose. He was a failure the rest of his days" (p. 22). It is unconvincing, Scott's portrait of Edward Fitzgerald's failure. Scott has turned failure into Failure; he needed to define his father as failure just as—*because*—he needed to define himself as failure. Dick Diver (*Tender Is the Night*) identifies with *his* failure of a father, ending like his father in "poor parishes." Fitzgerald himself saw his father as representative of *fallen glory;* of both—the glory and the fallen state. Like most of these writers, he had to flee his mother's power and his father's weakness and make himself over in his own image.

Hemingway's mother was more controlling than Virginia Woolf's, perhaps even more controlling than T. S. Eliot's. She gave or withheld her love like money in a bank account. Displeased with him, when he had just turned twenty-one, she wrote him a vicious letter: "A mother's love seems to me like a bank," and she warned him that "unless you, my son, Ernest, come . . . into your manhood, there is nothing before you but bankruptcy: *You have overdrawn*" (quoted by Lynn, p. 118).

Could Hemingway have gotten away with the youthful bohemianism that Faulkner practiced—practiced without having to leave his home? Hardly. Grace Hemingway was, of all these mothers, the most controlling, the most impinging. Like Maud Faulkner, disappointed in her husband, she ruled their house and made the decisions. While Faulkner loved his mother and stayed on good terms with her throughout her life, Hemingway hated Grace. John Dos Passos is said to have remarked that Ernest Hemingway was the only man he had ever known who really hated his mother (Lynn, p. 395). Hemingway's fiction bears out this hatred. According to Lynn, it was partly his mother's standards of beauty—elegant, inflated language supporting hypocritically held values—that Hemingway revolted against in his insistence on simplicity of style. Journalism, Twain, Anderson, Stein were the tools he used to create an aesthetic that would free himself from her and from those values.

Hemingway's hatred of his mother protected him. And so, too, did his connection with his father, who was erratic, sometimes violent, whipping him with a razor strop, but, like Lawrence's father, offering his son an alternative masculine identification. He gave him hunting and fishing as well as the possibility of an independent male identity. But, by his acquiescence to his wife, he became a model of cowardice.

To turn himself into another kind of man was for Ernest Hemingway a matter of life and death. In an autobiographical passage in *For Whom the Bell Tolls,* Robert Jordan thinks about his father, who, like Hemingway's, shot himself with his own father's pistol: "He was just a coward and that was the worst luck any man could have. Because if he wasn't a coward he would have stood up to that woman and not let her bully him" (p. 339). Even in his fifties, Hemingway told Charles Scribner he still "hate[d] her guts" for having "forced my father to suicide" (Lynn, p. 560). "Now I Lay Me" was written just after Hemingway received another of his mother's killer letters, this one attacking *The Sun Also Rises:* "a doubtful honor" to have written "one of the filthiest books of the year. . . . Have you ceased to be interested in loyalty, nobility, honor and fineness of life?" (p. 357). In "Now I Lay Me," discussed in Chapter 1, Nick recalls the importance of his father when his father confronts a castrating wife who had burned his Indian arrowheads.

Hatred was a tool for Hemingway. But under the hatred is the pain of a deep lack of nurturance. In a contemplative passage he added to *A Farewell to Arms,* but finally didn't print, Hemingway has Frederic Henry mourn, "But what if you were born loving nothing and the warm milk of your mother's breast was never heaven" (Lynn, p. 389). The anxiety of emptiness, of nada, in Hemingway does not come from a war wound or from a metaphysical condition made evident by war. If Conrad's vision of emptiness is grounded in the bare desolation of life with his shattered father, life without its sacred maternal center, the source for Hemingway, too, is in *family:* in Hemingway's need to flee impingement and moral destruction by his mother, to flee by cutting off emotion, feeling as little as possible, standing on his own, since his father could offer no support.[22] For Hemingway to grow, he had first to make the ground he stood on.

Like Forster, and even more like Lawrence, William Faulkner had to take the place of a husband for his "domineering and dominant" mother, to "live up to her high expectations" (Karl, *Faulkner,* pp. 31, 19). "Essentially a very cold person, somewhat immobilized by a marriage which was desperately unhappy, she tried to turn her eldest son into a surrogate for her attitudes and desires" (p. 213). Murry Falkner was a business failure, a social failure, a dullard. David Mintner notes that on her deathbed, Maud Falkner hoped for a heaven where she wouldn't have to talk to her dead husband (p. 7)! It was Billy she could talk to. "He was his mother's son rather than his father's," Karl writes. "Maud Falkner's intense devotion to her eldest son—and their similarities in size and taste—made it difficult or impossible for Faulkner to separate himself from her" (*Faulkner,* p. 19). An eldest son, believed in and loved by his mother, he grew up with a sense of his own specialness.

Murry, like John Arthur Lawrence, was increasingly pushed out of the family. In return, he showed little sympathy for or understanding of his son, making fun of his looks ("snake-lips") and his interests. But Faulkner was neither locked out of a masculine world nor deprived of male sources of support for his growing self. He hung around his father's livery stable, then around hunting camps, learning to drink and talk with men. His drinking repeats the drinking of his father and grandfather. Not just a way of handling the contradictions of his life, drinking also establishes him as his father's son. Much more fully than Forster, then, he was able to share, though not comfortably, not without role-playing, the life of his community, and to comprehend its partriarchal values.

Life in these families provided the right temperature and moisture for the growth of the culture of modernism. Different as they appear at first, they are actually quite similar and had similar effects. What are the conditions? First, a childhood lacking in nurturance, in empathy, in which the mother impinges on the child or is remote from the child, or both. Indeed, these seem opposites but are not different in source or in effect; in both cases, the mother is not responding to the child itself. She is either forcing the child to respond to her, to answer her needs, or she is emotionally withdrawn; there is in Daniel Stern's terms, a failure of "attunement," in Winnicott's language, there is a failure of "mirroring."[23] The controlled child—Hemingway is a case in point—may be as ignored in its own authentic being as the child whose mother is absent. A mother may lack empathy while still being very concerned with the child's life. Second, a childhood lacking a father who can offer support for the shaping of a strong self, who can serve as ego ideal and offer refuge from the child's anxiety of and wish for engulfment by the mother. When, in the late nineteenth century, those conditions were present, and especially since the surrounding community could not offer compensatory support, the child became that strange creature, the modernist.

I have to describe the creature first in terms of *lack:* it has no center, no sense that it has a coherent self; it is both hungry for nurturance and deeply afraid of being impinged on; it experiences itself as both special and despised. As I shall show in the next section, it feels cut off from family and community, needs to manufacture new sources of value, often, paradoxically, modeled on an invented past; ultimately, it needs to be its own god, to make itself up. Indeed, to defend itself, it invents a split-off, false self and struggles with schizoid tendencies. A troubled creature, it listens deeply to its own brain waves, aware of its own emptiness yet having nowhere to turn outside itself or its inventions. Yet as it learns to get along, its lacks become advantages, ways of knowing that in this strange world work *better* than earlier ways.

If it seemed at first an alien species, children were increasingly becoming this alien and understanding its peculiar language. After World War I, it seemed hard to speak in any other.

CHAPTER THREE

CHAOS

I HAVE BEEN TRYING to call up the ghosts for whom these writers were performing, ghosts who gave them a world in which the self couldn't be real, so that the world itself wasn't real. Certainly, they are *family* ghosts. But the world beyond the family is also part of the story. The world of these modernist novelists was in each case not *home* but—literally or figuratively—exile. It is the twenties we think of as the time of exile—Americans and British in Europe—adult exile. Only Faulkner and Woolf made permanent homes in their own countries. For example, as an adult Lawrence lived in exile, constantly moving from rented house to borrowed house to Italy, to Australia, to the American Southwest and Mexico, to England where he felt more at exile than anywhere else. James lived in London and traveled; Conrad lived in France and then England; Ford lived in Paris and the United States; Forster spent time in India and Egypt; Joyce, who never in a sense left Dublin, lived his life in Italy, Switzerland, France; Fitzgerald lived in Paris and in a catastrophic series of temporary residences in the United States; Hemingway lived in France, Cuba, and everywhere. But adult exile, I would argue, was a repetition of an exile these writers had already lived through as children. This condition of exile seems to me crucial in shaping them as modernists.

Henry James: a hotel child tossed between New York and Albany, Newport and Geneva, London and Paris. Under such conditions, even a stable family would have had a hard time bringing up children with inner stability. And Henry James, Sr., was himself unstable—tortured, insecure, confused. Jean Strouse calls their family "an impromptu laboratory for experiments in child-rearing and moral philosophy" (p. 17). The children couldn't determine what their father *was*, what he *did*. They were pulled out of school after school, ostensibly for pedagogical or financial reasons. What must it have been like to sail the Atlantic for an education only months after having sailed in the opposite direction for the same reason? Years later, Alice James wrote William, "What enrichment of mind and memory can children have without continuity & if they are torn up by the roots every little while as we were! Of all things don't make the mistake which brought about our rootless and accidental childhood" (p. 43). They grew up with an undirected, bewildering freedom. Edel notes that in his autobiography James omits one episode of moving back and then forth across the Atlantic—in order, Edel feels, to make the family seem less erratic than it actually was. James was a man without a country, a man with too many countries. He was American, but not comfortably American. His aesthetic relation to experience can be seen, partly, as the product of a childhood of perpetual tourism.

Joseph Conrad was in exile even from his real name, Teodor Jósef Konrad Korzeniowski (coat of arms, Nalecz). His name bears such patriotic, literary associations that it would be like calling a child from the South Robert E. Lee Faulkner. To anglicize his name was to confirm his loss of Polish identity, although throughout his life, even when in Britain, he signed his name very differently, depending on the context. Karl writes, "As Conrad he was English; as Korzeniowski, he was a Pole; as Nalecz he was holding on to the memory of his father and his father's family, even as he was indebted to his uncle, a Bobrowski. The division of allegiances boggles the mind."[1] Unlike James, whose roots were laid down thinly in a number of places, Conrad was an exile as rooted in Poland as James Joyce, another exile, was rooted in Ireland. The son of a hero, programmed like his father to patriotic self-sacrifice, Jósef Teodor Konrad Korzeniowski marched at the head of a huge patriotic parade in Warsaw in honor of Apollo, the father who died when the boy was eleven. "Both wandering exiles, we need each other" (Karl, *Conrad,* p. 70), his father had written. Conrad fled this intense connection of father and son, of son and culture. To become loyal to his uncle, Tadeusz Bobrowski, was already to betray his father. Then he left, age seventeen, for Marseilles. Partly he fled because not to flee would have been suicidal: as the son of a political convict, he would have been forced into extended military service. But inevitably, though he denied it, leaving Poland and the Polish language carried the meaning of infidelity and betrayal. He becomes the betrayer Razumov (*Under Western Eyes*), becomes Lord Jim, jumping from the ship and claiming it was something he hadn't willed.

Terror of penal exile, poverty, sickness, the death of both parents, the loss of status: no child could have gone through a more dislocating, insecurity-ridden childhood. Conrad's is not a childhood likely to produce an adult with a stable self. Rather, it is the grounding for inner exile—alienation, paranoia, schizoid distancing. It is no wonder that at twenty-one, Conrad tried to commit suicide—shooting himself through the chest and miraculously missing vital organs!—or that his fiction reveals at least fifteen suicides (Meyer, p. 274) and many, many more acts of self-destruction. It is no wonder that as an adult, married, with children, Conrad recreated the conditions of his own childhood. Frederick Karl quotes a letter to Galsworthy that, speaking of the trials of his ten-year-old son Borys, unconsciously echoes Conrad's own childhood: "He has not a very lively time; he plays the part of the devoted son to me coming in several times a day to see whether he can do anything for me—for I am very crippled and once anchored before the table can not budge very well" (*Conrad,* p. 47). What *is* a wonder is Conrad's power, the way he conquered his childhood by repeating it, reenacting it, in his fiction.

The childhood lives of the other modernists do not, of course, show as severe a dislocation as Conrad's. Ian Watt says that unlike other modernists, Conrad did not choose his exile (p. 32). But in a sense, no one chooses exile. Each of the writers is painfully dislocated almost from the beginning of their lives. Alienation becomes a strategy for dealing with a real condition.

Lawrence is dislocated by class and gender: caught between working class, uneducated father and middle-class mother with pretensions to culture and training as a teacher, he is at home neither in the male world of miners nor in the "female" middle class, which he grows to despise. Joyce is an oldest son in a family that is coming down in the world. They moved again and again because they couldn't pay the rent, and landlords, to get them out, gave them letters enabling them to rent again. Joyce's arrogance is in part the defense of a child from a family on the skids. Exiled from status, from class, they are, as Irish, already separate from the metropolis. "His language," Stephen thinks about an English priest, "so familiar and so foreign, will always be for me an acquired speech" (*Portrait,* p. 189).

As I suggested earlier, the anxiety of Joyce is different from that of other modernists, although he, too, was not of the center and his family patterns resemble those of the other writers. I think the difference lies in the Catholic church. It gave him a grounding for a self, something solid to rebel against. Henry James as a child visited many different churches as if they were theaters, but Joyce had *one* church, which he took seriously even while he struggled against it. And so, although his work expresses modernist defamiliarization and the self must be shaped out of chaos, Joyce is not, like Beckett, a writer of nothingness, emptiness, the void. Death-in-life results from guilt and repression; we see inner turmoil, not nothing. Still, Joyce remains a writer who grows up in exile.

None of these writers are of the center. They are peripheral in place, class, gender. It's strange: none are from either wealthy or very poor families, not even Lawrence; they tend to be shabby-genteel, fallen as a family (except for Woolf). Hemingway is the son of a doctor but not a successful doctor, and it was his mother's income as a singing teacher that provided most of their income. Leslie Stephen was always struggling for money, though the family had resources for travel, the boys' education, and the usual middle-class amenities. Fitzgerald, Ford, Joyce, James lived at the edge of their class; there was some hope of rising and some memory of a position of wealth, power, or status from which the family fell and against which it measured itself.

Forster's father, Edward, was descended from members of the Clapham sect, but Edward died when Forster was one year old; his mother, Lily, from a family much lower in status, was taken up as a girl by a well-to-do woman, Marianne Thornton, the aunt of her future husband, Edward Forster. Lily was essentially adopted. After her marriage and her husband's death—for which she felt subtly blamed—she was in a way poor relations. Morgan, loved by mother and great-aunt, was also poor relations. But at home, at least, he was "the Important One"; at boarding school he was unpopular, much more seriously than Fitzgerald. Homesick, he wrote his mother, "The worst of school is that you have nothing and nobody to love, if only I had somebody" (Furbank, p. 34). Bullied by the boys, whipped and beaten, and sexually abused by an adult stranger, he was removed from school under a cloud of shame and confusion and sent as a day student to Tonbridge School. As a day boy (he moved with his mother to Tonbridge to qualify for the reduced fees for the children of local residents), he was considered socially inferior to the boarders. Here, too, he was bullied. Half a century later, an old schoolfellow remembered Forster: "Forster? The writer? Yes, I remember him. A little cissy. We took it out of him, I can tell you" (p. 42). He cleaved to his mother, who devoted herself to him, refusing offers of marriage. It wasn't until Cambridge that he found good friends. There he lived what Furbank calls an "idyllic, sociable, intelligently-idle undergraduate existence" (p. 69). He had a home—it was the first time he had felt at home anywhere but with his mother. He was invited to become a member of the Apostles in his fourth year; it was through the Apostles that he became connected to the Blooms-bury circle.

At Cambridge, he understood that he was homosexual, though at the time he couldn't act on his feelings. He fell in love with his friend; it ranked in his mind as the second "great discovery" of his youth, along with his "emancipation" from Christianity. More than Faulkner, more than Hemingway, elvish Forster had a place, but it was his own strange place, one he made for himself.

How can it be said that Virginia Stephen's childhood knew anything of exile or dislocation? Of course, as a girl, brilliant, in a male world, she is already cut off from a center. She will never "learn Greek"—never be educated as a man is educated. She is cut off from the intellectual commu-nity and professional possibilities that men can take for granted. But until she is twelve, she cannot be said to be dislocated in the sense that Conrad and Joyce were dislocated. Her father was a respected, well-connected man of letters; until she was twelve, her family was complicated—chil-dren from two marriages, a psychologically damaged half-sister, a sex-ually aggressive half-brother—but intact. And yet the question of the self's coherence comes up again and again in her work. We feel the fragility, even unsubstantiality, and certainly lack of a rooted identity. Indeed, Woolf's fiction assumes, derives from, dislocation: "people feeling the impossibility of reaching the centre which, mystically, evaded them" (*Mrs. Dalloway*, pp. 280–81). In my chapter on Woolf, I will discuss at some length her longing for a center, a center derived from her experience of her mother. The mother whom she finally lost when she was twelve, she had lost psychologically much earlier. And then her breakdown, her helplessness against her brothers' sexual aggression, her loss of Stella, her loss of her father and finally of Thoby; in her teens and early twenties she becomes as dislocated, as terribly disoriented, as any of these writers. I have the sense of a child in terror, naked, exposed, trying to nest herself.

Fitzgerald, Hemingway and Faulkner all seem, at first glance, solidly located in community; Fitzgerald and Hemingway in the Midwest, Faulk-ner in Mississippi. All were comparatively well-off, all came from intact families, if not happy ones. Yet all were dislocated.

F. Scott Fitzgerald, an aristocrat in his imagination, struggled to keep up with the children of the rich. At the Newman School, an Eastern preparatory school, he was an outsider, considered "bossy and boastful . . . a coward and a bully" (Bruccoli, p. 33), when he wanted desperately to be accepted and admired. He was unable to live up to the glorious images of his imagination. It's hard to be in exile from (as he literally imagined) the royal Stuarts! But he was also unable to feel himself firmly rooted like the solid, responsible Nick Carraway, his "family . . . prominent, well-to-do people in this Middle Western city for three generations" (*The Great Gatsby*, p. 2). At school, indeed for all of his life, he hero-worshiped, and, just like Ford Madox Ford, modeled himself on, others. If none of these modernist writers had a firm sense of identity, Fitzgerald at least knew this about himself—and wrote about it in *The Crack-Up*. Even at the height of his success, he felt deeply that he was a poseur, a failure, an unacceptable member of society, never (in Conrad's words) "one of us."

Hemingway expresses in his fiction a prelapsarian time of connectedness to the natural world. It can be recovered, briefly, especially in solitude, but it gets easily spoiled, tainted, especially by women who suck at your talent and destroy your honest relation to the world, or by your own cowardice, or by your vanity. Ultimately, life is defeat and death, and what matters is the grace with which you endure it.

What a seductive, romantic, self-indulgent way of experiencing the world! When I was a young man, it gave me a way to be *serious* about my life. It was useful to me: it made me feel that the way I acted was crucial and that my life was art. But it also let me get away with posturing manliness; it rationalized my defenses. I lived a comfortable despair; I was disillusioned without having to undergo the experiences that would make me disillusioned. There is a great deal of power in disillusionment.

Hemingway's imagining of prelapsarian connectedness implies that one's ordinary relation to experience is one of dislocation. Recent biographies by Kenneth Lynn and Jeffrey Meyers, essays like the brilliant one by Millicent Bell, show that it wasn't the war that wounded Hemingway, that created the dark tones of disaffection and emptiness. His relationship to his mother was also his relationship to Oak Park: cello lessons and falseness. He never wrote a novel about Oak Park—but he threatened to. He is, before the war, like Krebs in "Soldier's Home" after the war. Krebs has to lie to his mother that he loves her and that he is the solid American boy she wants for a son—and he has to lie to townspeople about his war experiences; to keep from losing the experiences, he stops talking. Silence, exile, and cunning became Hemingway's weapons, as they became Faulkner's, as they became Joyce's. Hemingway added to these the posture of emotional deadness, permitting him to stay detached, outside experience, valorizing the psychological defense of keeping his guard up as a defense of integrity, of existential purity. Hemingway stands back, emotionally neutralizing experience.

Hemingway is so unlike E. M. Forster. Forster was an effeminate boy with a skinny body and sloping shoulders; Hemingway, a powerful boy as he was a powerful man, at home in the woods, at home—again, how different from Forster—*away* from his mother, in the world his father *should have* inhabited. But he is far more deeply than Forster in spiritual exile. Forster's world is one of human affections at war with conventions. It is conventions that do the emotional deadening. In Hemingway's work, emotional deadening is a necessary response to trauma, a means of survival in a fallen world, a tool of fresh perception, a guarantor of integrity.

Frederick Karl feels that, in 1925, Frazer's *Golden Bough* may have offered William Faulkner (as indeed it offered Eliot) a way of maintaining distance from his subjects even when they were close to him. But long before, Faulkner experienced himself as outside his community, and he intensified that distance as much as he could. As he grew older, he took on the persona of southern traditionalist, a writer rooted in his home world. But this was just one more persona, like the earlier ones of disaffected symbolist poet, dandy, wounded British aviator. He grew up with a deep familial connection to history and community—and yet as much as Joyce he rebelled against a rigidly defining culture in an attempt to redefine himself. Silence, exile, and cunning. Karl speaks about his "immense silences" (Faulkner, p. 212), about how unreachable he often was. He withdrew into silence just as he hid behind his personae.

Faulkner's situation is in many ways like Conrad's. No penal exile, of course. He grew up in security, grandson of an important man in Oxford. But there is the similar relation to a defeated, aristocratic culture, the same ambivalence toward a romantic, heroic idealism. Both come from families with stories of military glory and defeat. To be a southerner of good family, as to be an aristocratic Pole, was to be outside the center. And both Conrad and Faulkner were *outside that outside* as well, both accused of being traitors to their own people, both "isolatoes" (as Melville puts it) wearing the masks of tradition and the values of community. We might add James Joyce to this list; he is an outsider in a defeated colony, claiming to speak for the very people who see him as betrayer.

Unlike Conrad, Ford Madox Ford was born English, though his father was a German emigré in London. But Ford was never at home anywhere. According to Ford's biographers, Ford was clinically agoraphobic, felt "naked beneath the pitiless stars."[2] During his periods of weakness, he was unable to bear being in the midst of urban crowds or alone in the country. Only the sea assuaged him, but at times he needed support simply to board a ship. Agoraphobia is a kind of bodily metaphor expressing Ford's relation to the world; the world for Ford was anything but a holding environment.[3] He experienced himself as abandoned, the world as threatening his obliteration and as terrifyingly empty.[4]

As a very young man, he eloped with Elsie Martindale after considering for a time a suicide pact with her; for a while he lived with her the exile of a kind of bohemian farmer in the country. He lived much of his life in France; then, in the thirties, he moved to the United States and became an American citizen. But wherever he lived, he felt himself in exile. Throughout his life he had breakdowns and had to spend time recuperating at European spas; the worst was a severe psychotic break that occurred after he was traumatized in battle early in World War I.

In a sense, then, he was as much of an exile as his friend Conrad, and, as much as Conrad, was forced to reinvent himself. He grew up in a Pre-Raphaelite environment that was itself an enclave within and against bourgeois society. There were artists—and then there was everyone else. "To speak to anyone who made money by commercial pursuits," Ford hyperbolized, "was almost not to speak to a man at all. It was as if one were communicating with one of the lower animals endowed with the power of speech."[5] That becomes an even more shocking statement when you learn that Ford was under intense pressure to be an artistic genius—but he never felt good enough. As little children, his cousins, the Rossettis, wrote and performed in Greek. Ford felt he couldn't compete. He felt himself to be what his father called him, a donkey. A *donkey*, making him "one of the lower animals." And yet he had to become an artist. His beloved, fierce grandfather, the painter Ford Madox Brown, demanded it. After his father's death, when Ford was sixteen, he and his mother lived with Brown. His grandfather was good to him, but insistent. "God damn and blast my soul! . . . I will turn you straight out of my house if you go in for any kind of commercial life" (Mizener, p. 8). Ford was not at home in the world. As I shall show in my next chapter, he had to invent someone for whom the world was not exile, but home.

Each of these writers, then, lacked not only a relationship with parents that could support the development of the self; each also lacked grounding in a community. How could the self be stable? And in the absence of a stable self, how could the world be seen as coherent, meaningfully connected to the self? The self and the world are expressive of chaos, of a disorientation that is at the basis of the anxiety I have spoken of as modernist anxiety. It is out of this anxiety that they speak. It is not, as Terry Eagleton would have it, that the center had grown weak and that groups outside the center took its place;[6] rather, the experience of being outside gave these writers the vision to see the modern world, a vision that more and more people needed, especially after the Great War.

PART THREE

LIVING WITH CHAOS

IN MY LAST SECTION I explored ways that the "unthinkable anxiety" of ultimate disorientation—emotional and cognitive chaos—germinated and was cultured in modernist writers by their families and by their relation to society. I see this cultural dis-ease as the primary pain to which modernist writers responded in shaping their fiction. Now, I want to explore the pain. It intensified, made agonizing, three needs that all human beings share to some degree: (1) a need for shaping an identity; (2) a need for merger and a complementary fear of merger; (3) a need for an order in which the self can feel contained, held.

These are all really forms of a single need, a need for wholeness-in-relationship, for feeling whole and connected to the world. In response to a world which is not a holding environment but a terrifying void reflecting a nonself, the need for wholeness-in-relationship must become a terrible hunger, distorting a person's being-in-the-world. The self experiences itself as weak, isolated, fragmented, needy—in danger of being engulfed and yet longing to be engulfed.

Sometimes students will ask, "Why read the work of such tortured writers?" My answer is that their pain has become the pain of many in western societies and that they were peculiarly sensitive to the condition and struggled to cope with it. We see, passionately and beautifully revealed, the struggle to live in what we recognize as our own world. Indeed, as I shall show in Chapter 7, the pathological states described by modernist writers are analogues for the defamiliarized world in which people increasingly found themselves in the past hundred years.

But, along with the beauty and wisdom, I have to acknowledge the intensity of encoded pain and confusion. James, Conrad, Ford, Forster, Joyce, Woolf, Lawrence, Fitzgerald, Hemingway, Faulkner: all of them, growing up in conditions of instability, developed unstable selves. Depression, hypochondria, suicide, psychotic breaks. Lawrence expressed his instability in his wandering and especially in his rage. His rage and megalomania kept him in control of the chaos he otherwise would have faced. Woolf expressed her instability in her withdrawal and, of course, in her psychotic episodes. They all suffered breakdowns, in some cases repeatedly; Joyce and all three Americans were alcoholics; all endured confusion of identity and gender.

My own life and the lives of most of my friends show signs of instability—anxiety, depression, divorces, and on and on. If the lives of modernist writers were even more unstable than the lives of most of us, they expressed a growing instability in western society; they were pioneers in experiencing, expressing, and coping with chaos.

Look, just for instance, at the fluidity and confusion of sex roles.

Henry James retreated from a masculine identity, retreated into a vague crippling that he believed kept him from marriage, and into an asexual life. Late in his life, his homoerotic feelings began to surface; shaving off his beard, he opened himself to tender and passionate relationships, most likely never physically consummated, with Hendrik Andersen and other men.[1] E. M. Forster, of course, was actively homosexual. His sexual identification was probably less confused than that of the other writers, but we can see from his closet novel, *Maurice,* as well as from his relationships, what self-torture he went through as a young man. Virginia Woolf was married to Leonard, who loved her physically, but, as she told him before their marriage, she could not respond in kind (*Letters,* 1:496–97); she was in love with a series of women, her relationship with Vita Sackville-West the longest-lasting and most intense. The most explicitly erotic passage in Woolf's writing describes Clarissa Dalloway's sensuous apprehension of Sally Seton. Woolf's assertion of the androgynous nature of the artist, while it seems true to me, also seems to express her discomfort with clearly distinguished gender roles.

D. H. Lawrence, mythologizer of heterosexual love, had violently ambivalent attitudes toward homosexual love—at times believing the bond between men to be necessary, when he was under the influence of Edward Carpenter,[2] and then loathing it as beetlelike, corrupt.[3] He had, if any, only one physical homosexual relationship, with a Cornish farmer, William Henry Hocking.[4] But many critics have explored the homoerotic impulses that pervade much of Lawrence's writing.[5] The rejected prologue to *Women in Love* and Lawrence's absorption in describing the male body express *clearly* his *unclear* homoerotic feelings.

F. Scott Fitzgerald was disturbed by rumors that he was homosexual, and Zelda seems to have accused him of being homosexual (Bruccoli, p. 278). His fiction, too, especially *Tender Is the Night*, with its seemingly arbitrary obsession with homosexuals, indicates anxiety about homosexuality and its connection with incoherence in the self. *A Moveable Feast* tells of Fitzgerald asking for Hemingway's confirmation of his masculinity, showing him his penis, which Zelda had told him was too small to make a woman happy. Most likely, the story is (as Kenneth Lynn thinks) Hemingway's vindictive, self-congratulating invention, but it resonates with Fitzgerald's actual unease about his own sexuality and expresses as well Hemingway's own unease—Hemingway, who needed to be Papa, whose supermasculinity was seen as denial, as cover-up, even in his lifetime. It is, of course, only a joke to say that Hemingway and Fitzgerald were crossdressers: Fitzgerald, it's true, played the chorus girl in the show he wrote at Princeton, but Hemingway was, after all, only a small child when he was dressed as a girl. Still, it's not only a joke. Grace Hemingway kept her son in curls and pinafores to match Marcelline, part of an "elaborate pretence that little Ernest and his sister were twins of the same sex" (Lynn, p. 40). Lynn believes that both from his mother's obsession with twinship and from her own homosexuality come Hemingway's obsession with women who look boyish, mannish, and his persistent assertion of supermasculinity.

Frederick Karl points to the need of American writers—Hemingway, Fitzgerald, Faulkner—to insist on their masculinity. He speaks of "the need to present a masculine facade, undercut by compulsive drinking which made sexual performance weak or impossible" (*Faulkner*, p. 871). Of course, the drinking and the unease with gender role form part of the larger pattern of instability—the breakdowns, the alcoholism, the anxiety: inner chaos.

CHAPTER FOUR

THE IMPOSTOR

I T IS THIS LARGER pattern of instability that impels the first of the three needs I want to discuss: the need for identity. When Erik Erikson speaks about *identity,* he means different things in different contexts; I am using the term simply to indicate a continuous, coherent sense of self.[1] And that is what is at stake. For all these writers, identity is fluid, and the fluidity is both exciting and terrifying. The result is a need *to make oneself up.* Most of these writers are chameleon figures; they hide behind false selves; they are almost clinically *impostors.*

Most of these writers needed to invent themselves. An understanding that the self and reality both need to be invented is obviously crucial to modernist perception. This understanding, while attuned to the insights of Bergson, Nietzsche, and William James, emerges from the struggles of modernist writers to become whole, to feel the world as real. If we all shape ourselves into invented characters, the modernist writers do so obsessively as a way of combating (and at the same time expressing) chaos.

To an extent, of course, my own examining lens, itself a modernist lens, distorts my results. The biographers on whose work I am dependent are themselves particularly sensitive to self-fictionalization. The modernist insight that we invent ourselves as if we were creating fictional characters has become a common assumption. The figures in Genet's brothel in *The Balcony* or those in the portrait gallery that Sartre's Roquentin visits in *Nausea* have turned themselves into fixed ideas, fictional characters. Self-fictionalization is at the basis of Fowles's *The French Lieutenant's Woman:* "We are all novelists. . . . That is, we have a habit of writing fictional futures for ourselves." All our worlds are fictions and we ourselves are fictionalizations; we are *counterfeiters.* As Madame Irma tells us at the end of Genet's *The Balcony,* "You must now go home, where everything—you can be quite sure—will be even falser than here."

Similarly, psychoanalytic thinking has moved from a premodernist understanding of the past as something given, an archaeological substratum the analyst and analysand have to dig to uncover, to a modernist understanding of the past as alternative narratives, some richer, fuller, than others but none absolute. The past is not only *found* in the present, not only *repeated* in the present; it *exists* in the present. Narratives that can be *rewritten:* Roy Schafer, for example, sees analysands imprisoned in their own narratives.[2] As I have indicated in my first chapter, some analysts speak of "false" selves, implying that an authentic self exists. But then they describe this authentic self so fluidly—the experience of being in contact with one's own impulses—as not to be pinning down a fixed self at all. And their emphasis is not on the true self but on false selves, presentation selves. Inevitably, then, biographers like Bruccoli, writing on Fitzgerald, or Lynn on Hemingway, assume, as I do, self-fictionalization. And yet, even when I try to take into account my own tendency to see self-invention, I am amazed by the degree to which modernist writers have made themselves up—and have concentrated in their work on self-invention.

Clinical descriptions of the impostor and discussions of the relationship between the impostor and the artist have seemed fruitful to me. The descriptions shock me, so close are they to the self-inventions of modern novelists. And the etiology of the pattern of imposture surprises me still more; it is precisely the family patterns of the novelists of high modernism.

The one writer who was clearly not an impostor, though more than any other, she experienced the fluidity of self, was Virginia Woolf. And this agrees with my chief guides in this area, Phyllis Greenacre and Louise Kaplan,[3] who say that generally the impostor is male. As I scan the lives of the writers in this study, I find that all the male writers except for E. M. Forster are, if not extreme examples of the impostor, men with a strong tendency toward imposture.

"The artist," says Greenacre, "is at least two people, the personal self and the . . . creative self. These two selves are sometimes nearly as separate as they are in the impostor—the division not infrequently recognized in the use of different names" (p. 533). Kaplan, too, makes the comparison, noting mimicry, of course, but also "tensions between the real, ordinary self and the magical conjuring self, a fascination with dissembling" (p. 308). *Not* that artist and impostor are the same. Kaplan, more than Greenacre, differentiates the artist and the impostor, claiming that the artist is turned toward the world and "regards his marvelous simulations as a gift of love to the world" (p. 308), while the impostor's sense of reality is defective, and he has no love to offer anyone. Greenacre, too, in her chapter "The Childhood of the Artist," speaks of "the love affair with world which appears to be an obligatory condition in the development of great talent or genius" (p. 490).

But while they are not the same, analysis of the impostor can give us fresh, valuable ways of seeing the artist, especially, I would argue, the modernist artist. Greenacre and Kaplan both speak of artist and impostor as if they were ahistorical characters. And perhaps there must always be, in any writer of fiction, the quality of a chameleon. But the modernist writers in this study are, as we shall see, particularly close to the classical impostor.

The impostor is the fabricated individual who, talented enough to be successful through ordinary channels, finds himself driven again and again to create a fictional identity. He changes name and personal history, becoming a con man, a Titus Oates, a James Macpherson. Unlike the artist who creates the work of art, the impostor makes himself into his own work of art (Greenacre, p. 533).

The impostor, like the modernist novelist, suffers from a weak, fragmented self. Greenacre writes, "The well-developed career impostor appears to suffer from an incomplete development of the ego, involving grave defects in the ability to form object relationships, along with special disturbances in the sense of identity and reality." Like the novelists in this study but more intensely, impostors have sexual problems "and when they're potent, it's not serving libidinal but narcissistic aims" (p. 106).

Both Greenacre and Kaplan see the impostor as locked into the family romance. Like many children, impostors fantasize that they are foundlings, their true parents glorious; they are aristocrats in a mundane world. Most children give up the fantasy, but the impostor becomes absorbed in it and must live it out.

> The more typical family-romance scenarios are reflected in the Frog Prince, Dick Whittington, Snow White, Cinderella myths, in which a child has been temporarily reduced to a lowly and demeaned status, but . . . is at last rescued and restored to his or her legitimate status.
>
> Every imposture is an enactment of a Jack and the Beanstalk legend, the redemption aspect of the family romance. The impostor must impose his false personality and achievements on others again and again in order to maintain

the illusion that he is not small and insignificant, that he is worthy of his mother's admiration, that, moreover, he is entitled to trick the father, overthrow him and rob him of his powers. (Kaplan, pp. 295, 298)

Greenacre writes, "After reading a great many accounts of artists, I was struck with the prominence of the family romance in their lives" (p. 506). One explanation: "When a child feels different, the family romance furnishes a further rationalization for this sense of difference" (p. 529).

The model of the artist who can't let go of the family romance is Fitzgerald. An oedipal victor, a secret prince, Fitzgerald suspected as a child that he was actually a royal foundling, "imagined that he had been placed on the Fitzgerald doorstep wrapped in a blanket with the Stuart coat of arms" (Bruccoli, p. 20). As an adolescent, as an adult, Fitzgerald made himself into the gorgeous figure of his early fantasies. But always, feeling its falsity, he lived in anticipation of disaster. How long could he keep up the pretense? As I shall show, the other writers, too, played out some version of Jack climbing the beanstalk for his mother, turning himself into the hero of both their dreams.

Both Greenacre and Kaplan see a common etiology in artist and impostor. They emphasize the dynamics of the family, dynamics that are the same as those we have seen in Chapter 2, "Family Ghosts." Greenacre writes of the impostor:

> From birth, the mother had regarded the infant with extreme possessive and ambivalent concern and constant watchfulness. Whether this appeared as marked anxiety and guilt, or as great pride, seems less important than the fact that the attachment was extreme. . . . The parents were at odds, the mother frequently despising, reproaching, or attacking the father who either remained detached from the child or removed himself by death or desertion.
>
>   The intense maternal attachment to which the future impostor is subject . . . undermines his sense of a separate self and the development of his own identity. By placing the child in a position of definite superiority to the father . . . there is set a potentially serious imbalance of the oedipal relationship, the child being able to assume an uncontested supersedence over his father. This inevitable intensification of infantile narcissism favors a reliance on omnipotent fantasy in other aspects of self-evaluation to the exclusion of reality testing. (Pp. 101–2)

Similarly, Kaplan, speaking of the typical pattern in the development of an impostor, describes a "doting mother whose seductive possessive love of this marvelous, well-endowed infant impairs his ability to establish a firm sense of separateness from her. He remains not so much an extension of his mother but rather a mirroring reflection of her exalted ideal of masculinity. Contributing to the boy's difficulty in separating from the mother is an absentee or emotionally ineffectual father" (pp. 301–2). In the absence of father, the boy "can construct only a patchy image of some masculine self; without a father in his life to identify with, he must base his entire gender identity on a masculine ideal conveyed to him by his mother" (pp. 302–3).[4]

I find it necessary to quote at such length in order to emphasize how close is the relationship between the impostor and the novelists of this study. In both Greenacre's and Kaplan's descriptions, all the elements I have been discussing are present: the intensely attached, possessive mother who offers oedipal victory to a son; the father demeaned or removed. As Greenacre explains it, imposture "serves to give a temporary feeling of completion of identity . . . that can be more nearly achieved in this way than in the ordinary life of an individual so impaired from having been psychologically incorporated by his mother" (p. 104).

Ford is perhaps the most extreme case of the artist-impostor, and therefore he is worth examining in detail. Like his friend Conrad, Ford Madox Ford changed his name; in fact, he changed it twice. First, at the beginning of the Great War, Ford Hermann Hueffer needed to get rid of the Germanic "Hermann." Then, in 1918, he became Ford Madox Ford. Arthur Mizener sees this change, too, as practical, a change that allowed him to marry and give his name to Stella Bowen. Years earlier when he left his first wife, Elsie Martindale, for Violet Hunt, Elsie sued to prevent Violet from using the name Hueffer. "He was not going to risk another lawsuit by having Stella called Mrs. Hueffer" (p. 305). Thomas Moser, on the other hand, sees the change in name as a kind of symbolic suicide/renewal at a time of stress: "According to our theory . . . Marwood's determined rejection of Ford and Conrad's apparent withdrawal from him in 1913 so violated Ford's innate sense of blamelessness and so exacerbated his self-loathing that only one choice remained: to expunge Joseph Leopold Ford Hermann Madox Hueffer."[5] But while this reading interests me, I also see the change of names as simply Ford's constant making-himself-up. Denying his father, taking his grandfather's name, he created himself as fully as the fictional Jay Gatz turned himself into Gatsby—but Ford became many Gatsbys. H. G. Wells speaks of his "assumed personas and dramatized selves."[6]

Ford's sense of incompleteness, his need to find for himself an acceptable identity, was very strong. I am reminded of the case Erik Erikson cites in "The Problem of Ego Identity" of a girl of middle European descent who "secretly kept company with Scottish immigrants, carefully studying and easily assimilating their dialect and their social habits. With the help of history books and travel guides she reconstructed for herself a childhood in a given milieu in an actual township in Scotland." When Erikson asks about the invention, the girl explains: " 'Bless you, sir,' she said in pleading Scottish brogue, 'I needed a past'" (*Identity*, p. 141). Ford's deliberate reinventions of himself are almost that blatant. He said that Conrad had turned to him out of recognition that Ford was the greatest prose stylist in England. Yet at the time, Conrad was forty-one, Ford twenty-five—and barely known as a writer. And, after all, Henry James, whom Conrad admired enormously—and who admired Conrad—lived nearby.

Ford's elitist bohemian values subtly blur into elitist aristocratic values. He postured as the last aristocrat—but what aristocracy was he representing? When he was nineteen, Ford took trips to see his wealthy, aristocratic German relatives and, to court their favor, converted to Catholicism. And yet not just to court their favor—for he never formally disavowed the church, and the persona of aristocratic Catholic was one of the personae in his bag. But he was also a lordly Englishman with a vaguely ancient, aristocratic past, a gentleman who, like his idol Arthur Marwood, attended the best public schools—though in fact, he had merely attended, briefly, a school for the children of professionals in London.

He lied to puff himself up. In his autobiographical writing he acknowledges his distortions. "We wielders of the pen are not only adepts at misrepresentation of our motives; we are also adepts at self-deception."[7] Did Edward VII, when he was Prince of Wales, ever *really* pluck little Fordie out of his seat at a concert and sit there himself? And did his Queen Consort Alexandra then sit him upon her knees?[8] Hardly likely. It sounds like grandiose fantasy, a perfect Fordesque fantasy, of being nursed by a compassionate woman after attention-rejection by a powerful male. Neither are his observations of Lawrence or of Conrad to be trusted. He himself, openly contemptuous of scholars, spoke of being true to "impressions," not facts. It's unfortunate, because the observations are often brilliant when you can separate them from the lies, and because the lying has obscured the *real* importance Ford had for modern literature, as novelist but perhaps even more as editor of two extremely influential reviews—*English Review* and *Transatlantic Review*—and as discoverer of Lawrence and Pound and supporter of Hemingway, Joyce, and Conrad.

Ford was always an outsider. He never felt worthy, even though the other side of his representation of himself is of aristocrat and genius, greatest stylist in the English language, coauthor of some of Conrad's works, brilliant man of letters. Ford was, then, desperately weak, covering weakness in the self by typically opposing means. On the one hand, he asserted authority and greatness; on the other, he required constant reassurance and a need to fuse with idealized others.[9]

The psychoanalyst Masud Khan tells us that idealization is a common schizoid defense. The schizoid character creates a highly elaborate ego ideal, one specifically *not* based on primary parental objects (images of the parents that have been internalized) because these have not been adequate. This invented ego ideal protects the schizoid against "hopelessness, emptiness, and futility" (p. 23). But the protection is, as I have shown, incomplete. Ford lived his life desperately shoring up a false self. Even when he was able to function well, he seems to have lived outside his life—in the past, in romance, in fantasies.

In Ford's *Ladies Whose Bright Eyes*, originally written before World War I, the protagonist, a conventional, vulgar publisher, is knocked on the head and awakens in the thirteenth century.[10] He is forced to play out the identity in which he finds himself—a noble, heroic identity. At first he thinks he will take over the world because of his advanced knowledge; instead, he absorbs the values of that world and returns to a modern world as alien to him as home was to Gulliver. A double dislocation, then, expresses the constant sense Ford must have had of being an outsider, a stranger in a strange land. The blow on the head, the loss of identity, is an analogue of amnesia. How wonderfully strange!—because, years later, when Ford suffered shell shock in the war, he couldn't remember his name for thirty-six hours and for months could remember little else. That his trauma took the form of amnesia seems simply an exaggeration of what he must have always lived with. His response was to shape a fictionalized identity—well bred, Tory, brilliant, achieving victory by choosing not to compete, something like his friend Arthur Marwood, something like Christopher Tietjens, his protagonist in *Parade's End*.

Joseph Conrad writes the day before his wedding, "When once the truth is grasped that one's own personality is only a ridiculous and aimless masquerade of something hopelessly unknown the attainment of serenity is not very far off" (Watt, p. 71). The two parts of this sentence seem hopelessly contradictory, the serenity a vain wish. And indeed, in retrospect, Conrad's belief in the attainment of serenity is terribly ironic. His married life was full of hypochondria and periods of deep depression during which he could often do nothing but lie in bed, his head on Jessie's lap. But the first part of the sentence is true of Conrad's anxieties: personality as a masquerade covering over the unknown, the darkness. I think at once of Kurtz, the hollow man, of the manager, that "papier-mâché Mephistopheles," I think of Decoud's charm and inner emptiness, of the facade of the great DeBarral in *Chance*. I think of Conrad himself, lying about his romantic gunrunning and turning his suicide attempt into a "duel" until even he believed the lie. Bernard Meyer notes Conrad's identification, like Ford's, with heroic figures (p. 31). The character that Conrad, Polish exile, created of himself is, like Ford's persona, the English gentleman, "one of us," the phrase that echoes throughout *Lord Jim*.

The son of a posturing, idealistic father, Conrad rejected posturing and idealism. His vision of art was his vision of seamanship: "obscure and glorious toil." He was a "worker in prose" in the service of the truth of our commonality. But that vision had to combat Conrad's need to shore up a fragmented, incomplete self, and this combat shapes and fuels his fiction.

Jay Gatz turning himself into Gatsby is a common model for the self-fictionalizations of these writers. Frederick Karl, for instance, in *William Faulkner*, writes:

> Beginning with his slight name change, Faulkner fell into a pattern which Fitzgerald would limn with Jay Gatsby. It is a curious piece of Americana. Faulkner follows Gatsby's career, not in its illegalities, but in the desire to remake the past, gain the woman who rejected him . . . even to the renaming. (P. 124)

Like Conrad and Ford, Faulkner changes his name—changes it from the familial Falkner, although he grounds the change in his version of the family past. But even before he changes his name, he creates, like Gatsby, a splendid character who can, perhaps, give him permission to make himself an artist. A poseur, a kind of small-town dandy as a very young man, he returned from the war with a postured limp, a limp for which there was no physical cause. Postured—not like Conrad's hypochondriacal sufferings, for, as far as we know, Faulkner did not even imagine that he was hurt. It went along with the RAF uniform he wore, a uniform he had no right to wear, and the stories of flying escapades that never took place. He became a fraudulent hero, but that role was no more unreal than

his roles of good old boy or disheveled bohemian artist or landed aristocrat.

Fitzgerald himself is the model for his Gatsby. As an adolescent, he
wrote a journal, which he called a "Ledger"—wrote much of it in the *third
person!* Like his character Gatsby, he made lists of what he needed to
accomplish, his successes and failures. "If I couldn't be perfect," he writes
in his *Ledger,* "I wouldn't be anything" (Bruccoli, p. 57). At Princeton,
"observing that a tenor voice seemed to be one of the hallmarks [of a
campus figure], he tried to develop one" (p. 57). As a young man, he wrote
in his *Notebooks,* "When I like men I want to be like them—I want to lose
the outer qualities that give me my individuality and be like them. I don't
want the man. I want to absorb into myself all the qualities that make him
attractive and leave him out" (p. 35).

Fearing to be screen-tested as an actor, Dick Diver (*Tender Is the Night*)
says, "The strongest guard is placed at the gateway to nothing. . . . Maybe
because the condition of emptiness is too shameful to be divulged" (p. 70).
A defensive surface is put up to hide emptiness and so calm anxiety. That
is why in *Tender Is the Night,* as in Ford's *The Good Soldier,* as in so many
novels in the modernist canon, imagery of theater—roles, scenes, acting—
abound. If Fitzgerald gives us a Dick Diver as an actor guarding against
exposure of his own emptiness, a few years later, in *The Crack-Up,* the
series of sad, bitter essays he originally published in *Esquire* in 1936, he
gives us *himself* as actor, playing a number of roles but no longer being a
whole, "real" person. He speaks of "the disintegration of one's own
personality" (p. 76). "So," he says dryly, calmly, "there was not an 'I'
anymore" (p. 79). He has cracked into a hundred shards, none of which
are authentically him. In the second essay in the series, "Handle with
Care," he describes the pieces he has called his *self:* one man had been his
"intellectual conscience," another, his model for "the good life," a third,
his artistic conscience, a fourth, his model for human relationships, a fifth,
his political conscience. "It was strange," he says, "to have no self—to be
like a little boy left alone in a big house, who knew that now he could do
anything he wanted to do, but found that there was nothing he wanted to
do—" (p. 79). Now, he decided, "I must continue to be a writer because
that was my only way of life, but I would cease any attempt to be a
person" (p. 82).

It is Fitzgerald's almost good-humored, ironic acceptance of his condition that seems so unnerving. He accepts his loathing for other people, his
exploitation of other people, his isolation, and even his essential falseness.

(What about right now?—I want to ask. What is your relationship to me, your reader? You're making me uncomfortable.) What Fitzgerald never describes in any depth is the actual experience of his fragmentation. He stands far back from that condition, merely explaining that "in a real dark night of the soul it is always three o'clock in the morning" (p. 75). But the experience itself seems to be already a standing-back, a terrible indifference, an evacuation of feeling from the central ego. As Guntrip describes the process, "the ego of everyday consciousness experiences a progressively terrifying loss of interest, energy, zest, verging towards exhaustion, apathy, derealization of the environment, and depersonalization" (p. 64). Self-invention, then, as a way of handling anxiety, often intensifies the sense of falsity and emptiness that produced the anxiety.

A Portrait of the Artist as a Young Man is like a modernist textbook in the invention of identity. The world as it is offered to Stephen is one of confusion and contradiction. He has to remake the world, to make it his, and by doing so, make himself his. As critics since Dorothy Van Ghent have seen, the structure of the novel is the same from chapter to chapter: Stephen enters chaos; he experiences contradictions in the given world and in himself; he tries to integrate warring elements, especially (religious) obedience and (erotic) rebelliousness, so that the world feels harmonious. By the end of one chapter, he feels he has succeeded: the prostitute is the Virgin Mary or else the Virgin is eroticized; obedience is irradiated with passion and glory, or else rebellion is experienced as higher spiritual obedience. But by the succeeding chapter, the integration breaks down. The world and the self need to be reinvented; we experience the reinvention through the changing style of consciousness. Portrait of the artist—Everyman as artist-priest, "transmuting the daily bread of experience into the radiant body of everliving life" (Portrait, p. 221). Or, to step outside the mystification of reinvention, it is the portrait of the modernist (male) consciousness, reshaping an identity to protect itself from anxiety.

Joyce, unlike any of the other writers, doesn't express the anxiety of emptiness and the dissolution of the self but rather the anxiety of being flooded with uncontrolled life. In Portrait, Stephen's intense inner world protects him from dangerous encounters. Retreating from the possibility of a kiss, he creates a poem that idealizes the situation. His first sexual encounter with a prostitute becomes a religious rite. He turns people into religious symbols, shapes a world that, taming chaos, reduces his anxiety. He is superior, isolated, as if his real engagement were with the figures of myth or with God. This elite position keeps him safe, but it also dries him out until his language is reduced to the terse ironies of the notebook in section 4 and he is without lover or friend, cut off from even his family. For a failed living father he has substituted an idealized father from myth. Then, in *Ulysses,* he is unable to experience the encounter with a loving, human father-substitute. I would like to agree with Stanley Sultan that Stephen begins to reach out, to open his heart, but I cannot. Part of the sad comedy of the Ithaca section is that Bloom's satisfaction in his talk with Stephen seems unreciprocated. They urinate together under Molly's window; they share affinity as males in relation to Woman. But their connection remains slight.

Some years ago Ted Solotaroff wrote about his own defensive use of Joyce. Rather than see himself as a confused waiter with a family, Solotaroff saw himself as the Artist. He lived inside a myth borrowed from Joyce, and the myth protected him from degradation, confusion, anxiety. It protected him from his life. I would argue that it functioned in the same way for Stephen and for Joyce, although Joyce was, of course, aware of the strategy in a way that Stephen was not. Joyce could render in *Portrait* the explosive life of the scene at the Christmas dinner. Stephen could only suffer it.

The problem with this defensive strategy is that it *costs so much life.* It costs more and more, pressing the individual back into an increasingly empty half-life. Khan could well be describing Stephen: "Every good experience where he felt he could re-experience this ideal self . . . aroused in him the anxiety that he would go mad, disintegrate, or be annihilated" (p. 198). Exactly. As in the case of Henry James, art is used by Stephen as an idealized retreat, and yet art *flows from precisely those parts of his life from which he is in retreat!* The villanelle in section 5 of *Portrait* makes this explicit:

Your eyes have set man's heart ablaze
And you have had your will of him.
Are you not weary of ardent ways?

Above the flame the smoke of praise
Goes up from ocean rim to rim.
Tell no more of enchanted days.

Our broken cries and mournful lays
Rise in one eucharistic hymn.
Are you not weary of ardent ways?
(P. 223)

It is, of course, the artist, the priest, who is weary of ardent ways. The projection onto the "temptress" must be conscious on Joyce's part if not on Stephen's. The speaker in the poem, like its young creator, Stephen, desires, worships, and finally has to run from Woman. Part of the reason for his flight is to remove Woman from the possibility of touch by turning her into sacred object, Blessed Mother, Queen of Heaven. And yet it is the fire of the poet-priest's heart that creates holy incense, the incense that carries in it his art. And that art is inspired by the worship of the "temptress of his villanelle" (p. 223). Without her—without his own libidinal life—the poet dries up, like Stephen, who, fleeing, can write only dry, wry notebook entries. The villanelle is a poem to the muse—a poem asking the muse to depart!—a poem that ironically seeks to evade the frightening power the muse releases in the poet.

Although Stephen retreats to an inner world, in another sense his retreat is *from* inner life, that is, from libidinal life and, generally, life that interfuses the self and the world. Fantasies of merger with the mother and anxieties of abandonment and engulfment—these have to be transformed, mythologized, abstracted from actual inner experience, which more and more must be avoided. Inner experience needs to be transformed, mystified, mythologized; Stephen reinvents himself into the son of Dedalus. The confused child creates out of his own being an idealized father to whom he can dedicate an idealized self, a father who can let him fly above the muck of ordinary life, above chaos. It is this chaos, and the longing for chaos, that I am going to discuss in the following chapter.

CHAPTER FIVE

JOURNEY INTO CHAOS

I SEE THE NEED to compose a self as the other side of a need that is even deeper, one not permitted to be recognized: a need to *de*-compose the self, to regress into infantile fantasies of union with a maternal imago.

There is a hunger in all these writers for nurturance from a maternal figure—and a complementary fear of fusion.[1] All literature contains this longing and these maternal figures. But both the intensity of the hunger and the resulting ambivalence toward Woman seem extraordinary in modernist fiction. In Joyce, think of the maternal figures that his characters yearn for: the Virgin Mary, the dovelike girl on the beach, the temptress of Stephen's villanelle, and Molly Bloom. Mrs. Moore or Mrs. Wilcox in Forster's novels are figures that tantalize with promise of integration, wholeness, and that eventually disappoint and deprive the seeker. My chapter on Virginia Woolf discusses her longing for connectedness to a maternal center. It is as if each of the writers needs to provide images of the nurturance he or she missed.

Mario Jacoby sees paradisal longing as a manifestation of a kind of homesickness for primal connection with the mother. "Ultimately," he says, "it is a longing for the mother as the 'containing world.'"[2] Jacoby insists that there does not need to be any real experience of unity, or home, that the homesickness recalls; in fact, its intensity "is in inverse proportion to the amount of external fulfillment encountered in the earliest phase of life" (p. 8). The result of infantile deprivation, he feels, is intense longing for a home that never was. In its absence, "adults may go through life with a basic sense that there is absolutely nothing to rely on, neither out in the world nor inside themselves" (p. 46). This is the anxiety that I find in the works and lives of all the modernist novelists. Erikson would call it "ontological insecurity." Kohut would speak of it as an incomplete self, one which never experienced empathy and ideals on which to grow. Object-relations analysts would speak of maternal deprivation leading to schizoid emptiness and falseness. It doesn't matter; for such adults, a *paradise* exists to fill the void with memory or imaginings of primal unity and wholeness.

"What if," Hemingway once wrote, in a bitter passage deleted from *A Farewell to Arms*, "the warm milk of your mother's breast was never heaven" (Lynn, p. 389). But while he hated his own actual mother, Hemingway's fiction reveals the longing for that heaven, for nurturance by a "good" mother—a nonimpinging, selfless, nursing figure—Catherine in *A Farewell to Arms*, Marie in *To Have and to Have Not*, Maria in *For Whom the Bell Tolls*. In "Now I Lay Me," the narrator *tries* to regress to a prelapsarian wholeness and simplicity by repeating his childhood prayer and fishing, in memory, his childhood river; Hemingway sees him warding off the trauma of war and the loss of wholeness with these inadequate rituals. Inadequate, because home has been broken up, broken long before the war, when the grandfather dies and the father's masculine power is destroyed by the mother. In other fiction—uncritically, sentimentally, without irony—Hemingway imagines moments and places of innocent wholeness outside the destructive adult world—times of fishing, of lovemaking with a woman who is one with the man, times beyond time— "Oh, now, now, now, the only now, and above all now, and there is no other now but thou now and now is thy prophet" (*For Whom the Bell Tolls*, p. 379).

The longing for paradise is even more transparent in Conrad. Even before he fails in his responsibility, Jim longs for retreat and collapse. Conrad speaks of "the bewitching breath of the Eastern waters. There were perfumes in it, suggestions of infinite repose, the gift of endless dreams" (*Lord Jim*, p. 11). Jim imagines himself the hero of romances. But the "gorgeous virility" that he fantasizes about is a cover for infantile regression. This is Jim's true wish—to be a nestled infant: "He was a little sleepy, too, and felt a pleasurable languor running through every limb as though all the blood in his body had turned to warm milk" (p. 17).

Going to Patusan equals retreating to the jungle of a fantasy mother. In discussing *Heart of Darkness*, Meredith Skura says, "No outright sexual encounter with the mother could be so open a representation as this jungle river voyage, this internal voyage, because there was none in the infant's fantasy in the first place; the mother *was* the entire landscape, the lush jungle with its river entry. Conrad is not hiding a fantasy but going back to the most open, literal version of it" (p. 86). The lush landscape of Patusan, with its deep cleft of jungle river, is another representation of the mother. The mud from which Jim has to extricate himself is the mud of a re-birthing. "Slime up to his breast"—he is blind, beplastered with filth, he makes "one mighty supreme effort in the darkness to crack the earth asunder, to throw it off his limbs." (*Lord Jim*, pp. 182–83). Running, he falls at the feet and is put into the bed of Doramin's old wife, who makes "a to-do over me as if I had been her own son" (p. 183). And so he gets his opportunity for action—but his opportunity is seen as "an Eastern bride" (p. 175); connected to the yearning for repose, for mother, that he experienced on the sea.

Here is Jim, before he becomes Lord Jim, apprehending the ocean: "Jim on the bridge was penetrated by the great certitude of unbounded safety and peace that could be read on the silent aspect of nature like the certitude of fostering love upon the placid tenderness of a mother's face" (p. 15). Nature as mother, as "holding environment." But the calm surface is illusion. The "certitude of fostering love" is false; the mother cannot be trusted to foster, as the father cannot be trusted to offer strength: Jim's kind, loving father "possessed such certain knowledge of the Unknowable as made for the righteousness of people in cottages" (p. 6). In cottages, perhaps; but on the sea, that is no knowledge at all.[3] "Trust a boat on the high seas," Marlow tells us, "to bring out the Irrational that lurks at the bottom of every thought, sentiment, sensation, emotion" (pp. 88–89). Immediately after Jim feels that he is in a mother's care, the gentle waters change into the captain's "torrent of foamy, abusive jargon that came like a gush from a sewer" (p. 18)—an explosion of anality; then the ship rides over the unknown thing from underneath the calm surface—perhaps a submerged wreck, but it's better, richer, that we never know for sure. The surface of duties, of prescribed relationships, of values, is broken, and Jim descends. He jumps into an abyss.

Seen in the light of his longing for merger with a maternal imago, Jim's plunge represents a letting-go. His need to let go is Conrad's need as well.

When he began to write *Lord Jim*, Conrad felt the terror of falling beneath the surface of his life. The terror, not the relief, but I think I can show that relief was there too. In a painful letter to Edward Garnett, he writes:

The more I write the less substance do I see in my work. The scales are falling off my eyes. It is tolerably awful. And I face it, I face it but the fright is growing on me. My fortitude is shaken by the view of the monster. It does not move; its eyes are baleful; it is still as death itself—and it will devour me. Its stare has eaten into my soul already deep, deep. I am alone with it in a chasm with perpendicular sides of black basalt. Never were sides so perpendicular and smooth, and high. Above, your anxious head against a bit of sky peers down—in vain, in vain. There's no rope long enough for that rescue. (Watt, p. 254)

Stillness, fallenness, a chasm. Jim also feels himself in a "chasm without bottom" (*Lord Jim*, p. 76). After he jumps, the ship "seemed higher than a wall; she loomed like a cliff over the boat. . . . there was no going back. It was as if I had jumped into a well—into an everlasting deep hole" (p. 82). My point is that Jim enacts, dramatizes, the spiritual condition in which Conrad found himself in 1899.

Conrad had recently been accused of jumping ship—of deserting Poland. What must such an accusation have meant to this man for whom fidelity and solidarity were the highest good? The earliest notes for "Tuan Jim: A Sketch" were composed on blank pages in an album of his maternal grandmother. Frederick Karl is right: this can surely be no accident.[4] If the "real terrors" or the "Dark Powers," "always on the verge of triumph, are perpetually foiled by the steadfastness of men" (p. 89), then Conrad must have questioned his own steadfastness, his own ability to defeat the "Dark Powers."

But of course, to limit the nightmare of that letter to his unease over his desertion of Poland is to trivialize it. The terror of falling into the abyss, into the monster-laden jungle of the self, the terror of finding himself in a place without boundaries or guides, a place from which he cannot extricate himself—I find this terror, its secret seductiveness and the defenses against it, everywhere in Conrad.

In defense, Jim goes to Patusan to become more than human. In defense, Conrad turns to the genre of the romance. I mean that the stylistic shift into romance is Conrad's form of an acceptable regression as the retreat to Patusan is Jim's. Conrad was aware of the division in his novel between realism until Patusan and romance following Patusan. He called it the "plague spot" (Watt, p. 308). Karl sees the split as the confrontation between the Don Quixote and the Sancho Panza sides of Conrad (*Joseph Conrad*, p. 497). Watt sees the Patusan adventures in a related way: "If *Lord Jim* is the most romantic of Conrad's works, it may be because he began it as a sad and affectionate farewell to an earlier self, but then discovered that the parting would be too painful unless he first granted that romantic self some of the satisfactions it had dreamed of long ago"

(p. 346). Perhaps this formulation makes the choice too conscious, too much like an indulgent father giving a child free rein. Conrad needs the romance to express his longing for regression. He does not need Patusan as a stage on which the realism and the romance in his nature can struggle; the earlier part of the novel has already been that stage. He needs to let the child live out his fantasy—and then to kill him off.

In his switch to romance, Conrad is obeying Stein's dictum:

> Very funny this terrible thing is. A man that is born falls into a dream like a man who falls into the sea. If he tries to climb out into the air as inexperienced people endeavour to do, he drowns—*nicht war?* . . . No! I tell you! The way is to the destructive element submit yourself, and with the exertions of your hands and feet in the water make the deep, deep sea keep you up. (*Lord Jim*, p. 153)

If the dream is "the destructive element," and if it is by submitting yourself to that element that you can be saved, then Conrad, by turning to romance, is doing just that, making "the deep, deep sea keep you up".[5] It is as if the dream—the sea—were to be made a holding environment by your own efforts, "the exertions of your hands and feet in the water."

But can the dream support anyone? Not according to the novel. For the dream is, secretly, not to act, but to sink into the bath of life. Bernard Meyer, discussing Conrad's fears, speaks of "phobias characterized by fear of falling, drowning, entrapment, and even dying" as "derivatives of an unconscious desire to re-experience a child's blissful pleasure in sinking sleepily within the warm encircling arms of an all-powerful loving mother" (p. 182). It is Gerald's secret dream in *Women in Love*. It is Lord Jim's, too. The dream seduces one to infantile regression. Marlow speaks of his very different faith. While he acknowledges his secret affinity with Jim, Marlow is a "member of an obscure body" (not a solitary dreamer, not an egoist), "men held together by a community of inglorious toil and by fidelity to a certain standard of conduct" (not personal heroics or romance). In *Lord Jim*, as in *Heart of Darkness*, that is the sort of faith that saves him.

In *Heart of Darkness*, Marlow goes almost deep enough into dream to die from it. But it is his shadow self, again, who dies. Acknowledging that "the mind of man is capable of anything," that he feels affinity with the beat of the drums, he says that what saved him was not a more humane nature but will, consciousness, "deliberate belief" as against "principles." "An appeal to me in this fiendish row—is there? Very well; I hear; I admit, but I have a voice, too" (p. 37). And *work:* "I had no time. I had to mess about with white-lead and strips of woolen blanket helping to put bandages on those leaky steam-pipes—I tell you. I had to watch the steering, and circumvent those snags. . . . There was surface-truth enough in these things to save a wiser man" (p. 37). Exactly: *surface*-truth. If the leaky steamboat, with its Freudian pipes putting out too much pressure and needing support, is the ship of the self, then Conrad's response to the darkness, to the "unthinkable anxiety" of psychic disintegration, of infantile chaos, is to carefully steer the boat. It is the very opposite of Lawrence's response: it is close to Freud's—"where id was, let ego be."

At one stroke, Jim's suicide, Conrad can have it both ways: he can kill off the child hungry for ultimate regression and luxuriate in that regression. At the moment of Jim's death, Marlow imagines that Jim again "beheld the face of that opportunity which, like an Eastern bride, had come veiled to his side." He enacts a "wedding with a shadowy ideal of conduct" (*Lord Jim,* p. 300); that is, his death satisfies both his need for infantile regression to primal union with a fantasy mother *and* his job as a "hero." "The dark powers should not rob him twice of his peace," Marlow says as he describes Jim's refusal to fight, his final self-sacrifice (p. 294). But in fact, the heroic fantasies are already a form of regression— schizoid flight into inner, dissociated reality.

In *A Personal Record,* Conrad speaks of the very start of his writing career, the day he began the first page of *Almayer's Folly.* He hesitated to "take the plunge into my writing life," because "my whole being was steeped deep in the indolence of a sailor away from the sea. . . . For utter surrender to indolence you cannot beat a sailor ashore when that mood is on him, the mood of absolute irresponsibility tasted to the full" (p. 73–74). The implicit choice is between a plunge into life—and we have seen how dangerous it is to plunge—and indolence. And yet, there is an odd contradiction. To plunge, to fall, is to lose control, to fall into a dream as a man falls into the sea. In one sense, writing *is* action. Just as Lawrence shapes his writing to be a kind of *mining* in the darkness, a way of identifying with his father, so does Conrad take on his father's work, writing, and identify with the childhood father who vacillated, in writing and in political life, between action and depressed passivity—that tragic, tubercular, destroyed idealist, a martyr, yet a man guilty, as he himself partly felt, of the death of his wife. As Bernard Meyer shows, his life followed a pattern of intense energy alternating again and again with indolence to the point of absolute inertia and collapse.[6] Joseph Conrad, like his father, wrote to defeat depression. But he wrote, too, to reach down (safely) into regressed depths of the self.

For it is the yearning to collapse that underlies the fear of collapse. Yearning to sink into the abyss underlies its terror. Meyer is right, I believe, in emphasizing the desire for merger with primary objects in Conrad's oscillation between energy and "a passive yielding up to their engulfing embrace." Meyer writes, "almost without exception Conrad's heroes are motherless wanderers, postponing through momentary bursts of action their long-awaited return to a mother, whose untimely death has sown the seeds of longing and and remorse, and whose voice, whispered from beyond the grave, utters her insistent claim upon her son's return" (p. 69). The return is to paradise.

But it is a strange sort of paradise. Harry Guntrip, discussing schizoid pathology, speaks of regression to the breast as defense against a more severe regression to the womb. "Return to the womb," he writes, "is a flight from life and implies a giving up of breast and incest fantasies which involve a struggle to go on living" (p. 53). In Conrad, as in many of these writers, *desire for union with a maternal imago hides a deeper desire for union with that "Eastern bride"—for the darkness, for death.* While Conrad valorizes responsibility, work in the world, sanity, and restraint, while his novels defend against regression, they are fueled by desire for regression, for darkness. The energy for the writing comes from the dream, from Conrad's need to slip away into the jungle, into formlessness, into fusion—dissolution of boundaries—into libidinal fantasy, but just as much into infantile dependence. But the dream is dangerous, especially because it threatens identity. Entering the dream through Kurtz and Jim and Almayer and Razumov and Leggett, Conrad takes risks comparable to those that Virginia Woolf takes by flowing from point of view to point of view, also dissolving boundaries. Conrad's narrative strategies, then, arise from the need to express and at the same time cope with the dream, to contain it.

The secret beneath the longing for union with a maternal imago is, for Hemingway as for Lawrence as for Woolf as for Conrad, *the darkness.* Making love with Maria, Robert Jordan descends into a fusion that becomes darkness: "For him it was a dark passage which led to nowhere, always and forever to nowhere, once again to nowhere, always and forever to nowhere, heavy on the elbows on the earth to nowhere, dark, never any end to nowhere, hung on all time always to unknowing nowhere, this time and again for always to nowhere" (*For Whom the Bell Tolls*, p. 159). Darkness, like the darkness in Lawrence or the darkness in Woolf or the darkness in Conrad, is a darkness that blurs boundaries, that descends below the ego, and that is associated with a desire for death. Kenneth Lynn speaks of Hemingway's obsession in *For Whom the Bell Tolls* with self-destruction (p. 485). It is no accident that Hemingway's fictions, like Conrad's, increasingly end in suicide or in romantic denouements of unintended self-destruction. In the darkness is rest, in the darkness is home.

Guntrip writes: "The barrier between the conscious and the unconscious may be very thin in a deeply schizoid person and the world of internal objects . . . may flood into and dominate consciousness very easily" (p. 42). Fitzgerald provides an example. We don't see this flooding in *The Crack-Up*—but we do see it in *Tender Is the Night* in the character of Nicole. I have come to see Nicole and Dick not as separate characters so much as aspects of a single psyche, like Clarissa and Septimus in *Mrs. Dalloway*. Nicole, through the language of psychosis, expresses the chaos in the psyche. Just as Nick Carraway in *The Great Gatsby* retreats from the moral chaos of the East into his childhood of the Midwest, Dick Diver retreats into the obscurity of the "poor parishes" where his father had struggled.

Yet chaos is what he wants! It is the madness of Nicole that seduces Dick just as Zelda's madness must have seduced Scott. Nicole's mad language of breakdown, culled from Zelda's actual letters, crackles across the gaps, so different from the cool detachment of *The Crack-Up*:

> They said you were a doctor, but so long as you are a cat it is different. My head aches so, so excuse this walking there like an ordinary with a white cat will explain, I think.

> And now when I know and have paid such a price for knowing, they sit there with their dogs lives and say I should believe them what I did believe. Especially one does but I know now. (P. 122)

Dick's "repose," his mask, his charm, finally grow too difficult to sustain (as he can no longer exhibit his skills as a water skier, lifting a man to his shoulders). He retreats into masochistic failure. Masud Khan and others explore the way schizoid patients may need tension, "even masochistic pain, to sponsor a sense of self in them" (p. 21). That seems close to what happens to Dick as his surface cracks and he dives deeper and deeper.

But there is something stranger, more sinister, closer to Conrad, Hemingway, Woolf. The title, *Tender Is the Night,* from Keats's "Ode to a Nightingale," hints at it: the yearning for rest, for death. For Guntrip and Fairbairn, this is the ultimate schizoid retreat. But death in the novel is somehow associated with sensuality. The paradox is already there in Keats: "Now more than ever seems it rich to die." In *Tender Is the Night* the paradox accounts for the seduction of Dick by *the infantile,* represented first by Nicole, still a child when Dick meets her, and later by Rosemary. It is the music of a dark romance: Nicole sings to Dick, "thin tunes, holding lost times and future hopes in liaison," then "minute by minute the sweetness drained down into her out of the willow trees, out of the dark world." The conjunction of romance and death: "On the pure parting of her lips no breath hovered." She is, for him, a "waif of disaster bringing him the essence of a continent" (pp. 135–36). The essence is in the music and in Nicole's own sweet darkness, calling him away from work, acting, effort, to "easeful Death." The pull is regressive, relating to the call of childhood in the novel, of lost youth, an Edenic, fantasy youth like that implied in the Daisy of Gatsby or in the maternal, erotic, "fresh green breast of the new world." Leaving Nicole at the end of the novel is *not* leaving her in darkness, which she has by this time pushed away from her; it is regression, Dick's return to the dark obscurity of America.

The structures of the psyche are outside of time. In *Tender Is the Night,* Dick begins as a success and then learns to fail. Or at least, so it appears. But in the darker story—and in Fitzgerald's own life—the strategy of failure is there from the start. Bruccoli and others have noted that after Fitzgerald's father lost his job with Procter & Gamble, his son saw him as a failure. At thirty-nine, Fitzgerald remembers, "That morning he had gone out a comparatively young man, a man full of strength, full of confidence. He came home that evening, an old man, a completely broken man. . . . He was a failure the rest of his days" (Bruccoli, p. 21). I would suggest not only that he structured on his father's failure his own sense of life as loss and disaster but also that the way he saw his father was already mythologized, a fictionalized structure through which he saw all experience. How bizarre it is to hear a grown man say about his loss of eligibility for president of the Triangle Club at Princeton, "A man does not recover from such jolts" (p. 60). He remembers that already, sitting on top of a taxi driving down Fifth Avenue, celebrating his success in publishing *This Side of Paradise* and in winning back Zelda, he is already mourning, "bawling," that he "would never be so happy again" (p. 135).

The drama of Fitzgerald's life, like that of Dick Diver's, was shaped by a sense of irretrievable glory and inevitable decline. Both Fitzgerald and his character defend against this with hard work—the hard work of keeping up a facade of charm—while underneath, death whispers seductively.

No wonder, then, that there is such ambivalence about the longing for nurturance, for mother, for merger, for engulfment. I believe this ambivalence is largely responsible for the intensity of fear of woman-as-destroyer and the resulting misogyny of all of these writers, except perhaps for Woolf. But even Woolf, as I shall show in Chapter 11, expresses revulsion for the controlling mother. Think of Lily Briscoe's complicated relationship to Mrs. Ramsey, Lily hungry and resisting, wanting to be held, yet demanding self-containment.

Conrad's landscape is feminized; his jungles and his sea are eroticized, they are expressions of longing. But landscape and woman herself are ambivalently charged. Conrad idealizes woman-as-nurse, but he also perceives woman-as-destroyer. If Jim feels in the sea "the certitude of fostering love upon the placid tenderness of a mother's face" (*Lord Jim,* p. 15), he feels *false* certitude. In *Nostromo,* the two daughters of the old revolutionary Giorgio Viola represent the dual aspects of woman in Conrad: Giselle, the faithful, tender, and childlike; Linda, the hungry woman who leads Nostromo to destruction.

Meyer speaks convincingly about the fantasies of oral sadism, even of cannibalism, that Conrad attributes to women characters (pp. 168–75). Such fantasies combine fear of a longed-for engulfment by the mother with projections of aggression and rage that, I would assume, Conrad experienced and repressed as an abandoned child. The result is intense misogyny. At times this misogyny is expressed by vicious characters like Mr. Jones in *Victory,* who loathes women as unclean and detestable. But the narrative structure of *Victory* betrays a more fundamental unease about women. Of course the book is a *critique* of someone who thinks he can live in an idealized, self-created world, someone like Conrad's own father, or like Lord Jim at Patusan. Evil seeps in. But the novel undermines this reading, since it is by *leaving* the walls of his castle, by introducing a woman to his island, that Axel Heyst is destroyed. In *Lord Jim,* it is partly the girl, Jewel, mistaken for a rare gem, who leads Gentleman Brown to Patusan.

At times, increasingly after his breakdown in 1910, Conrad expresses his misogyny directly. In *Chance* Marlow, often Conrad's spokesman, speaks of women contemptuously, as lacking "masculine decency" and hungry for power. Of course, Marlow's view is criticized in the novel by the frame narrator, but it is never fictionally undermined. Even earlier, in *Heart of Darkness* (*Blackwood's*, 1899), Marlow portrays women as living in illusion, "out of touch with truth." But Marlow's attack goes even deeper, and is directed against that faithful woman, Kurtz's Intended.

> "His last word—to live with," she insisted. "Don't you understand I loved him—I loved him—I loved him!"
> I pulled myself together and spoke slowly.
> "The last word he pronounced was—your name" (*Heart of Darkness*, p. 79).

A lie to protect fragile womanhood? Partly. But suppose we take it as also *not* a lie. I like to read the scene as *dark comedy*. The last words Kurtz spoke were, of course, "The horror! The horror!" Is there any way in which the Intended can be equated with the Horror?

I believe so. Although Marlow says of women, "We must help them to stay in that beautiful world of their own, lest ours gets worse!" (p. 49)—yet it is illusions that have left Kurtz unprepared to face the Darkness. It is Intentions. Intentions are a facade for the repressed, demonic hungers within everyone. The Intended, who believes utterly in that facade, represents, then, the disowning of those hungers. Far from keeping our world beautiful, such disowning is what disarms us. We have to know and to consciously defend against those hungers. The Intended is a living lie, and Marlow says a lie is tainted with "mortality." Look at the Intended: "all in black, with a pale head, floating towards me in the dusk" (*Heart of Darkness*, p. 75). She isn't of flesh and blood. She denies flesh and blood. In fact, Marlow uses her, needs her, to deny flesh and blood. And yet she is, curiously, like her terrible Kurtz. She echoes his ego hunger. "My Intended, my station, my career, my ideas," Kurtz says; and his Intended: "He needed me! Me!" For all her self-sacrifice, she is in her way, as Kurtz in his, a parody of the western ego, denying reality, secretly craving power. The horror.

Then there is the dark, sensual, "savage" woman. This is the other side of Conrad's anxiety, for beautiful and fleshly as she is, she is associated with the dark underside of Kurtz; she wants to possess him for the darkness.

> She was savage and superb, wild-eyed and magnificent; there was something ominous and stately in her deliberate progress. And in the hush that had fallen suddenly upon the whole sorrowful land, the immense wilderness, the colossal

body of the fecund and mysterious life seemed to look at her, pensive, as though it had been looking at the image of its own tenebrous and passionate soul. (P. 62)

She is the soul of the darkness, the landscape that is the body of the mother. The Intended is death by denial; she represents repression of the horror. The savage woman is connected to Kurtz's savage rites that seemingly relate to human sacrifice and cannibalism; she represents regression to oral sadism and loss of individuation. She, too, wants to possess Kurtz. Woman in all her guises is terrifying to Conrad.

And not only to Conrad. Woman-as-Destroyer is a central fantasy for all the male modernist writers I am discussing. As I consider the fiction of James, Ford, Lawrence, Fitzgerald, Hemingway, and Faulkner, I see men terrified of women, enraged at women. Lawrence is at war with the woman in himself, and he is terrified of the Magna Mater, the great mother goddess whom men serve. Women possess men and demand service; for Lawrence they are the goddesses of the industrial machine. The fantasies of Joyce and Forster are more complex, but for them, too, women are figures of terror.[7] Often men fantasize women as nurturers who are in fact predators. American women "have made a nursery out of a continent" (*Tender Is the Night*), they are "the hardest in the world; the hardest, the cruelest, the most predatory" ("The Snows of Kilimanjaro"). British or American, they are the destroyers: Ford's Florence and Leonora and even the innocent Nancy among them destroy Edward Ashburnham, simple, idealistic knight. Ford saw himself as a feminist and he expresses decency and gallantry toward women in *Parade's End*. But surrounding the noble Christopher Tjietens are women ready to do him in. The essential fantasy is one of mild male dignity betrayed by women. Mary Gordon may speak about Ford as a man who loved women: "No one makes a woman so welcome as Ford Madox Ford" (p. 208). But it is a strange welcome; beneath neofeudal, pseudofeudal graciousness is a grotesque picture of woman as either nurse who saves or vengeful, mad destroyer. The best example remains *Ladies Whose Bright Eyes,* with its absolute dichotomy between the vicious, monstrous Lady Blanche and the utterly benign Dionissia, who turns—quite literally—into the hero's nurse when the hero returns from the Middle Ages to the present day. In *The Good Soldier,* Leonora changes in midstory from nurse-protector to vengeful destroyer. Mary Gordon has been seduced by Ford's pretense of gentle male innocence.

Women in Hemingway's fiction, when they are not selfless, nursing figures, lead men into chaos and destroy their souls. The bitch goddess. The devouring mother. As in Fitzgerald, women's power is often compounded by money. While in *Tender Is the Night,* Fitzgerald knows very well that Dick Diver longs for immersion in darkness, that he is responsible for his own destruction, Nicole is still the seductress, her wealth part of her power. Beneath the sophisticated psychological study is a simple fantasy of innocent midwestern boy seduced and destroyed by glamour and wealth. It is "Diamond As Big As the Ritz" in more complex form. In the same way, Hemingway shows us, in "The Snows of Kilimanjaro," a writer who betrays his own talent, gives up his calling, slips into painless ease. He destroys himself. But the *fantasy* is of the artist with integrity seduced to his destruction by a woman with money.

In *The Ambassadors* Strether tells Jim Pocock that Mrs. Pocock hasn't shown her claws: "She isn't fierce." Jim answers:

> "They aint fierce [Sally and her mother Mrs. Newsome] . . . ; they let you come quite close. They wear their fur the smooth side out—the warm side in.
>
> "They don't lash about and shake the cage . . . and it's at feeding-time that they're quietest. But they always get there."
>
> "They do indeed—they always get there!" Strether replied with a laugh that justified his confession of nervousness. (Pp. 215–16)

Throughout James's late novels roam wild beasts like Sally Pocock, women who threaten to ensnare, to claw, to control, to devour. The erotic and aggressive are essentially what James shuns; women only lead one into the maelstrom.

In Joyce women *are* the maelstrom. Sexuality is for Joyce both the primary threat that Stephen needs to fly from on Daedelus's wings—and the source of art. Women set man's heart ablaze, inspiring his art; they also betray, leading man into mud and slime. Even Bloom, that "womanly man," is terrified of engulfment by women.[8]

Each of the male writers has, in disguised or overt form, a painfully enlarged, distorted, grotesque image of women. It is, of course, a *cultural* sickness, this picture of half the human race. But it seems even more intense in these writers than in the larger culture. I believe that the terror and hatred come from childhoods in which the father was not there to provide a foundation of strength for the self. The cultural expectation of the father as the model of absolute independence, courage, power, was, of course, dangerous nonsense, and partly it is the measuring oneself against this expectation that is so shattering. But on the contrary, these fathers were models of weakness or absence. They provided no alternative to the desire to be reengulfed by the mother. The mother became both intensely desired and intensely feared. There was no one to turn to for protection and for help in achieving individuation, in becoming a separate person. The mother was simply too powerful, particularly when she impinged, controlled, overwhelmed, as in the lives of Hemingway, Lawrence, and Forster. So there arises a yearning to fuse with her, be engulfed by her, a yearning to regress not just to the paradise of infantile fusion but to return to the dark, the dark with no boundaries, with no self, a darkness associated with the peace of death.

PART FOUR

ORDER AND CHAOS

CHAPTER SIX

THE AESTHETICS OF ORDER

W E ARE ALL SO afraid, we are all so alone, we all need from the outside the assurance of our own worthiness to exist" (*The Good Soldier*, p. 115). Facing this anxiety, people retreat into the "they," live an in-authentic life. They create an identity that can protect them. They may long to sink beneath the false surface into fusion and rest, but life below the surface terrifies. After all, I'm speaking about fear of the loss of individuated being, a merger both longed for and engulfing, disintegra-tion, explosion of impulse, and the seductive call of death.[1] The call from beneath is powerful—and it is a call to fuller life as much as it is a call to chaos. The terror of that call forces people to protect their fragile selves with an external order that can heal their inner chaos.

I have spoken of the needs for identity and for merger resulting from modernist anxiety; a third need is for a created external order that can support the self. Modernism is the art of chaos. But while modernist writers did experience and express chaos, they also searched for various protective orders against it.

Lacking a father who can offer support, most of the modern novelists I have been considering looked back one generation to a family figure who represented past glory or strength. This is true of Faulkner, of Heming-way, of Lawrence. In Conrad's case it was his great-uncle, an aristocrat who had fought with Napoleon. I can find no record of James mythologiz-ing his father's powerful father, but that old tyrant played a terribly important role in James's life: Henry James, Sr.'s, weakness, which helped create the dislocation and deracination of his son, must be seen in relation to his own father's power. It is as if in rejecting commercial aggression, action in the world of affairs, Henry James, Jr., is identifying with his father's oedipal struggle with his own father—Henry James, Jr.'s, dead grandfather. Fitzgerald, through the stories of his father, looked back on his southern ancestors, distantly connected to Francis Scott Key, as charmed, glorious, aristocratic. It is no accident that two of his first four stories are about the Civil War. Joyce, like Faulkner and Fitzgerald, lived inside the myth of a fallen family, a family fallen from wealth and status.

Ford used his real and wonderful English grandfather, as well as his European Catholic ancestors, as sources of strength and of identity. Perhaps it was providential that his father died when Ford was an adolescent, for his father ignored or shamed Ford; his grandfather loved and supported him. When Ford wrote down one of the fairy tales he made up for his sister, his grandfather illustrated it and got it published as *The Brown Owl*. Ford was nineteen. At twenty-three, he published a biography of his grandfather; in *Memories and Impressions*, he wrote about him again at loving length.

I have already spoken of Faulkner's admiration for his grandfather and great-grandfather, the "Young Colonel" and the "Old Colonel." In *The Sound and the Fury*, Quentin imagines his grandfather and Colonel Sartoris on a high place. "Grandfather wore his uniform and we could hear the murmur of their voices from beyond the cedars they were always talking and Grandfather was always right" (pp. 218–20).

But the grandfather who was always right is only one version of the heroic model used to shore up the self. "What has become of all the once-glorious ones?" Ford asks (*Memories and Impressions*, p. 82). His hero worship—not only of his grandfather, but also of Conrad and Arthur Marwood—was intense. Fitzgerald, in *The Crack-Up* (see Chapter 4) tells how he substituted various heroes for a self of his own. Hemingway did not identify with actual heroic others; instead, he created an *initiate*, knowing, courageous, ultimately undefeatable even if defeated, and he gradually became this figure. The threatened son became Papa.

This desperate need for support for a threatened self, it seems to me, is the meaning of the pathological insistence on the leader, the great man, the powerful race, in the work of D. H. Lawrence, especially from the middle of the war to 1925. "You will know that any creature or race is still alive with the Holy Ghost, when it can subordinate the lower creatures or races" (*Phoenix*, p. 471). How revolting! He writes, "Every lower order seeks . . . to serve a higher order" (p. 473). This sounds like that pathological narcissist, the hollow Gerald from *Women in Love*. Lawrence, who understood so well the pathology of control, was afflicted with it himself.

Dying, and having written the three versions of *Lady Chatterley's Lover,* he was at last almost finished with the fantasies of leadership. Salvation would come not from the leader-follower relationship but in the relationship of man and woman, each dropping encumbrances to meet, nakedly, the other. But in Lawrence's "heroic" phase, the period of *Aaron's Rod, The Plumed Serpent,* "The Woman Who Rode Away," and so on, he was responding to various narcissistic blows, intense humiliations. Here was a tubercular man, bitter about the slaughter of millions, forced to stand naked all day at a draft board; here was a frightened male married to a woman more powerful than he—what a joke to go from his spiritual, possessive mother to the much more difficult, demanding, passionate, brilliant Frieda. Here was an impoverished writer, a great writer, his masterpiece (*The Rainbow*) destroyed by the censors, a writer unable to publish, having to take bread from the people he saw as the sickness of England. And here was a man who deeply loved England, suspected to be a spy and forced to leave Cornwall.[2] That in his humiliation and narcissistic rage he should identify with the natural leader, the great man, is no mystery. Identify he did.

And not only Lawrence—many of the modernists (though not all, not William Carlos Williams, for example) by the 1920s played "Follow the Leader." Modernists' disgust with ordinary people, with ordinary life, a disgust that Saul Bellow attacks so brilliantly in *Herzog,* seems to me a pathological response to an inner world of chaos—elitism as defense.

If it wasn't a great man, a substitute father, like Mussolini for Pound, it was a mythologized past or a mythologized moment of consciousness— Provence, the Renaissance before the "dissociation of sensibility," or Ford's lost medieval aristocracy. Bruccoli speaks of Fitzgerald's "aristocratic individualism" (p. 124); the same phrase could be applied to most of these writers. Aloofness and a sense of privilege became a powerful defensive tool: Joyce, the priest of art, James, the Master. And for a number of them, as for Ford, the metaphor or fact of aristocracy served as a weapon as well. Lawrence, working-class boy, saw himself as naturally aristocratic and the strong in general as essentially aloof, superior. Like Woolf, and more comfortably than Woolf, who was embarrassed by her own snobbery, Lawrence felt his superiority confirmed by the company of actual aristocrats. Faulkner, for all his ambivalence, for all his complex, ironic understanding, turned into the landed aristocrat of his own mythologized past.

No one understood better than Faulkner the siren call of the idealized past, the destructive power of the mythology of the South on actual life. We think of Emily, "married" to a skeleton, or of Hightower, whose life ended in a cavalry charge that took place before he was born, or of Quentin and Caddy, both imprisoned by a fantasy about the southern lady. And yet the stubborn rigidity of the aristocratic past is fused with this mythologized glory.

The values of an evoked past: Faulkner's Nobel Prize address, like Conrad's preface to *The Nigger of the "Narcissus"* half a century earlier, affirms the universality and eternality of values that Faulkner and Conrad undermine in their fiction, assertions of a wish to believe in solidarity and traditional values—assertions by exiles, deeply withdrawn isolatoes with dark, anarchic impulses. If modernism is art that expresses the phenomenology of chaos, these writers did what they could to fend off the chaos—to fend it off with a manufactured political or religious order.

The most significant order with which modernist writers shored up the self against chaos was, of course, the order of Art. Not works of art but Arts as a tradition and discipline with which individuals could identify—which could keep them safe. Charles Newman, in *The Post-Modern Aura,* quotes a letter from Flaubert to Louise Colet in which, Newman says, "the basic assumptions and contradictions of modernism are already in place." According to Newman, Flaubert's letter implies:

> Aesthetic (and ascetic) moralism. . . .
> Art as a sanctuary (perhaps the only one) for the individual.
> The imagination transcendent as it becomes depersonalized. . . .
> Elitism. . . .
> The autonomy of technique. (P. 25)

These attitudes permeate James's prefaces and his stories of artists. They are also taken up by Joyce. The artist becomes a priest not really in the sense of spokesman for the "uncreated conscience"—the soul—of a community (as Stephen claims), but as hierophant of an unworldly higher order. As Newman says, "the task of art . . . is its *own* self-realization, outside and beyond the established order" (p. 25). Outside and beyond, I would add, the tortured individual self. "The artist, like the God of creation," Stephen Dedalus tells Lynch, "remains within or behind or beyond or above his handiwork, invisible, refined out of existence, indifferent, paring his fingernails" (p. 215). Although Stephen claims that, as an artist, the "disorder, the misrule and confusion of his father's house" was "to win the day" in his soul (p. 162), in fact he runs from disorder and from his father's house to the refuge of the esoteric, solitary, priestly order of art.

Tradition and the individual talent, artistic tradition as a fabricated holding environment to support the creature floating in psychological space. What tradition? A tradition invented by the artist and his friends (say, Eliot, Hulme, Pound), the fact of that invention then conveniently forgotten. That shaping of tradition, an imposition of the present onto an invented past, is not unusual. Eliot was doing no more than any poet in nailing together for himself a tradition to serve as a platform on which he could stand. But this reifying of capital *T* Tradition was more than that. It permitted the individual to merge with something larger, something separate from contemporary reality and culture, thus letting her, letting him escape from the chaos of the individual life. Tradition served as a device for distancing, for permitting artists to separate themselves from anxiety over inner chaos.

Distance through detachment; distance through impersonality; distance through an emphasis on tradition; distance through an emphasis on point of view, and an emphasis, more generally, on technique. Not Lawrence, of course; in fact, my critique is close to that of Lawrence's own critique of modernism.

Modernist aesthetics are like a subtle machine for coping with personal confusion and anxiety. That is the psychological seduction of Ortega's dehumanization of art. James F. Miller, Jr., demonstrates how T. S. Eliot's aesthetics permitted Eliot to hide the pain of his sexual conflicts, his tortured marriage, his struggle to recover from a breakdown.[3] The personal agony gets encoded, mythologized, distanced. And the aesthetic theory both protects him from the need to express his tortured self and also protects his poetry from those who might see the suffering human being underneath. How comforting to think that a "poet has, not a 'personality' to express, but a particular medium," that "poetry is not a turning loose of emotion, but an escape from emotion; it is not the expression of personality, but an escape from personality," or, as Eliot puts it in most extreme terms, "a continual extinction of personality."[4] Miller quotes Randall Jarrell:

Won't the future say to us in helpless astonishment: "But did you actually believe all those things about objective correlatives, classicism, the tradition, applied to *his* poetry? Surely you must have seen that he was one of the most subjective and daemonic poets who ever lived, the victim and helpless benefici-ary of his own inexorable compulsions, obsessions?" (Pp. 45–46)

More than anyone, Eliot established authoritatively the aesthetic princi-ples that would protect generations of writers from their own confused selves.

Of course, in some ways what Joyce and James and Eliot were arguing is valid: the "personality" is a superficial social construction. To "express personality" is to express what is least deeply true about ourselves. But my argument is that these elements of modernist aesthetics gave writers an order which protected them from the chaos of their own lives. The insis-tence on formal order is a gesture not of healing, but of burying anxiety deep enough to permit a gesture of healing to take place at all. For Freud, "order is a kind of compulsion to repeat."[5] To repeat what? Painful, conflictual—therefore repressed—material. The repressed returns and is magically made safe by the ordering impulse. Modernism is an art whose content is darkness and chaos; its emphasis on formal order is a way of coping with danger.

For of course we are not talking here about mental patients who create elaborate constructions out of wood or words to continue to avoid pain; rather, we are looking at explorers, warriors, courageous enough to take terrible emotional risks by facing the darkness, then returning and trying to handle what they find there. In Conrad's words, the artist "descends within himself" to a "lonely region of stress and strife." Modernist writers might be compared to a contemporary of theirs, Madame Curie, who died from the accumulated effects of the radiation that she'd been investigat-ing. No wonder, then, that these writers hunger for order and create an aesthetic that emphasizes order.

In modernist aesthetics the work of art is a separate reality, a created world, not an imitation of the ordinary world; it is, in fact, an alternative to the ordinary world. And that is exactly the point: the creation of a separate reality under the control of the real-izer. Lawrence parodies the attitude of his modernist compeers; in *Women in Love,* the modernist Loerke sneers when Ursula tells him that his statuette of a horse is not at all horselike.

"Wissen Sie," he said, with an insulting patience and condescension in his voice, "that horse is a certain *form*, part of a whole form. It is part of a work of art, a piece of form. It is not a picture of a friendly horse to which you give a lump of sugar, do you see—it is part of a work of art, it has no relation to anything outside that work of art." (P. 420)

I said *parody;* and yet Loerke's words are not exaggerations at all. *Flaubert:* "from the standpoint of pure Art one might almost establish the axiom that there is no such thing as subject, style in itself being an absolute manner of seeing things" (see Ellmann's *The Modern Tradition,* p. 127); *Picasso:* "nature and art, being two different things, cannot be the same thing. Through art we express our conception of what nature is not" (p. 25); *Apollinaire:* "real resemblance no longer has any importance, since everything is sacrificed by the artist to truth, to the necessities of a higher nature whose existence he assumes, but does not lay bare. The subject has little or no importance any more" (p. 115). Roger Fry, an important aesthetic guide for Virginia Woolf, writes in his preface to the catalog of an exhibition of postimpressionists he organized in London that these artists "do not seek to imitate form but to create form; not to imitate life, but to find an equivalent for life."[6]

Lawrence attacks the idea that—again in the despicable Loerke's words—"It is a work of art, it is a picture of nothing, of absolutely nothing. . . . It has no relation with the everyday world . . . they are two different and distinct planes of existence" (*Women in Love,* p. 421). Through Ursula Lawrence replies, "As for your world of art and your world of reality . . . you have to separate the two because you can't bear to know what you are." And she calls art "only the truth about the real world" (p. 422).

What is the psychological function of the modernist aesthetic of the autonomy of art, its creation of a separate world? Its function is control. If the modernist experience is one of disorientation, the anxiety of being not-held, psychological chaos, the modernist answer is an aesthetic that offers the artist control over experience. The artist can make solid what is fluid even while recognizing that there are (like cookie molds) infinite makings. Perhaps the "figure in the carpet" in James's story is not a particular design but instead the existence of designing, the presence in art of a principle for ordering chaotic life. D. H. Lawrence, exactly because his own need for control was so great, was sensitive to people shaping external order to ward off the devils of internal chaos and emptiness. His Gerald in *Women in Love,* his Clifford in *Lady Chatterley's Lover,* keep away inner anarchy by exercising control over their mining operations. In my chapter on Lawrence, I treat this pathology at some length, indicating the connection between Stephen Dedalus's artist who is the figure of God and Lawrence's control-hungry, empty industrialists, like Gerald who "was the God of the machine, Deus ex Machina" (*Women in Love*, p. 220).

Hemingway, very much the artist of control, shows us again and again men who, in danger of imploding upon their own nothingness, create modes of order. The *right* way to backpack and to fish—or to hunt—or to drink—are essentially disguised rituals to keep the world safe.

Style keeps Hemingway's world safe. Obsessive alertness, prayers from childhood, terrible self-control all serve as defenses against inner chaos and emptiness. The Hemingway protagonist will not let himself be like Williamson ("The Snows of Kilimanjaro"), who spills his guts on the barbed wire. Williamson had been "addicted to fantastic shows," and, cut loose, he screams to be killed, and the protagonist has to give him all his morphine. As afraid as Henry James of "the terrible fluidity of self-revelation,"[7] Hemingway fears loss of control, inner chaos. And so his protagonists deaden, damp down, feelings—even at the cost of atrophy. "The Snows of Kilimanjaro" begins: "'The marvelous thing is that it's painless.'" The cost of painlessness in this story is death by gangrene, a cutting off of circulation. In Hemingway's work in general, painlessness is an image of the psychic economy that Hemingway practices. His prose style doesn't lie—it lets us intuit the pain of chaos that is being defended against—but it functions, too, as a built-in anodyne against anxiety.

And that, I am saying, is unconsciously and generally true in modernist aesthetics: of the emphasis on formal order, a separate order, which resulted in the creation of a fictional world like that in *Ulysses*, in which each chapter is written in a different style, focused on a different organ, and correlated with a different art and a different episode from *The Odyssey*. In shaping a novel in this way, a coherent, separate world with its creator everywhere and nowhere, Joyce casts aside the armor of an intact narrative self; he risks disappearing. But the control protects him, the control of an aesthetic of distance and impersonality, a reality firmly governed by its creator. Such aspects of aesthetic control are culturally valorized forms of obsessional orderings, needed to handle the emotional risks of their work, to keep off the anxiety of disorientation, even of disintegration.

Modernist fiction seems to me like a battleground. Novelists with unstable selves experienced intensely the falsity of surfaces—the presented self and the professed values of their culture. This experience of falsity—epistemological doubt, an unease that nothing is out there to guide and support the self, no ordered world in which to live—threatened the artist with psychic disintegration. Hungering for a world that could be home but fearing merger and loss of individuation, the artist invented an order, invented a self for whom the world could be home. For all these writers, their art and the aesthetics that guide their art are the most complete answer to chaos.

CHAPTER SEVEN

THE AESTHETICS OF CHAOS

F YOU APPREHEND chaos in your self, you can deal with it by finding some form of external order to identify with—an ego ideal, an ideology, a mythicized construction of past and present. Or you can enter that chaos and try to locate there some principle of order, try to shape a self out of the "foul rag-and-bone shop of the heart."

> A mound of refuse or the sweepings of a street,
> Old kettles, old bottles, and a broken can,
> Old iron, old bones, old rags, that raving slut
> Who keeps the till. Now that my ladder's gone,
> I must lie down where all the ladders start,
> In the foul rag-and-bone shop of the heart.
> (W. B. Yeats, "The Circus Animals' Desertion")

But of course all of us do *both*. I have spoken of the intense pain that modernist writers grew up and had to cope with and how that pain intensified the ordinary human need for a sense of wholeness-in-relationship. Writers responded to this need by identifying with external order. But at the same time—and this is the burden of the present chapter—they took extraordinary emotional risks in descending within the self, "that lonely region of stress and strife," as Conrad puts it. I want to explore ways in which they sought healing in the chaos itself and how they used the reader in their search.

Their anxiety of chaos was of course growing widespread. Walter Houghton, Morse Peckham, and many others have described the terrible experience of doubt, of the breakdown of traditional frameworks of thought in the last half of the nineteenth century. By the end of the century in the West, the surface of society and of the individual was felt to be a laminate, a veneer pulling away from what lay beneath. Descriptions for reality have, of course, never fit experienced reality, but increasingly the split was becoming more visible. It is this split to which modernism responded—a new sense of the problematic nature of reality, a reality in which everything—values, categories of meaning—was thrown into doubt.

Modernist writers (Conrad, Joyce, Sartre, all) looked at the laminate and because of the ways that their own dislocation and disorientation had honed their vision, they saw its falsity, its status as a covering, a covering-over, a covering-up; when they looked *beneath,* they saw chaos. Sometimes, as I showed in Chapter 1, it is the *falsity* they emphasize and therefore the experience of hollowness, the void, nada. The manager's spy in *Heart of Darkness* is a "papier-mâché Mephistopheles, and it seemed to me that if I tried I could poke my forefinger through him and would find nothing inside but a little loose dirt, maybe" (p. 26). Hemingway's old waiter in "A Clean, Well-Lighted Place" prays to . . . nothing: "Our *nada* which art in *nada.*" Beneath the laminate, reality is meaningless, unstructured. Language about experience inevitably falsifies reality.[1] This is chaos as emptiness.

Sometimes, on the other hand, it is what the laminate *hides* that these writers emphasize: darkness, horror. For modernist writers, as for Freud, beneath the (false) surface of society, of the self, lies a rough beast slouching to Bethlehem. Matthew Arnold longs to express "The Buried Life." But what if it's buried for good reason? What if it's not benign and in need of protection as it is in Arnold but rather the dark self of Stevenson's *The Strange Case of Dr. Jekyll and Mr. Hyde* or of James's "The Jolly Corner"? What if, when the true self is expressed, it turns out to have a heart of darkness like Kurtz?

Writers have always understood that experienced reality is covered over by official versions of reality. But until the late nineteenth century, they could seek to discover and name the true version of reality. Houghton has pointed out the difference between the high Victorians' loss of faith in received truths and the late Victorians' relativism: Arnold, who actively sought reconstruction, versus Pater, for whom the world is subjective and absolute truth is not even to be sought (pp. 14–18). Now, for modernist writers, the only true experience was one of ultimate disorientation—darkness and chaos, chaos in the self as well as in the world—and they need to defend themselves.

I have spoken about some of their defenses: protection of a false surface, "flight," regression, and withdrawal. But what makes these writers *modernists* and *artists* is not their defenses against but their plunge into chaos. *Modernism is an aesthetic of chaos.* Even at the moment that modernist writers are most completely asserting traditional values, traditional—even reactionary—forms of order, they are dancing their dance on a high wire over no net. And we are led into their dance.

It is a kind of dance therapy or even a magician's dance to channel energies from outside the center, illicit energies. Malcolm Bradbury refers to a "confrontation with anarchy," of writers feeding on "springs outside or beyond civilization" (p. 90). Modernist art, even when apparently reactionary, even when dressed in elitism and stripped of human feeling, is a dangerous art, an art subversive of established forms of feeling and expression. Frederick Karl writes, "the constant in all Modernism is defiance of authority" (*Modern and Modernism*, p. xxi). Again, "Modernism is synonymous with freedom, however well the latter is submerged in discontinuous elements or technical experimentation" (p. 41). This is Modris Eksteins's basic vision of modernism, too, in his fascinating *Rites of Spring*. Modernism was freedom (p. 43). Using the Nijinsky-Stravinsky-Diaghilev ballet *Le Sacre du Printemps* to illustrate the central thrust of modernism, Eksteins writes,

> The ballet contains and illustrates many of the essential features of the modern revolt: the overt hostility to inherited form; the fascination with primitivism and indeed with anything that contradicts the notion of civilization; the emphasis on vitalism as opposed to rationalism; the perception of existence as continuous flux and a series of relations, not as constants and absolutes; the psychological introspection accompanying the rebellion against social convention. (P. 52)

Not only is this anarchic, dangerous, exploratory aspect of modernism real; it is the reason why modernism so demands formal order and tradition. Michael Levenson, in *A Genealogy of Modernism*, explains that modernism, at least in Britain, moved from an emphasis on personal revolt to an emphasis on escape from personality, from change to tradition. But both elements are constantly present and both are part of the enactment of healing that I find in modernism. Modernist literature heals, or, rather, gestures towards healing, both for the writer and the reader. It enters into chaos in order to heal chaos, not merely for the self but for the culture. Modernism was the last great expression of a cultural myth of the artist as teacher, reaching radically, in spite of personal risk, toward new wholeness.

The word *chaos* seems hyperbolic, romantic, but for me it captures the feeling—what it means to have no grounding, no orientation. Recognizing that the effort is self-contradictory, both because chaos is by definition outside human orderings and because we can't speak about chaos without assuming the potential existence of order in the first place, let me try to describe the phenomenology of modern chaos.

In Chapter 1, I used *chaos* to describe the condition of utter disorientation, loss of a coherent self. Chaos in that sense leads to psychotic breakdown and can heal no one. And yet the breakdown of psychic structure *has* been seductive to modernist artists. There is a romantic valorization of madness as risk, as exploration. Even self-destruction, including alcoholism and suicide (Plath, Sexton, Berryman), is honored as evidence of artistic intensity and integrity, the cost of the enterprise.

But "unthinkable anxiety" produces little that is creative. Indeed, Winnicott tells us that a patient fearful of breakdown is unable to play, and so, unable to create (*Playing and Reality*, pp. 54–55). There is, however, a related form of chaos that is very important in modernist exploration—that is, the emphasis on the rending of traditional surfaces, on the irrational, on the breaking of rules, on the breaching of boundaries. There is enormous energy in disorientation—not disorientation of psychic structure to the point of schizophrenic breakdown, but dissolution of conventional modes of apprehending reality, of fixed boundaries, of static descriptions.

There is the actual risk—it is not just romantic mythology—that in entering defamiliarized reality, world without names and borders, the artist may fall through the grid that orients us to everyday reality, fall into the abyss. And when they found themselves in the abyss, Virginia Woolf, Joseph Conrad, and Henry James could produce nothing. Winnicott says that "clinical fear of breakdown is *the fear of a breakdown that has already been experienced*. It is a fear of the original agony."[2] I believe that for each of these writers there was an "original agony"; that in exploring chaos they were visiting home territory, their home world. Indeed, it is this memory of an early "acute confusional state that belongs to disintegration of nascent ego structure" (*Playing and Reality,* p. 97) that fuels, that necessitates, their exploration of chaos. Again: in madness, in the state of psychic disintegration, there is no healing, no art. But the "original agony" is a paradigm for modernist explorations of chaos, explorations that do have value.

Robert Musil's city in *The Man without Qualities* is a good metaphor for modernist experience.

No special significance should be attached to the name of the city. Like all big cities, it consisted of irregularity, change, sliding forward, not keeping in step, collision of things and affairs, and fathomless points of silence in between, of paved ways and wilderness, of one great rhythmic throb and the perpetual discord and dislocation of all opposing rhythms, and as a whole resembled a seething, bubbling fluid in a vessel consisting of solid material of buildings, laws, regulations, and historical traditions.

Blur, evanescence, confusion of boundaries, loss of traditional ordering principles. There's no center; there's not even a name. No one can map such a city, for it is fluid, self-transforming. But note: there is also energy in this experience: "throb," "seething," "perpetual discord."

Hemingway has given us, in the beautiful short story "A Way You'll Never Be," the experience of chaos in its more terrifying, malign aspects. Nick Adams sees the dead left after an attack: "They lay alone or in clumps in the high grass of the field and along the road, their pockets out, and over them were flies and around each body or group of bodies were the scattered papers." The narrator goes on to describe the scattered paraphernalia of the dead, then focuses on the scattered paper. There are "group postcards showing the machine-gun unit standing in ranked and ruddy cheerfulness as in a football picture for a college annual; now they are lumped and swollen in the grass" (*Stories*, pp. 402–3). It is not so much the horror of death as the chaos—meaninglessness, randomness— of the aftermath of battle that Hemingway emphasizes. Letters are strewn all over the field. Pockets are out. The bodies are swollen "all alike regardless of nationality." Identity is lost, order is lost. The affect is anxiety over the loss of control—the anxiety that I have explored in the first chapter.

It is this chaos that produces Nick Adams's climactic speech to the Italian soldiers he has been sent to convince that the Americans are coming. The speech is a parody of a military briefing by a speaker who has lost control. He describes grasshoppers and distinguishes them, uselessly, from locusts, as if the distinction bore military significance. The grasshoppers accrue unconscious metaphorical power:

> But I must insist that you will never gather a sufficient supply of these insects for a day's fishing by pursuing them with your hands or trying to hit them with a bat. . . . The correct procedure, and one which should be taught all young officers at every small-arms course . . . is the employment of a seine or net made of common mosquito netting. Two officers holding this length of netting at alternate ends, or let us say one at each end, stoop, hold the bottom extremity of

the net in one hand and the top extremity in the other and run into the wind. The hoppers, flying with the wind, fly against the length of netting and are imprisoned in its folds.

In a style that reminds me of Beckett's, Nick's speech parodies the attempt to impose military order; listening to it, we remember the chaos of the dead. Here, too, the grasshoppers become like soldiers, sacrificed indiscriminately, without individuation. Then, in the final passage of the speech, the traumatized Nick Adams makes a final parody of military order: "In the words of that great soldier and gentleman, Sir Henry Wilson: Gentlemen, either you must govern or you must be governed." Nick Adams is out of control, he cannot govern himself let alone prescribe meaningful governance.

The result is helplessness and terror and in an attempt to hold down terror, arbitrary, invented order is employed. Dignity in the face of chaos. But what Hemingway does first is to undermine false order, to find in himself the giddy, crazy place in which civilization and the voice of reason seem to be lies.

Reading Hemingway for the first time as an adolescent, I remember the power I felt in identifying with him, with his courage at stripping away false conceptions of the world. Like all the great modernists, Hemingway takes a heroic stance as solitary explorer, self-exiled from the mapped and named, finding sustenance in a desert. It left me feeling not helpless and anxious but strangely energized, empowered. Partly, I turned him into an orderer, a surrogate father, as if he could initiate me into manhood. Partly, I used him to help me wall myself off from my own surcharged feelings. But most of all, I identified with his teaching of courage.

Paradoxically, of course, the power of this heroic isolation has cultural roots and cultural support. The culture of Europe in the nineteenth century, at the time of its own intensifying self-doubt, had sanctioned the model of the culture hero who was able to break through the mask, to discard "Hebrew old-clothes" (Carlyle), the artist as transforming prophet. Faust breaks the visible world and is told it is up to him to rebuild it; Zarathustra tells people that in a world in which God is dead, they themselves must assume the function of gods. Modernism is the last expression of that heroic stance. The last, I would add, so far; the hunger for wholeness and truer life will not end simply because literary intellectuals have decided that life is a web of floating signifiers without ultimate signification.

What's left after nothing is left? "The priest departs, the divine literatus comes," Whitman said. For postmodern readers the "divine literatus" has also departed. But in the period of high modernism writers could still be cultural priests, still seek truth, wholeness, healing. It is an assertion of enormous power for the artist. It is a dangerous calling.

I remember walking down the street reading Dostoyevski, Conrad, Lawrence and only barely avoiding collision with lampposts. I felt that the received world was broken and that in the next few pages I was going to learn how to reimagine it. I remember, some years later, sitting on a train reading the "Time Passes" section of *To the Lighthouse* and finding myself weeping at its vision of loss and survival; *no*—of loss that, in the very moment of its assertion, in the voice that asserts, convinces me of "something central which permeates."

Conrad, at times too sick to walk to his desk, would crawl to his labor, seeing it as agonizing, solitary *labor*. He thought of his work as duty, not as self-therapy, as a way of refreshing our understanding of the solidarity of human beings. Perhaps more than any of these writers, *he performed a radical quest into chaos to sustain a conservative moral vision of order.*

It is into what most of us would call chaos that D. H. Lawrence reaches for healing. Of course, for Lawrence "chaos" is a negative term; paradoxically, he applies the word "chaos" to mechanical organization, which most people would consider *order*. For example, Gerald Crich, in his organization of the mines, created a "perfect system that subjected life to pure mathematical principles."

> It was the first great step in undoing, the first really great phase of chaos, the substitution of the mechanical principle for the organic, the destruction of the organic purpose, the organic unity, and the subordination of every organic unit to the great mechanical purpose. It was pure organic disintegration and pure mechanical organization. This is the first and finest state of chaos. (*Women in Love*, p. 223)

It is, on the other hand, in the unconscious unfolding of organic life that Lawrence, following the nineteenth-century tradition of Blake and Goethe and Carlyle, finds true order, including the order of the true self.[3] It is in the smashup of the falsely ordered self, in self-obliteration, in what most people would think of as chaos, that healing arises:

> At last came death, sufficiency of death,
> and that at last relieved me, I died.
> . . . and I am dead, and trodden to nought in the smoke-sodden tomb;

dead and trodden to nought in the sour black earth
of the dead; dead and trodden to nought, trodden to nought.

The speaker enters Hemingway's nothing, nada, but rather than defending himself against it, he finds himself redeemed:

For when it is quite, quite nothing, then it is everything.
When I am trodden quite out, quite, quite out,
every vestige gone, then I am here risen, and setting my foot on another
    world
risen, accomplishing a resurrection
risen, not born again, but risen, body the same as before,
new beyond knowledge of newness, alive beyond life.

("New Heaven and Earth")

It is the traditional Christian paradox—dying in order to be born again—though not in the service of a traditional Christian rebirth. What dies is the dead, false self. Lawrence is not talking about the loss of self that results in ultimate disorientation and schizophrenic fragmentation. He is talking about loss of self in a *religious* sense.

Is that compatible with a psychological reading of transformation?

I believe it is. The "self" that needs to be destroyed is Winnicott's "false self," the shell of personality, that which armors the person against deep anxiety. According to Winnicott, the true self hides in order to stay alive. Lawrence believes in the possibility of restoring that original self. What is "born again," then, is authentic being.

Lawrence undermines surfaces and boundaries. The famous "carbon" letter, of which I speak at greater length in my chapter on Lawrence, shows him as a miner, like his father, digging beneath the surface of personality for the carbon that makes up the essential person: "(Like as diamond and coal are the same pure single element of carbon. The ordinary novel would trace the history of the diamond—but I say, 'Diamond, what! This is carbon!' and my diamond might be coal or soot, and my theme is carbon)" (*Letters*, 1:281–82).

What he seeks in his aesthetics of fiction, he seeks in human beings. Always, Lawrence sees dissolution as necessary precursor to healing. "Her heart was gone, her limbs were dissolved, she was dissolved like water" (*The Rainbow*, p. 488). The destruction of the isolated woman, even her sacrifice, as in "The Woman Who Rode Away," may indeed express Lawrence's pathological fear of and rage against women. But much more important for me, such destruction uses the woman as metaphor for the self—any self—that needs opening, purging, breaking, renewing. It is the three strange angels. Admit them, admit them. Connie, Ursula, Kate are best seen, I feel, as the aspect of the psyche that needs to stop seeing itself as Self, as isolated *I*.

Lawrence enables me to imagine my own bursting forth into truer life. In this passage from *Women in Love*, I identify strongly with the rhythm of destruction-creation that Ursula is undergoing: "Her active living was suspended, but underneath, in the darkness, something was coming to pass. If only she could break through the last integuments!" (p. 3).

These integuments for Lawrence are like the nets that Stephen Dedalus must try to fly past. For both, the "voice of my education" ("The Snake"), the given world, is experienced as impinging, and it needs to be rejected so that the true self may be born.[4] But Lawrence's "integuments" are much more integral to the individual—his husk or shell or skin—not merely nets thrown out by an external "society." For Joyce and Lawrence, the self must bear living in chaos and then out of chaos arrive at new being. But for Joyce the self must impose its own order on chaos; for Lawrence the self must wait until its true form can grow forth from within: "There is nothing to save, now all is lost, but a tiny core of stillness in the heart like the eye of a violet" ("Nothing to Save"). From this emptiness of self comes new life.

Even in his descriptions of landscape Lawrence bursts form, destroys outline; I think of the "tiny amber grains" of the blackthorn "burning faintly in the white smoke of its blossoms" (*Women in Love*, p. 39). Earlier, in *Sons and Lovers*, Paul Morel tells Miriam about his sketch: "It's . . . shimmery, as if I'd painted the shimmering protoplasm in the leaves and everywhere, and not the stiffness of the shape. That seems dead to me. Only this shimmeriness is the real living. The shape is a dead crust. The shimmer is inside really" (p. 152). Similarly, Birkin, in *Women in Love*, demands of Ursula not external attractiveness but "that golden light which is you" (p. 242). Over and over we see beneath the social mask, beneath what characters would be able to say about themselves, to the deeper, often darker part, that the narrator, as seer (see-er), knows. The narrator has no epistemological doubt. Modernist doubt is itself part of the false surface that needs to be broken.

And under the false surface, in the darkness, through touch of an Other, the new life comes into being.[5] In the place in which exact outline is lost, in which the bounding-off of the isolated self dissolves, in a place of merger, which Lawrence both longs for and fears, the self does not merge with a mother imago; it meets an Other and knows itself for the first time.

Modernist writers break boundaries and seek wholeness in the unknown regions, indeed, in the chaos, derived from childhood, which fuels their art.

I am thinking of E. M. Forster, sensitive, gentle, timid—no subversive, certainly—whose fiction is so often about the breaking of boundaries or conventional orders. In each novel and in the stories, characters want—sentimentally, unthinkingly—to break down barriers, to cross boundaries. And the reader feels for them, identifies with their desire. But Forster doesn't lie about the results. When someone crosses into forbidden territory, the result is destructive and grotesque, not beautiful. He or she loses nearly everything. In *Where Angels Fear to Tread,* his characters' sentimental, aesthetic response to disordered foreignness leads to death; the attempt to bridge the gap between the rigid English and the loose Italians ends with a mother dead, a baby dead, and the protagonist tortured and guilty. In *The Longest Journey* the attempt to break out of the stultifying, life-denying role of the English gentleman and to trust the earth ends in the protagonist's death. In *Howards End* Helen Schlegel tries to bridge the gap between classes just as her sister Margaret tries to bridge the gap between cultures. Helen's gesture leads to an illegitimate baby and to the death of the baby's father, the lower-middle-class Leonard Bast; Margaret's gesture leads to the destruction of the family she joins. And in *A Passage to India* the various attempts to make a "bridge party," to break out of the rigid boundaries of rulers and colonial subjects, English and Indians, end in near-ruin, personal collapse, destruction of friendship.

Yet the urgency in Forster's essential fable is toward unity, even at the risk of inviting chaos: "Only connect."[6] The English with the Italian; the upper classes with the lower; the cultured Schlegels with the pragmatic Wilcoxes; the colonizer and the colonist. The sky and the earth. Rarely does Forster show us actual unity; instead, he offers us the *longing* for unity. Professor Godbole sings to Krishna, and when Fielding asks for an explanation, Godbole says,

"It was a religious song. I placed myself in the position of a milkmaiden. I say to Shri Krishna, 'Come to me only.' The God refuses to come. I grow humble and say: 'Do not come to me only. Multiply yourself into a hundred Krishnas, and let one go to each of my hundred companions, but one, O Lord of the Universe, come to me,' He refuses to come."

"But He comes in some other song, I hope?" said Mrs. Moore gently.

"Oh no, he refuses to come," repeated Godbole, perhaps not understanding her question. "I say to Him, Come, come, come, come, come, come. He neglects to come."

But Godbole, no modernist westerner, is far from waiting for a Godot. When Fielding accuses him of preaching that good and evil are the same, Godbole says no, they are different, but

> "Both of them aspects of my Lord. He is present in the one, absent in the other, and the difference between presence and absence is great, as great as my feeble mind can grasp. Yet absence implies presence, absence is not non-existence, and we are therefore entitled to repeat, 'Come, come, come, come.'" (P. 80)

There is a constant, inevitable strain on language in Forster. Language creates divisions and requires divisions in order to name, to produce meanings. But meaning, unity, is beyond categories, divisions, and in reaching toward unity, language stretches beyond its possibilities. Unity is at moments intimated—that is all. Especially in *A Passage to India* Forster reaches for larger and larger, more encompassing perspectives, often imaged in the shape of an arch or vault. But, as Mrs. Moore felt even before discovering nothing in the cave, "Outside the arch there seemed always an arch, beyond the remotest echo a silence" (p. 52).

The *urge* toward unity is, however, finally, *blessed* in Forster's fiction. The destruction is creative; in each novel it is chaos that generates the possibility of new life. *The Longest Journey* ends with the new life of Stephen, Rickie's illegitimate half-brother. In *Howards End* the new life is the farm life of the two sisters, who will bring up the baby—a baby who is an image of the bridge between classes and of the blessing that can come out of the terrible breaking of boundaries. A child will be raised, without a father, by two women, as Forster himself was, brought up by his mother and his great-aunt; in fiction as in life the women are strong and the husband sick, unable to breathe, though not tubercular as Forster's father was. I mean that Forster generates an image of healing in a near-reproduction of his own chaotic childhood life.

In *A Passage to India* there are many images of chaos, but especially two: the cave and the penultimate episode, "Temple." Mrs. Moore experiences her own emptiness in the emptiness of the cave, and it kills her. To break the boundaries of class and culture and values seems, here as in all of Forster, romantic, noble; but it costs; it destroys. "Visions are supposed to entail profundity, but—Wait till you get one, dear reader!" (p. 208). Leave the clean, well-lighted place at your peril. And yet—it is in chaos, through immersion in chaos, that joy can be found. The Hindu festival of rebirth is muddle as much as mystery, confusing time, place, actor, meaning. But it is also a joyful noise unto the Lord: "There was still only a little light and song struggling among the shapeless lumps of the universe" (p. 310). It is a "divine mess," a "benign confusion" (p. 290). The boats collide on the lake.

> The four outsiders flung out their arms and grappled, and with oars and poles sticking out, revolved like a mythical monster in the whirlwind. The worshippers howled with wrath or joy, as they drifted forward helplessly against the servitor.
>
> . . . . The oars, the sacred tray, the letters of Ronny and Adela, broke loose and floated confusedly. Artillery was fired, drums beaten, the elephants trumpeted, and drowning all an immense peal of thunder, unaccompanied by lightning, cracked like a mallet on the dome.
>
> That was the climax, as far as India admits of one. (P. 315)

As far, too, as Forster himself admits of one. Fielding and Aziz are close again, they ride together, but Aziz says they can never be friends. And yet the fall into the lake amid the din of a ritual of rebirth is an image of joyful confusion, of triumph through immersion (a literal immersion) in chaos.

And why triumph? Because it says that the cave is not final; the need for compartmentalized reality can be transcended. We can survive in the Defamiliarized Zone.

In Forster's essential fable, an innocent with good intentions enters a world that becomes defamiliarized. "How can the mind," Forster asks, "take hold of such a country?" This is "passage to more than India," as Whitman said; passage to the country in which there are no names for things, in which a chestnut tree (*Nausea*) is *not* a "chestnut tree," in which Magritte can label the painting of a pipe, "This Is Not a Pipe." Language breaks down.

> I was always embarrassed by the words sacred, glorious, and sacrifice and the expression in vain. We had heard them, sometimes standing in the rain almost out of earshot, so that only the shouted words came through, and had read them, on proclamations that were slapped up by billposters over other proclamations, now for a long time, and I had seen nothing sacred and the things that

were glorious had no glory and the sacrifices were like the stockyards at Chicago if nothing was done with the meat except to bury it. (*A Farewell to Arms*, p. 184–85)

All modernist artists destroy the given world, the world taught to the child through structures of language. Defamiliarization has been described by the Russian formalists as part of the strategy of any art, forcing a widened gap between signifier and signified. Certainly, it is crucial to modernism. Welcome to the Defamiliarized Zone! The characters—and the reader— are immersed in a blurred world. It is a world without names. The world that *can* be named is always a false, hand-me-down world. The language for things is a net to be flown past.

Marlow sits on the deck of a ship in the dark and tries to communicate to representatives of the establishment. Frustrated, he gropes for language. The language shaped by those in power is worse than false; it rationalizes barbarism. But what is the language of real experience? The reader is immersed in vague profundities, the kind of language that so annoyed F. R. Leavis. But that cloudy language is, in fact, a precise linguistic version of the fog on the river, the dense bush, the fever through which Kurtz speaks and Marlow hears. Real experience is defamiliarized experience—blurred, incommunicable. Marlow says: "I did not see the man in the name any more than you do. Do you see him? Do you see the story? Do you see anything? It seems to me I am trying to tell you a dream—making a vain attempt. . . . No, it is impossible. . . . It is impossible. We live, as we dream—alone" (pp. 27–28). For Conrad the job of making the reader see—not see physical reality, but truth—is almost a sacred duty.[7] It is how Conrad maintains solidarity with humanity. What we hear in *Heart of Darkness* is a storyteller—a "worker in prose"— struggling and struggling vainly to use language to communicate truth and therefore make a gesture of solidarity, while feeling the falsification of language and experiencing defeat in a world of isolated subjectivities.

We are as readers immersed in the destruction of conventional language and the defeat of any attempt to use language to capture reality. The world stays unfamiliar. The reader can't know. Indeed, the reader *mustn't* know, for a world that can be known is a world falsely described! The early and persistent bourgeois attacks on modernist art, that it intentionally confuses its audience, are correct. The reader of a modernist text must be oriented to disorientation, led into an altered perception of the world as unfamiliar and unknowable. To see Lord Jim from all sides is to see a confusing cubist portrait. To see through the eyes of the narrator of *The Good Soldier* is to see through the ground glass of impressionism—or expressionism. Perspective collapses; everything is foregrounded. The reader *falls into* the Benjy section of *The Sound and the Fury*. When, what, who? Why make me enter the perceptions of an idiot? Not simply because Benjy's hunger is the most naked form of the family's need, not simply because his dependence lets me see beneath asserted cultural values—but mostly because to make me see through Benjy's perception is to make me experience a defamiliarized world and force me to grope for meaning. And the reader's disoriented groping is an analogue for (1) the Compson experience of disorientation and (2) their need for the holding environment they call Caddy. To read a modernist text I have to become a modernist perceiver.

In *Portrait,* Joyce uses style after style to show us that the world Stephen sees is not ever simply *there;* Stephen always sees through the thick glasses of a style. But while Stephen has to make his own orientation, style giving way to style, lens to lens, the reader is at least oriented by Stephen. In *Ulysses,* the reader is forced to *see through* (in both senses) one style after another, with no narrative authority. It is a funhouse of disorientation.

Virginia Woolf's characters are like Musil's fluid city—identity blurring into identity. We are "never, never to desert Mrs. Brown," the unique individual in her particular living spirit, but how hard it is to be true to her, for she is of "unlimited capacity and infinite variety; capable of appearing in any place, wearing any dress; saying anything and doing heaven knows what."[8] And besides, as we know from Woolf's "An Unwritten Novel," Mrs. Brown is unknowable. How much is the writer merely seeing himself, herself, in Mrs. Brown? How *can* anyone know anyone else? To see clearly is to see nothing; to see with modernist vision is to see a blur and be unsure whether the blur is merely in the lens or in the world seen. But what I want to emphasize about Woolf is the half-secret delight she takes in the blur, in the loss of boundaries. The most rapturous passages in Woolf are, beneath the anxiety, passages of self-obliteration, diffusion of the self into the air, erasure of the edges of characters, moments of selflessness. At times in modernist writing, moments of salvation are not moments of containment and recaptured selfhood, but their opposite. If loss of self and loss of orientation produce anxiety, they also produce freedom and, more to the point, bliss.[9]

The aesthetics of chaos: The artist takes us into defamiliarized reality in which chronology is broken; we see fragments, shards, from unfamiliar angles. The real is problematized—it is always a fiction, a human creation.[10] *Vertigo.* The modernist plunge into chaos was a desperate heroic effort of artists growing up in chaos to explore chaos and find there a place to stand—or learn to float.

PART FIVE

GESTURES OF HEALING

CHAPTER EIGHT

GESTURES OF HEALING

WHY SHOULD MEN AND women who have grown up with fragmented selves—grown up dislocated, alienated—enter their own chaos in their writing? Why do these writers take on themselves the emotional risks and costs? Why not avoid them? How is it bearable? What are the benefits? How, for God's sake, is it experienced as healing?

As I have indicated, these modernists (even D. H. Lawrence) are not consciously using their art to heal their own personal splits, to fill their empty places. They are explorers of a chaos that belongs to the culture—or, as they might have said, to the human condition; they are attempting to heal all our lives, to render and make readers experience the terror of spiritual chaos, and to shape a model for survival. And yet, I am arguing, it was in their own lives that, unconsciously, they found that chaos and the need to create order.

In a sense, it is their own childhoods they are entering—their home worlds. They create spaces in which their internal objects, transmuted, walk again.[1] The phenomenology of their particular chaos, with its particular dynamics, is expressed. Virginia Woolf sketches on the page a landscape of her pathology, derived from her childhood. It is a Bloomsbury painting (I am thinking of the paintings by Duncan Grant, by Vanessa Bell) with blurred boundaries, faces without definition. Her fiction is of a world without clearly separated selves. No wonder she satirizes the novels of Edwardian gentlemen who knew precisely the identity of each character, knew by external circumstances. Yet separation is also terribly painful for her. If the voice of the fiction longs to know who people individually "are," it also longs to find what connects people, what enables them to communicate, what holds them together. It yearns for rest, stability, a maternal giver-of-meaning, longs for things to come together and to last.

She paints the fragmented world I myself sometimes inhabit, but the fragmentation in Woolf is deeply intensified.

And that makes sense for a girl growing up in a family in which she was not permitted to express the helplessness, outrage, and anguish she had to feel,[2] a family in which she experienced her father as (partly) a tyrant and her mother (before and after she died) as an absence, an absence of, really, her own center and ground of being. Her fiction repeats—and repeats— her childhood world of internal objects. It is a world that does not give back an image of the self.

But then where is the healing? Partly, it is in the strange positioning of herself, living dissociated in her imagination, hovering above the wreck. I suspect some strategy like this was what held her together as a child. But it is far more powerful in her fiction. It is the power of *naming*. For Woolf, for all these writers, writing fiction that immerses the writer and the reader in chaos can be experienced as healing when it names the chaos. To name the monster is to gain power over it. Vague and diffuse anxiety is transformed into anxiety that is bearable because concrete and focused.

After the 1989 earthquake in San Francisco, as after all such traumas, children and adults told stories of their experiences. Why do people tell stories of disaster and thereby relive the pain? Because the narrative structures offer a way of controlling, placing, the anxiety raised by the event; because the act of narrating brings the terror out of the dark; and because the narrator positions himself, herself in the role of survivor, master of the experience. The same can be said when the experience to be mastered is not a traumatic episode but a childhood experience of a terrifying world in which the self has no home.

The writer, in this case, Woolf, is not as helpless as she was in her childhood. She can re-present in her fiction the experience of doubt, of blurred life, of helplessness and confusion. I see it as more a child's diorama than as a landscape. The figures are easily held in the fingers, placed here—no . . . *here*—to get them right. The writer, using her narrative voice like a giant hand, as expression of her adult power, is larger than these figures from the world of internal objects; they are not so dangerous to her. From this vantage point, she can love them.

The world represented by modernist writers—all except Lawrence—is one without a ground for one's being; one of its features is its lack of narrative authority. But if there is no omniscience in such a world, if the nineteenth-century omniscient God, father, and author are gone, there yet remains omniscience in the narrative voice. *In the act of creation*. Indeed, the writer is responsible—what a culturally and psychologically powerful position—for the creation of the world! It is easy to point to narrative omniscience in Woolf's fiction.[3] There is a voice that you can hear through all the other voices, offering loving reassurance of wholeness and continuity even as the world represented is one of fragmentation and evanescence. That voice names and by naming lights up the darkness or, rather, finds comfort in the darkness. The voices of Rhoda and Bernard and the others in *The Waves* cry for both separate identity and real connection, but the voice under their voices is our assurance of wholeness, of healing.

In the 1908 "The Poet and Daydreaming," Freud writes that "imaginative creation . . . is a continuation of and substitute for the play of childhood." He speaks in *Beyond the Pleasure Principle,* of play as a child's means of mastery. Robert Wälder, in a 1933 paper that depends on these essays and especially on Freud's concept of the repetition compulsion, asks why a child should play, again and again, with imaginative materials which were originally painful. He argues that a child may repeat in play his painful experience at (for instance) a dentist until he has overcome and mastered the pain. "It is eventually mastered because of the playful repetition itself" (p. 218). He emphasizes, as does Freud, the transformation of passive experience of childhood trauma into assertion of an active role. Finally, having mastered the experience, the child no longer has to play it out. This paradigm is an important part of the theory of play therapy (see Virginia Axline's *Play Therapy*), in which a child, too young for psychoanalytically oriented therapy using language, dramatically plays out a conflictual issue, finding in play mastery of affect and solution of the conflict.[4] D. W. Winnicott, whose *Playing and Reality* has affinities with the work of Axline, believes that "playing is itself a therapy" (pp. 50–51).

In some ways it is the same for the adult artist: the repressed returns, and the artist names and "solves" what was once helplessly suffered. Ernst Kris, in *Psychoanalytic Explorations in Art*, speaks of mastering what was formerly a danger by incorporating it into a work of art (p. 52). I open the door of my closet in the night, I gain power over the monsters. Now I tell you about them, and in the telling, put the monsters under my control.

But there is a serious problem with this. "Eventually mastered . . ."? If a writer could master painful childhood reality by telling about it, or, rather, by reenacting it, he or she should be able to stop—stop writing, at least about that. But in fact writers tend to tell a very few stories, to re-present a very few emotional landscapes, their whole creative lives. Perhaps they describe them more precisely, more intensely—perhaps not. We recognize in the early work of Virginia Woolf the psychic drama of her more complex later work. In Hemingway's later work the tension seems reduced, the fiction weaker, but the components within that body of work, of the early *In Our Time* are recognizable; the voice is recognizable. *The writer never masters the originating condition. The gesture of healing never heals.*

If it is the experience of loss of self and of a real world that requires healing (see Chapter 1), then for these modernist artists the self is never found, the world is never made real. While Winnicott believes in the efficacy of play, he also asserts, "If the artist . . . is searching for the self, then . . . in all probability there is some failure for that artist in the field of general creative living. The finished creation never heals the underlying lack of sense of self" (*Playing and Reality*, p. 55).

There is a paradox at work here: in repeating and mastering (in transmuted form) the home world, in seeking a place of healing within the nightmare, the writer also has to reexperience its pain. Hemingway has to return to the experience of childhood impingement, humiliation, and rage and to his original defenses of walling off, deadening, and withdrawing. He is not able to actually "work through" the experience; he enacts it over and over. Each writer of fiction or poetry knows that along with the sense of harmony from shaping chaos comes the turmoil raised by return to the originating condition. There is no one, after all—no analyst or friend—to help. The writer can perhaps discover new, formal containers for the pain, but the internal world has not been transformed.

What does the work of art do, then, for the artist? As I have said, it keeps the originating condition, the home world, in the light, keeps it safe, under control. It can't haunt me when I tell about it! And then, in each fiction, the modernist writer explores the chaos and in the form of play temporarily exorcises the ghosts, creates images of wholeness and order. Phyllis Greenacre, whose work on the impostor I discussed in an earlier chapter, has a useful qualification of Wälder's thesis:

> That play does serve to diminish anxiety after trauma seems definite, but it may be doubted whether the anxiety is so thoroughly and generally reduced, and the originally disturbing experience so nearly mastered as Waelder's theory suggested. It seems to me that frequently some residue of the anxiety contributes to the fun and excitement of play; and that this is made tolerable not by the fusion of fantasy and reality . . . but rather by the opposite, the child's ability to

separate fantasy and reality and his tacit realization that his play is not real reality after all.[5]

Similarly, it is the reenactment of the drama of anxiety in the form of play that is satisfying—the enactment, not the solution. I need my nightmare; I need to enter and reenter it to feel its danger safely, to absorb the energy out of that danger.

Then, too, this play, this art, *does* shape a solution—but it is a solution that the writer can only *wish* for, can only live in while "playing." At the end of *Mrs. Dalloway,* and at the end of *To the Lighthouse* Woolf establishes peace and order. Fragmentation, evanescence, death are merely notes in a final harmony. Clarissa fears no more the heat of the sun; she can look with composure on the dying old lady across the street. Lily Briscoe is able, using the figure of the dead Mrs. Ramsey, to cohere the composition of her life. And the narrative voice soothes Woolf; I know that by what it does to me. It offers me a resolution that transcends all the pain of the novel. "For there she was" (*Mrs. Dalloway*). "I have had my vision" (*To the Lighthouse*). But Virginia Woolf herself, finishing these novels, was exhausted, nearly broken. And she went on to explore the originating chaos again in *The Waves,* in *The Years,* in *Between the Acts,* until finally the chaos became too much for her.

Chaucer's Troilus, who has lost his inconstant love and given up his life, is lifted up to the "eighthe sphere," from which he looks down upon pained humanity and sees the place of battle (Chaucer must have been imagining England itself): "This litel spot of erthe that with the se[a]/Embraced is." From that distance, the agony is transcended and the tension of earth and sea becomes an embrace. How beautiful! So many works of fiction, modernist and premodernist, end in that kind of resolution. I'm thinking of Bellow's Herzog in Ludeyville, somehow no longer tortured, "pretty well satisfied to be, to be just as it is willed, and for as long as I may remain in occupancy."

Often (certainly not always) modernist writers work toward moments that don't deny, yet do transcend, chaos. Eliot's narrator ends *The Wasteland.* "Shantih   shantih   shantih." Fitzgerald's narrator steps back from carnage and moral debacle to childhood, to aboriginal innocence, to the America "that flowered once for Dutch sailors' eyes—a fresh, green breast of the new world." Hemingway's Harry, the writer in "The Snows of Kilimanjaro," dies in a fever of gangrene poisoning, but spiritually, in dream, rises to the top of the cool mountain. Lawrence's Paul Morel, whose bent is surely toward death at the end of *Sons and Lovers*, suddenly turns: "But no, he would not give in. Turning sharply, he walked towards the city's gold phosphorescence. His fists were shut, his mouth set fast. He would not take that direction, to the darkness, to follow her. He walked towards the faintly humming, glowing town, quickly."

Paul's solution does not resolve Lawrence's conflict, just as the novel does not cohere Lawrence's split world nor heal his wound. But the novel does map the psychic-social landscape and give Lawrence power over his own ghosts. And something more, something true for each of these writers; as Winnicott writes, "It is creative apperception more than anything else that makes the individual feel that life is worth living" (*Playing*, p. 65). In this sense, the gesture is experienced as healing. The writer is trying to create a home-that-never-was in the representation of the home-that-was, trying to find a self that has become unavailable. If these homes are impossible, it is still possible to live in a healed state *on the page*. The writer feels the torn edges knit. The world feels whole and temporarily radiant. In the act of writing, the writer becomes whole and in connection with his or her true self. *The song is home.* The state that the writer can reach while writing, the condition that Winnicott speaks of as "creative apperception," permits the writer to create a voice that can sing itself into wholeness, no matter how broken a world it describes. Who does the writer become in the act of writing? That person he becomes—*that's* the healed, the (temporarily) whole person.

One way to see the work of art is as a transitional object in Winnicott's sense, a cultural object that is neither an internal object, inside, nor an object in the external world, but an object that resides in an "intermediate area," experienced by the artist as both his or her creation as well as a real object. For Winnicott the transitional object "is a symbol of the union of the baby and the mother" (*Playing and Reality*, p. 96). And he sees the cultural object in the same terms, "the adult equivalent of the transitional phenomena of infancy and early childhood."[6]

The basic paradigm is that of play. "If play is neither inside nor outside, where is it?" he asks (*Playing and Reality*, p. 96). He speaks of it as taking place in an intermediate area, a potential space. "The place where cultural experience is located is in the *potential* space between the individual and the environment" (p. 100). If the originating condition for modernist narrative is the absence of a world as holding environment (see Chapter

1), the creation of narrative is partly the attempt to create, in the intermediate area, a linkage between the self and the world. In healthy development, giving up maternal provision isn't really giving up, but rather finding a way to let the world provide continuity from earlier conditions.[7] Or, to change metaphors, it's the child who provides, by taking the mother inside, so that there's a safe place wherever the child is.[8] In the absence of such continuity, the modernist artist creates his or her own holding environment through the creation of the art work as transitional object. *Even though the object may express the absence of home, it can itself be home.* I think most of all of Conrad, for whom the creation of fiction was a gesture of solidarity with the community denied by that fiction. But I see all of these writers shaping an object in which they can become whole, through which they can be, temporarily, at home in the world.

Memory is an expression of love, and love is partly a search for wholeness.[9] The writer repeats as an act of obeisance an incantation that will carry him or her home, even if home is pain. Maybe especially when home is pain. Has this always been true? I think so, but it is more noticeable now that wholeness is so difficult to achieve. For these writers home itself was, as we have seen, the *absence* of home. Their art is partly the representation of that absence.

Christopher Bollas, a contemporary analyst practicing in London and a follower of Winnicott, describes what he calls a "transformational object."[10] If a *transitional object* represents a union of the baby and mother, permitting the baby to be "held," in the absence of the mother, a *transformational object*

> is experientially identified by the infant with processes that alter self experience. . . . Not yet fully identified as an other, the mother is experienced as a process of transformation, and this feature of early existence lives on in certain forms of object-seeking in adult life, when the object is sought for its function as a signifier of transformation. Thus, in adult life, the quest is not to possess the object; rather the object is pursued in order to surrender to it as a medium that alters the self. (P. 14)

Bollas connects the aesthetic experience with this process, as "an existential recollection of the time when communicating took place primarily through this illusion of deep rapport of subject and object" (p. 32). Bollas differs from Winnicott here in that the rapport is not simply a holding but a changing, an experience of integration. "The Transformational Object seems to promise the beseeching subject an experience where self fragmentations will be integrated through a processing form" (p. 33). The artist, then, may be seeking to create a form that models a state of half-remembered, half-longed for, integration. It is only a modeling, as a prayer is a modeling of a relationship between the worshiper and the sacred. But it helps explain the relationship of the work of art to healing. I am reminded of a beautiful passage by Saul Bellow (in "Distractions of a Fiction Writer"): "The page in the typewriter describing a certain conversation that never actually took place is an offering placed on the altar of certain gods who—who aren't around just now." At the moment of beseeching, through the vehicle of the art, the memory-longing for integration is temporarily called up and answered.

But their art is not just the re-creation of home, or the creation of an object in potential space in which they can be held, or the creation of a state of transforming integration. It is also an act of linkage, a denial of alienation and an assertion of connectedness with a listener, who must, then, become a powerful presence, must enter the writer's world of internal objects as a psychoanalyst enters the internal world of a patient. Bollas writes, "A patient does not simply represent his internal world to the analyst in narrative. He **uses** the analyst as a transference object and this usage is further articulated through the analyst's countertransference" (p. 9; Bollas's boldface). Over the course of an analysis, the hope is that there is a new object created through the new relationship, that the analyst is not merely a transference figure but someone who can become a new figure shaping a new environment. But the reader is not, after all, able to play that role; the writer has created the listener, the reader. While for the reader, the writer can represent a new dialogue, all that the reader can do for the writer is represent old relationships.

And yet psychoanalytic process is a useful model for seeing the relationship of writer and reader.[11] Like the analyst, the reader is brought into the encoded internal world of the writer. The listener is turned into an actor in that world and is asked to establish a variety of links with the narrator. All narrative is performance art. It is not merely the creation of an object that is experienced as healing; it is the creation of a relationship to an invented listener. As reader, I am built into the gesture of healing.

To read sensitively, then, I need to ask, Who am I for this writer? How am I being used in the longing for healing? And to answer, I have to turn to my own "countertransference" responses: How do I feel used? Whom have I become in my reading?[12]

It is easiest to see how a writer uses me as a reader by examining consciously "unreliable" narrations, cases where a writer invents a narrator who is defending him- or herself in the text. In these cases, the writer is creating a character who is using me as reader. John Dowell in *The Good Soldier,* Humbert Humbert in *Lolita*—these characters need me in ways I can more or less clearly specify. I am meant by the writer to watch them try to charm me, seduce me into their vision. The unreliable narrator is a special case, an interesting model of a narrator using a reader. But whether the narrator is unreliable or reliable, my question in this chapter is not "Who am I for John Dowell or for Marlow or for Nick Carroway or for Frederic Henry?" My questions are How has the writer *used* this narrator? What is the voice behind the voice? How am I being moved? Why does the writer need to move me in this way? The question is the same when the narrative voice is simply an unnamed narrative voice, asking me secretly—largely unconsciously—to share a vision of the world. Necessarily, the answer to the question "How am I being used?" differs with each writer and may differ from fiction to fiction and even within a fiction. I have to examine what happens to me as I read. What makes the search problematic is that the answer also differs with each reader, as with each therapist, and yet there is only one patient, one writer. I accept and enjoy multiple readings of a text; but how do I know that my perception of a *writer's use of me as reader* responds to the writer's own dynamics? How do I know that I'm not engaging in countertransference in the old, negative sense—my projections getting in the way of what's out there?

One could argue that it's hardly different from the problem facing an analyst. Roy Schafer has argued just that.[13] An analyst, he says, like a reader, has to choose what to take in as data and how to see it. A Kohutian reading of text or patient will differ from a Freudian reading. Schafer downplays the differences between analyst and reader, and yet they are important. First, as reader I have less data. I have only a written text, its defenses polished smooth by a wordsmith. Suppose that an analysand were to come into an analytic session with a typed text or a tape-recorded script. That would be a gesture an analyst might confront. But for the reader there is always, only, that voice, taped and retaped until all the flaws—stammers, contradictions, revealing shifts in style—are removed. Of course, like an analyst, I may know other texts—other fictions, letters, memoirs, journal entries—and I may know biographical data. Still, my data are limited. Second, I get no feedback from a writer's responses to my interpretations. I can't see the writer's body language or expression, and I can't hear how he or she answers me or what associations my responses raise. My chances of distortion are great. Meredith Skura, discussing the use of the psychoanalytic exchange as a model for the process of reading, says, "It is still not clear whether these theories can be usefully applied to specific texts, as opposed to the creative process in general" (p. 173).

In trying to apply a model of transference and countertransference, a model of reading based on the psychoanalytic exchange, I am stuck with these limitations, stuck with insufficient data, a rehearsed, polished voice, my own shaping preconceptions, my own ear, and my own sensitivity.

In general, cultural terms it is easy enough to say who I am and how I am used by most writers. I am needed to affirm the writer's experience and vision; indeed, to affirm the writer's *self*.[14] In a sense, I am made by most writers into the image of the good Winnicottian analyst, who gives "the patient back what the patient brings." Winnicott says, "I like to think of my work this way, and to think that if I do this well enough the patient will find his or her own self, will be able to exist and feel real" (*Playing and Reality*, p. 117). Of course, as reader, unlike as analyst, I *cannot change* the writer. The relationship with the reader whom the writer creates can never be more than a temporary imaging of such a relationship of change. As reader, I am also asked to affirm the writer's defenses and, more generally, his or her strategies for validation. I become someone the writer creates with whom to share his or her shaped world, a kind of "chorus," in Berger and Luckmann's sense, helping in the process of reality maintenance.[15] *The shaped text shapes a reader who confirms the orientation to reality that the text expresses.*

These functions of a reader are particularly significant at a time of such dislocation, confusion, change—such an experience of chaos—as I have described in these chapters. The writer uses me—the created me—as a soul in affinity. In a sense, I hold his or her hand as we walk into chaos.

Conrad sometimes uses me this way.
I remember his letter to his editor and friend, Edward Garnett:

My fortitude is shaken by the view of the monster. It does not move; its eyes are baleful; it is still as death itself—and it will devour me. Its stare has eaten into my soul already deep, deep. I am alone with it in a chasm with perpendicular sides of black basalt. Never were sides so perpendicular and smooth, and high. Above, your anxious head against a bit of sky peers down—in vain, in vain. There's no rope long enough for that rescue. (Watt, p. 254)

Here Garnett is the particular reader to whom Conrad appeals at the same time that he despairs of receiving help. He imagines Garnett as some kind of male mother offering an impossible umbilical cord out of some terrible, cold womb. The appeal in his fiction is very different from the appeal in this letter—but still it is an appeal. The voices in the fictions also ask for rescue.

Marlow struggles to clarify but he is unable to do so. I hear this struggling narrator in *Heart of Darkness* and *Lord Jim*, although not in *Chance*. In *Chance* the voice pontificates but does not struggle; modernist readers, better able to identify with a struggling narrator, have rejected the once-popular *Chance*, but they feel close to Marlow as narrator of the Defamiliarized Zone. *This* Marlow does not seem to look for help from his listeners; indeed, he feels that little help can be offered: "We live, as we dream, alone." And yet, as Bouson has argued, "While Marlow's detached, idol-like appearance suggests that he is autonomous and self-contained, his interactions with his audience reveal his need to be understood and acknowledged. . . . As a storyteller, Marlow acts out his own need for self-rescue" (p. 103).

In *Heart of Darkness* and *Lord Jim* Marlow acknowledges his identification with figures who have gone under, Kurtz and Jim. Marlow stays safe by not denying his connection with these figures. Denial is dangerous, as in the case of Captain Brierly, who judges Jim, then himself, and finally commits suicide when awareness of his denied self breaks through. But Marlow *admits*, and I identify with his flawed humanity and so rescue him from his identification with Kurtz and with Jim. He is not solitary because I am made safe by his safety. He has steered the ship; he comes back to affirm traditional values, which feel necessary and precious and fragile—yet supportable.

But how does Conrad *use* Marlow to speak to me? To answer, I begin from my identification with Marlow the teacher, who experiences chaos but is not disintegrated. Marlow is the container for Conrad's own risk. Conrad, too, is made safe by Marlow's survival, his condition of calm, wise teacher. As a listener, affirming Marlow, I affirm Conrad's fragile world. Marlow is not Conrad, but his voice is being used by Conrad to create a link to a listener, to many listeners, so that Conrad may feel less terribly alone. I become the supporter of the moral universe that seems so shaken. I am, after all, "one of us." I give Conrad reassurance of a community in the absence of community; I permit him to descend into moral chaos and to return to steer me, as Marlow steers his ship through a jungle.

The narrative voice of Conrad's fiction can talk about desperation, but whether Marlow or omniscient narrator, the voice itself is not desperate. I sense that at times I am being asked to mirror Conrad's self-representation of calm and solidity while he takes me into chaos, the chaos of Razumov or Kurtz or Decoud. Yet I see in the appeal to Garnett a model for Conrad's general relationship to any reader. To *me* as a reader. Like Garnett, I am being used to hand Conrad a rope, to reassure him that someone remains above the chasm, that there is a place above, a place of rescue.[16] I rescue by confirming that the solidity of the speaker is real. Conrad creates the reader into a transitional object if not a transformational object, and the speaking-listening situation into a holding environment in which his self can feel healed.

I recall all the fantasies of rescue in Conrad's texts: Marlow rescuing Kurtz, Marlow rescuing Jim, Jim rescuing the natives of Patusan, the Captain rescuing Leggett, Heyst rescuing Lena, Captain Anthony rescuing Flora—the list goes on and on. I think of Conrad himself, rescued often by his Uncle Tadeusz, most importantly after Conrad's suicide attempt.

As a reader, I am rescued as well. By being created into one who affirms moral solidity and permanence, I am able to take the plunge with Conrad into moral chaos; and I can experience myself as strong and coherent enough to do the rescuing, as "one of us," though God knows Conrad would never have seen a deracinated, cosmopolitan, middle-class Jew as "one of us." I bracket my particular social identity to assume the identity he needs me to have in order to support his own.

Henry James, more openly than Conrad, I succour in his loneliness.

James experienced himself as very much alone, and he longed to be understood. His stories of artists and writers show us an isolated creator, devoured or ignored by the ignorant, occasionally worshiped by a kindred spirit. Which kin? James's father? His mother? His brother? Mostly, I think, his brother was the model for the reader, though rather the brother he longed for than the one he competed with. The actual William James became increasingly impatient with Henry's prose, and sending William his work must have been for Henry an acting out of the drama of his isolation. The true reader is the way out of that isolation. In an 1891 essay, "Criticism," Henry James defines the perfect reader:

> One sees the critic as the real helper of the artist, a torch-bearing outrider, the interpreter, the brother. . . . When one thinks of the outfit required for

free work in this spirit, one is ready to pay almost any homage to the intelligence that has put it on; and when one considers the noble figure completely equipped—armed *cap-à-pie* in curiosity and sympathy—one falls in love with the apparition. It certainly represents the knight who has knelt through his long vigil and who has the piety of his office. (*The Art of Criticism*, p. 235)

James's metaphors give us a fascinating beloved object, part figure of "maternal provision," as Winnicott puts it, and part male defender—helper, brother, finally knight whom one "falls in love with." Why thank you, Henry, I blush as critic. But of course, this is an outrageously idealized figure, and if James seeks this kind of reader to complete him, he is in serious trouble.

In his stories of artists and writers, there is often such a reader, although he or she may not write criticism. In "The Middle Years," this worshiper gives up his financial security to serve the dying artist, whom he, almost alone, understands. In "The Figure in the Carpet," the act of understanding a particular writer's work becomes important enough to organize one's life around. And in nearly all the fiction I can think of there is a comparable figure—a sympathetic listener, whose job it is to understand the protagonist. James may speak of a figure like Maria Gostrey as a "ficelle," someone who simply serves as confidante so that information can be passed and ruminated upon. But the listener is too common and crucial a figure to be seen as a purely technical device. Listeners not only "sympathetically understand"; figures like Maria, like May Bartram in "The Beast in the Jungle," like Alice Staverton in "The Jolly Corner" are, indeed, the protagonists' only way out (though they may not realize it) of their isolated condition.

Not only do these readers succour and sympathize; often, like the worshipful knight of "Criticism," they reflect back to the protagonist his most grandiose vision of himself. It is as if Henry James, through these readers incorporated within his fiction, were creating his own holding environment. And as a reader I become like these fictional readers. I "rescue" a Strether (*The Ambassadors*), connive with James to focus not on Strether's evasive withdrawal but on his civilized sensitivity. I become maternal and fraternal at once—a mother who really holds and a brother who is not a rival. And I feel myself encouraged as a reader to vibrate in attunement with this subtle, difficult intelligence. We share what I refer to in my chapter on James as the "contemplative space" which he creates. I am flattered to be taken inside this space, to be handed this precious object, and if I fail in being sensitive enough to appreciate it in its complex brilliance, my sense of failure seems to me part of James's success in using me in his self-affirmation.

I hear Virginia Woolf's voice in *Mrs. Dalloway, To the Lighthouse, The Waves,* and other fictions as the voice of a mother, and I become the child. She, who hungered for mothering, who in letters to Violet Dickinson or, later, Vita Sackville-West, can sound so childlike, dependent, in much of the fiction speaks with the voice of the mother she longed for. Under the spell of that music, the world is radiant with meaning and beauty. The "something central which permeated" that Mrs. Dalloway feels she lacks resides in the narrative voice. The world is *not* bare, *not* fragmented; its tonic key is *not* loss. The voice is what reassures me, soothes me, as Mrs. Ramsey, covering up the boar's skull, reassures James so he can sleep and reassures, wordlessly, Mr. Ramsey when he fears that he is a failure.

It is not, of course, Mrs. Ramsey's voice or Mrs. Dalloway's voice that holds me. It is the voice that we hear under all the others weaving the same set of images, a lyrical protector—the voice constant under all the changes of point of view in *Mrs. Dalloway,* the voice of the "Time Passes" section of *To the Lighthouse.*

I find my own sentences changing as I write, becoming a little *affected;* I find myself not exactly imitating her voice but relating to my own listeners as Virginia Woolf's narrative voice relates to me. I suppose I am enacting what is known as *parallelism.* Gail Reed speaks of parallelism as "reenactments in supervision by the supervisee of current aspects of his patient's affect, behavior, or conflicts of which he is not consciously aware." Reed examines such reenactments in the writing of criticism:

> Just as the structure of the supervisory situation places the therapist in a situation similar to the patient's in therapy, thereby facilitating transient identification, so the critic writing about a text places himself in a situation similar to that of the original author of the text. The critic repeats the author's act of writing.[17]

In reading Virginia Woolf's created voice I feel that I am the protected child that Virginia Stephen never felt she was. She has made that voice into what Winnicott calls the "environment mother" and the reader into the protected child. And so in my own writing about Woolf, I take on the other role in the drama, *I* protect *her* and I speak to *my* listeners as her invented mother-voice speaks to her listeners—in other words, as her voice speaks to *me.*

Of course, in creating a voice of maternal provision, I the reader am no more than a split-off part of Woolf herself, the needy child she was, in danger of fragmenting, dissolving. During the time of writing she can create a mother for that child. And in doing so, she touches chords in me of my own pained childhood, touches the child in many people. I—we—experience the healing, the being-made (temporarily) whole.

Each of the writers I am concerned with in this study needs to make me someone else. I mirror Hemingway's grandiosity and elevate his protagonists; instead of seeing them as characters expressing bitter withdrawal hidden by a mask of Stoicism, I am supposed to see them as characters expressing the truth about life. And I also experience Hemingway's hostility, his competition. Fitzgerald, on the other hand, is often trying to charm me, to butter me up. For D. H. Lawrence, I am the longed-for *Blutbruder*, the friend he never found; I also feel seduced, entered, a sexual object.[18] Each is different; to examine my relationship as reader to any one writer in any depth would require an essay in itself. The same writer may be using me in opposed ways—as authority and challenger and father. But it is clear to me that the relationship of writer to reader is central to the gesture of healing. The modernist writer needs me in order to face the chaos in which he or she finds both danger and new life.

CHAPTER NINE

HEALING THE CULTURE

HERE ARE TWO different things often confused: (1) the shaping of modernism in the hearts of a few artists and writers and (2) the absorption of modernism by a persuasive cultural elite who enshrined it in the universities and gained its admission into the popular media. World War I and conditions of postwar social fragmentation are frequently seen as the cultural context for modernism. And they are—for its reception and enthronement. But as I have tried to show, for its *origins* we have to look into particular childhoods at a particular cultural moment. My question now is this: What is the relationship between the shaping, or sources of modernism, and its absorption or social acceptance? I have spoken about modernist art as an attempt to heal, to make whole, the artist. Now what about the audience? What did or does modernist art, specifically the fiction of the writers in this study, do for its readers? Why was it canonized, why did it get to be seen as *the* literature of its time and grow to influence popular media in this century?

One way to explain modernism, partially valid but incomplete, is to see it as the expression of a class trying to handle the difficulties and contradictions of capitalism. Frederic Jameson sees "modernism and its accompanying techniques of 'estrangement' . . . [as] the dominant style whereby the consumer is reconciled with capitalism."[1] Gerald Graff speaks of modernist media as redescribing "actual alienation as 'a revolutionary form of freedom and potency,' thus furnishing 'a model by which social powerlessness can be experienced as gratification'" (Robbins, p. 236). How can this be, when modernist art was from its beginnings subversive art, despised by the bourgeoisie, despised by every totalitarian government of the Right or Left? or when Trilling tells us that "the characteristic element of modern literature . . . is the bitter line of hostility to civilization that runs through it"?[2] Robbins's answer is typical: "There is no doubt that [modernist] sacrifice of respect for the present has been energizing for criticism but only at the cost of keeping it away from overwhelming questions about contemporary society and the possibilities of action within it" (p. 236). The critical element in modernism is tempered by its distaste for the common life and its isolating distance from all battles. Modernist disgust with the present is palatable to those in power, for they are left unimpeded.

And there is truth to this critique. Modernism is, paradoxically, subversive but quietist; it undermines conventional orders, but often only to shape an alternative order into a place to rest. "For poetry makes nothing happen: it survives / In the valley of its saying where executives / Would never want to tamper" (W. H. Auden, "In Memory of W. B. Yeats"). When modernist writers have turned actively political, they have tended to be seduced by visions of political authoritarianism. Michael Levenson, in his brilliant *A Genealogy of Modernism,* shows the anarchic individualism of early stages of modernism as perennially in tension with a hunger for order and reads the career of the critic T. E. Hulme, for example, as precisely a movement from Bergsonian subjectivity to classicism and finally to a distanced, shaped, geometric order. The point is that modernism became acceptable not so much in its revolt as in its emphasis on form, on created order, on impersonality, on tradition—in short, it became acceptable through Eliot, not through Williams.

In an explosive recent study of modern American poetry, Cary Nelson discusses the politics of literary criticism. He points to the fact that the conservative Fugitive group gave the New Criticism its impetus.

> In doing so, they drew on some of Eliot's critical essays and thereby reinforced a disciplinary inclination to view the fragmented modernist text as a purely aesthetic object, its linguistic fragmentation purified of social influence and critique. In a remarkable reversal of the revolutionary strain in modernism . . . literary theory thereby covertly fused the disjunctive modernist poem with the idealized view of poetry in the genteel tradition.[3]

Nelson sees official literary modernism, academically approved modernism, as part of the cultural mechanism promoting an idealized self-image. The division between literature and history, "one eternal and idealized, one temporary and debased, is entirely a disciplinary fiction, one however, also entirely in the service of the real world power the discipline considers unseemly and tries to believe it has surpassed" (p. 244). This analysis cannot—and does not try to—explain why modernist writers wrote as they did, but it does help to explain why a certain way of selecting, defining, and valorizing moderism was so attractive to influential conservative critics.

In Britain, the impact of F. R. Leavis and *Scrutiny* has come under examination in the same way. As Robbins says, "If history is atrophy, then initiative passes from society to the Scrutineer, one of the happy few who recognize and nourish the sacred remnants of earlier and better ways of life preserved in the canon. Thus the modernist move against modernity was embodied in an institution" (p. 240). Leavis's Lawrence was a Lawrence of health and cultural continuity; his darkness, his contradictions, his status as someone outside the center, were buried.

The audience for modernism, according to this view, was shaped by sociopolitical needs and was made comfortable by the emphasis in modernism on distance, ambiguity, ambivalence. Nelson speculates that radical American poets have been dropped because their poetry

> does not generally display the surface indecision and ambivalence that many critics since the 1950s have deemed a transcendent, unquestionable literary and cultural value. From that perspective, the ideal political poem is W. H. Auden's 1937 *Spain,* a poem tortured by the impossibility of making a clear commitment to either side in an imperfect world. Because it reinforces the English profession's ruling ideology of political indecision lived out in uneasy inner anguish and external inaction, Auden's poem is often taken to be *aesthetically* superior. (Nelson, p. 44)

I agree—indeed, I have myself argued—that the stance of distanced awareness, contemplation and acceptance of pain, loss, emptiness, is seductive for the modernist writer. It is seductive for the audience, too. It puts the reader into the position of a privileged elite observer, like God on a hillside watching trains approaching each other on the same track around a bend.

Modernism, while it struggled with the language and conventions of the dominant culture, provided the means to lift its readers above the world of social struggle into the private world of spirit. Readers identified with Rilke, with Kafka, with Hesse; they entered the contemplative space that James created for himself and for us. With Joyce, they shaped worlds of language. Modernists didn't produce the exile of its audience, but they *furnished it with attitudes,* they made it home. In keeping distance from the present in which "a savage servility/slides by on grease," one cannot hope to find the strength of a Colonel Shaw; one can only watch what is happening, watch on TV "the drained faces of Negro school-children," and comment bitterly on the ironies of vulgarity, on moral loss and defeat. Lowell wrote "For the Union Dead" before the civil rights movement, the peace movement, and the opposition to the war in Vietnam had shaped an alternative community. During the 1960s, the community of modernism was overlaid, for many of us, by a more active comradeship in political struggle. Like intellectuals of the 1930s, we attacked modernist art—at least modernist art as it was taught to us—because it represented retreat.

There is, of course, another aspect to the selection and definition of modernist literature by the New Criticism. New Critical tools work especially well on materials that are self-contradictory, complex, ambiguous. If its tools were forged earlier by a conservative social vision, those critical tools then shaped what was worth discussing, indeed, what was considered literature and what was not. Passionately political literature, infused with a social vision, was *not*. Modernist literature of a certain kind became necessary to critics as a field on which their tools could be employed. Then, in turn, the power of a profession shaped the taste of two generations of educated readers.

But I cannot accept as complete this view of the cultural absorption of modernism. I agree that the arts of modernism have been "co-opted by market capitalism." Or, to replace this hideous reifying language with the language of ordinary experience, people who have to sell things will use any exciting cultural vocabulary. We see bastardized hand-me-downs from modernism, for example, in Coca-Cola commercials or in the discontinuous, fragmented, explosive music videos on MTV. And I agree that New Criticism, invented partly to serve modernist art, was used to propagate a way of life emphasizing submission to tradition and formal order. But there are other necessary ways to see the relationship of modernist art and its audience. While the powerful will always try to strengthen their hegemony by using the most persuasive cultural vocabulary available, I would argue that modernism served real, psychic needs in the community that took it up; it served such psychic needs in my teachers, in my friends, in myself.

The conditions that created the modernists created their audience. These conditions were already present and already being commented on again and again in the nineteenth century in Britain and the United States. I have already described some of these conditions; they are generally well understood. Reality felt increasingly unreal, without foundation, without external authority for its values. In the United States as in Britain, the Victorian era was self-consciously an age of doubt.[4] Religion was attacked by the new mythos of scientism and scientific history, but the dynamo was incapable of substituting for the Virgin. Popular novel after popular novel, like Mrs. Humphry Ward's *Robert Elsmere,* show us the Victorians' passion and pain for their loss. Walter Houghton says, "Those who have never been disinherited because they have never known the absence of doubt can only imagine the distress of the first, sudden catastrophe."[5] Houghton asserts that the Victorian longing for a hero was related to the lack of an underpinning for social beliefs. "The truce from cares which the Victorians found in contemplating the hero is a truce from the cares of living in a world where one feels an acute sense of weakness" (p. 340).

Rationality was also under siege by thinkers as different as Nietzsche, Marx, Freud, and Mannheim. Rationality was a veneer, a coded expression that hid reality while secretly expressing it. It disguised self-interest, class interest, unconscious impulse. I have argued that the intellectual conversation of the end of the nineteenth century and the beginning of the twentieth was not responsible for the creation of modernist artists; that conversation did, however, shape the openness of an audience *to* those artists. Intellectuals taught generations not to doubt but to *name* doubt, to give it an intellectual framework.

Doubt about the social fabric was endemic as well. As E. P. Thompson, among others, has shown, class harmony, even in the eighteenth century, is a myth equivalent to that golden age in which you could find good servants. But in the Victorian period not only was there conflict, but the myth of class harmony had itself been exposed, and class struggle had become a competing, anxiety-producing model of the way society worked. Everyone was stepping out of their places: Agricultural workers and their families were forced to migrate to cities; in the United States, most of society had recently immigrated. Workers in all countries were making increasingly intense political demands; socialist parties were forming all over Europe and the United States. The traditional leaders of Britain were giving way to at least the upper levels of the bourgeoisie. Women in Britain and the United States demanded suffrage and equality under the law. At the moment of colonialism's greatest success, its injustices, as well as the injustices of capitalism itself, were being bitterly attacked by intellectuals. Scientific and technological progress was being attacked. An opposing culture that fostered the development of *modernism* took root in opposition to modernity.

All this is well known. There is no point in contributing another analysis of late nineteenth-century doubt and confusion. And yet it is necessary to remember that these conditions, which I have spoken of with regard to the modernist writers of this study, were present in the culture at large and helped produce the audience that needed the therapy of modernism.

I have argued that the families of modernist writers had a great deal to do with shaping the sensibility of which modernism was an expression and against which it was a defense. If such families were crucial for the shaping of modernist artists, they were increasingly typical in Britain, Europe, and the United States. The fast pace of change intensified generational conflict, so that it became difficult for sons to accept their fathers as models; not only were oedipal issues exacerbated but the establishment of identity grew increasingly problematic. The James family was an extreme example of a new freedom. But by the late nineteenth century, more and more families were forced to permit greater individual expression or risk incapacitating their children in a society that demanded initiative and the ability to adapt to change.[6] Such families had weak structures of traditional authority; the mother became central and the father was weak and often absent. The family was forced into itself centripetally by social forces; yet its center was not strong, and it tended to fly apart at the mercy of unstable economic forces. If the family increasingly permitted self-direction on the part of the children, without grounding in coherent cultural and familial authority, these children experienced a lack of coherent selfhood. Jackson Lears writes, "the autonomous self seemed no longer Promethean but fragmented, defined according to the needs and demands of others. By the turn of the century, more than a few Americans had begun openly to declare that independent selfhood was an illusion" (p. 34). It was these children of the new families who became the audience for modernism.

What of the influence of the Great War? The war did not produce modernism nor, as Fussell has pointed out, did the language of modern irony derive from the war; it was already found, for example, in Hardy's "Channel Firing."[7] Certainly the arts of disjunction and discontinuity, of the problematizing of language and value, did not wait for the war. The modernists were already formed and all the gestures of modernism were in place by the time war began—began in such enthusiasm. Futurism was being debated, postimpressionist and expressionist art were well developed, cubism had already run its course; in England vorticism was the most publicized form of experiment in literature and the visual arts, with the appearance of *Blast* just before war broke out. Ford's *English Review* (which published Lawrence, Pound, and others) had already come out and Ford had departed as editor; *The Egoist* was under way. *But the audience was not in place.* The Armory Show in New York, Roger Fry's exhibitions of postimpressionist art, the performances of *Le Sacre du Printemps* in Paris and London, were avant-garde expressions directed at a small audience of followers plus an even wider audience of the hostile. What the war did was to make the anxieties and defenses embedded within modernism everyone's anxieties and defenses, and out of that *everyone,* a much larger audience for modernism was shaped.

The period before World War I in Europe, Britain, and the United States was not (as it has long been clear) the belle époque it was once touted to be, a period of dreamlike innocence before catastrophe. Rather it was a period of (1) a denial that change had occurred or (2) a longing for social and religious coherence (Jonathan Rose points out that words like *wholeness, unity, synthesis, connection* were heard again and again [pp. 27–40]); or (3) revulsion toward bourgeois forms with rage and a desire for explosion.[8] Modris Eksteins connects the dance of ritual sacrifice and rebirth in Nijinsky's ballet to the ecstatic celebration of the onset of war among all classes and in all countries in August 1914. It seems as if Lawrence, in "New Heaven and Earth," is expressing—bitterly, ironically, horribly—a longing for purgation and renewal that spoke for millions who never heard his name: "War came, and every hand raised to murder; very good, very good, every hand raised to murder!"

When the murder came, it was hardly a ritual for rebirth; it solidified disillusionment; the war prepared the generation that suffered through it to become the audience for modernism. Peter Loëwenberg, in his brilliant essay, "The Psychohistorical Origins of the Nazi Youth Cohort," shows how the deprivation suffered by children growing up in Germany in World War I created the longings for security that, ironically, re-created (in World War II) the same deprivation.[9] I think we can make a comparable connection for the entire generation growing up in Europe and America around the time of the Great War. British and American children did not suffer the terrible deprivation—starvation, infantile abandonment, experience of powerlessness—suffered by the German children; they did not live in such absolute want and finally suffer reunion with fathers who had undergone defeat and were helpless to support their families. Still, children and young adults had to cope with a trauma to their picture of reality: to their relationship to leadership, to their faith in the meanings offered by the culture. Perhaps the best short expression of the resulting moral chaos may be Mann's story, "Disorder and Early Sorrow," in which traditional values are breaking up in the midst of a family whose authority structures are dissolving in the midst of a society that is coming apart.

A Farewell to Arms and *All Quiet on the Western Front* do not express the actual disillusionment suffered by soldiers at the front; Eksteins writes that to an extraordinary degree soldiers on both sides maintained high morale and loyalty: "The soldier had been sustained by social values in which he genuinely believed, but . . . those values had been subjected to such grievous attack in the course of the war that his attitudes towards society, civilization, and history were indeed irreparably altered" (p. 190). He sees Remarque's best-seller as a description *not* of trench warfare but of postwar disillusionment. We have come to see Hemingway's fiction in the same way: the trauma of war is not a cause but a metaphor, an "objective correlative," for Hemingway's vision. That vision is rooted in Hemingway's childhood. It felt true to its audience because it described the condition of childhood that was growing increasingly common and the disillusionment that so many people experienced after the war.

Disillusionment developing out of the war and the social and economic turmoil that followed may have helped shape the choice of directions within modernism—its audience's emphasis on order and tradition rather than on revolt. Disillusionment also explains better than either the economic needs of market capitalism or the machinations of political conservatives the tendency of modernism's audience to emphasize the formalist, traditionalist directions within modernism. The same needs that led Eliot to declare himself an Anglican, a Royalist, a classicist, led its audience to emphasize Eliot's version of modernism.

Modernism gained its audience, then, an audience that in turn decided which tendency within modernism would be emphasized, because modernism accurately described the feelings of a postwar generation: the absence of credible authority, the absence of a family structure in which you could be grounded, the sense of inner chaos and outer meaninglessness. But there is something else, *something positive*, going on. Or perhaps what I am about to say is simply a positive statement of the same phenomenon. Modernist art—specifically, modernist literature—gave people an orientation to modernity, an orientation to a disorienting reality. In doing this, modernism served a quasi-religious function. In expressing and naming for its audience the experience of emptiness, alienation, and anxiety, modernism ironically assuaged the condition by creating a community in which such feelings are held in common. Trilling speaks of a "second environment,"[10] an environment of art and freedom alien to the dominant culture. Artists and their audience found in this environment a fellowship in which their aloneness and pain was confirmed, and by being confirmed, diminished. We were in the same lifeboat. It was a holding environment for anxiety and disillusionment. While I feel overdramatic making the comparison, it seems like a civilian version of the comradeship under conditions of terror that Fussell and others describe as taking shape in the trenches. If modern reality was defamiliarized, we learned through modernism how to make the defamiliarized familiar; disorientation became our orientation.

Again ironically, modernists, who themselves had no fathers, became *our* fathers. A student of mine who recently graduated, a young writer, alienated from the contemporary world and from his own family, told me in my office how lost he felt, how rootless, weightless, directionless. "I'm reading Woolf, Joyce, Lawrence," he said with a shrug, as if he were a little embarrassed.

"You identify with them?"

"Well, they went out and did it. They faced it. You know—alone. Maybe," he laughed, "I'm looking for a father."

Flaubert, I told him, once said, "Bohemia is my Fatherland." And what a strange country to come from! In a sense, the modernists this young man reads *are* surrogate fathers, providing, in their lives and writing, a model of courage, an ego ideal. *Postmodern* writers might see with irony that lonely spiritual struggle, might treat it as a gambit to pluck out of the museum collection of spiritual stances and try on—remembering always to keep quotation marks around it. But modernists were the last of the heroic, romantic artists. James Baldwin, in his magnificent story "Sonny's Blues," expresses in the figure of the jazz artist this spiritual courage:

> Then Creole stepped forward to remind them that what they were playing was the blues. He hit something in all of them, he hit something in me, myself, and the music tightened and deepened, apprehension began to beat the air. Creole began to tell us what the blues were all about. They were not about anything very new. He and his boys up there were keeping it new, at the risk of ruin, destruction, madness, and death, in order to find new ways to make us listen. For while the tale of how we suffer, and how we are delighted, and how we may

triumph is never new, it always must be heard. There isn't any other tale to tell, it's the only light we've got in all this darkness.

My student was being fathered, in a sense, by the figure of Creole, the artist who teaches that it is necessary to risk emptiness, loneliness, darkness, in order to shape something true about life. It is what Allen Ginsberg meant when he called Walt Whitman a "lonely old courage teacher."

I've spoken about the modernists' gestures of healing. In a sense, these writers were *my* healing. You grow up (I grew up) in a culture that offers no moral assurance let alone certainties, that gives you (that gave me) no place to stand, no way to be a person; and modernist novelists, poets, visual artists act as courage-teachers, explorers, fathers teaching you to face the darkness and survive.

The contradictions! Courage, retreat. Modernism was from its beginnings an art of personal rebellion. It broke conventions, artistic forms. It was fueled, as Eksteins shows, by the release of underground sexual energies. Its heroes are Nietzsche and Bergson. The artist destroys the given world to remake it for him- or herself. But modernism is also an art that emphasizes formal relations, tradition, dehumanized order, that is impersonal, that examines its own activity and creates a harmonious inner order as an alternative version of reality.[11]

Both. While later, in the academy, modernism may have emphasized formal order, aesthetic pattern, what its contemporary audience needed and found in it was both personal expression, regeneration, support for the shaping of an alternative self, a self in opposition to conventional models, as well as wholeness, harmony of inner relations.

Each writer named, mapped, some problematic aspect of our reality. Feeling it named, we, like the writers, felt in control of it and felt connected to others who experienced it. We were also offered strategies of handling the experience. Fragmented experiences could be subsumed into a pattern and connected by means of myth, as Eliot taught us, as he taught us to distance ourselves from the condition of cultural emptiness and confusion by naming it. The trick was to dive into the wreck yet keep some part of the self to stand above the wreckage. That's one value of the use of myth.

These writers were spiritual guides for their audience—guides in Creole's way of diving into the wreck. The audience was taught how to dive beneath the surface of cultural falseness and the superficial ego and bring up an alternative vision and an alternative self. These writers were also spiritual guides—and this is less obvious—in revivifying and making palatable a kind of religious humanism.

One of the paradoxes of modernism is that while the modernist writers taken into the canon were explorers of the falsity of the cultural surface, they were also defenders of the traditional values of the culture. Saul Bellow's Nobel Prize address (1976) pays homage to Conrad's preface to *The Nigger of the "Narcissus."* He quotes the passage in which Conrad speaks of descending within himself and finding "the terms of his appeal . . . to that part of our being which is a gift, not an acquisition . . . to the latent feeling of fellowship with all creation—and to the subtle but invincible conviction of solidarity . . . which binds together all humanity." Bellow comments,

> We may want to take it with a few grains of contemporary salt. I belong to a generation of readers that knew the long list of noble or noble-sounding words, words like "invincible conviction" or "humanity" that had been rejected by writers like Ernest Hemingway. . . . I told myself . . . that Conrad's rhetoric must be resisted. But I never thought him mistaken. He spoke directly to me. The feeling individual appeared weak—he felt nothing but his own weakness. But if he accepted his weakness and his separateness and descended into himself, intensifying his loneliness, he discovered his solidarity with other isolated creatures.

Bellow is not considering—and does not need to consider for his purpose—that this formulation by Conrad is a prayer more than a conviction. It represents the distillation of a terrible struggle in Conrad's soul, and that is why, knowing Conrad, we respect it. But it surely expresses a heroic, religious humanism that speaks for Bellow as much as for Conrad.[12]

In that same speech Bellow does not refer to another Nobel Prize address that must have been on his and everyone's mind at the gathering in Stockholm: the speech by William Faulkner. When Bellow asks "Can it be that human beings are at a dead end?" and wishes for an art addressing the question of "mankind determining . . . whether it will endure or go under," the audience must be remembering Faulkner's ringing, "I believe that man will not merely endure: he will prevail." Faulkner proposes "problems of the spirit" as the true subject for writers. His own life's work, he says, was done "in the agony and sweat of the human spirit." Bellow speaks of the true being under the false, glimpses of "true impressions" under the false: "We never seem to lose our connection with the depths from which these glimpses come. . . . We are reluctant to talk about this because . . . people would have to say, 'There is a spirit,' and that is taboo. So almost everyone keeps quiet about it, although almost everyone is aware of it." All three writers have earned these celebrations of the human spirit in struggles that make it possible for their audience, like Baldwin's, to take them seriously.

Each of the writers in this study—James, Conrad, Ford, Forster, Joyce, Woolf, Lawrence, Fitzgerald, Hemingway, Faulkner—expresses the emptiness, the falsity of the cultural surface. But each one of them is at the same time a struggling defender of traditional values of the culture. By that I'm not referring to the fact that each (except, of course, for Woolf and possibly Forster) unfortunately asserts what it's become conventional to call the values of the patriarchy; I'm not referring to the fact that each (except for Joyce) unfortunately asserts traditional values of race and class. I mean, rather, that having explored the falsity, the nothingness, of the social surface and the lonely, terrifying place beneath that surface, these writers give their readers fictions in which there is the possibility of true life, in which the fictional world manifests that truer life. "Why read the work of such tortured writers?" my students have asked. One reason is that they offer us visions of possibility for our lives within the wreckage.

I have named and explored some of these visions in the course of this study. In the style of Woolf's fiction we are offered an antidote for the isolation and ephemerality, the darkness of human life. In Lawrence's passionate language we are given a model of connection between spirit and world; it is a language of being-in-the-world, and it revivifies the world of being for us. Hemingway shows us nothingness, but in the simple dignity of his style he offers us a model for being true to our experience of the world. He gives us the concrete world and a style of being that permits us to savor it. Joyce describes modern paralysis but gives us a way of experiencing the world in wonder and ecstasy.

They are, as I have said, the last of the heroic, romantic artists. Robbe-Grillet, condescending to Albert Camus, says, "The world is not absurd. It simply *is*." What was absurd, for Camus, was the contradiction between the world and the longing of the human heart. The implied figure of the artist-everyman is of one doing battle with the absurd, and, paradoxically, in that very battle making it meaningful. But Robbe-Grillet and the postmodern writers who surround us do not experience—or at least do not ask us to experience—this heroic struggle. The world simply *is*. For modernist writers, for the audience of modernism, the world is still a battleground, and the victory is the possibility of the making of meaning, the making of a world expressing spirit.

PART SIX

INDIVIDUAL STUDIES

CHAPTER TEN

THE PSYCHOLOGICAL STRATEGY OF HENRY JAMES

T HIS IS A STUDY in chaos, its sources lying in childhood experience and adult defenses against it. It is also a study in the transformation of psychological defenses into a literary strategy. James served as the Master for a literary culture that needed, as he did, to valorize as an aesthetic defenses against psychological chaos.

But they are not merely "defenses." And he was truly a master, able to shape in language a contemplative space that he used as a refuge, but that extended beyond refuge, too—a place of transformation, of healing, making whole. It wasn't simply a place in which creativity was possible but a representation of the creative imagination in its war with chaos.

William, Henry, Garth Wilkinson, Robertson, and Alice James: if you did not know the stories of their adult lives, you would envy children brought up in such freedom within a rigid Victorian America. A kindly philosopher father, a loving mother and aunt, opportunities for travel, contact with the best minds of the age, concern for education. And yet four of the children were invalids for extended periods; the two younger sons were failures; Alice was "neurasthenic," depressed, unable to take care of herself. She suffered intense psychosomatic symptoms and was essentially an invalid for her adult life. Robertson, like Henry and William, was sick with back trouble—and also kidney trouble, poor digestion, constipation, and depression. William was as a young man almost suicidally depressed; according to Leon Edel, he and Henry passed psychosomatic illness back and forth between them. Henry had at least two serious breakdowns, first when he couldn't find an audience for his plays, then more severely, when his New York Edition was a commercial failure. And, while he had good friends, he was essentially and deeply alone.

In 1910 James went through a dark night of the soul. It is not the fact of his despair but its particular quality that interests me here. In a painful letter, Edith Wharton, James's close friend and student, tells Morton Fullerton about James's breakdown:

> When I entered, there lay a prone motionless James, with a stony stricken face, who just turned his tragic eyes towards me—the eyes of a man who has looked on the Medusa! the good nephew slipped out, and I sat down beside the sofa, and for a terrible hour looked into the black depths over which he is hanging. . . . I could hardly believe it was the same James who cried out to me his fear, his despair, his craving for the "cessation of consciousness," and all his unspeakable loneliness and need of comfort, and inability to be comforted! "Not to wake—not to wake—" that was his refrain, "& then one *does* wake, & one looks again into the blackness of life, & everything ministers to it—all one reads & sees & hears." And London is a torture—and the thought of the return to Rye intolerable . . . ; solitude suicidal; & companionship excruciating. . . . At the end . . . after pleading me to stay—"Don't go, my child, don't go—think of my awful loneliness!" he wanted me no more and could hardly wait for me to be out the door![1]

This is so painful to read about a novelist whom I admire as much as I admire James that I feel something close to shame in quoting it, as if it were too intimate and might distort my experience of a great writer. On the other hand, to remember this breakdown helps me see an unapproachable Master—the persona that James himself gave shape to—as a struggling person. And what are the terms of that struggle? We are witnessing a man whose defenses have broken down, who is terrified of isolation and of connection both, the response of someone whose self has failed. We are witnessing regression to pre-oedipal anxieties of abandonment and engulfment.

It makes me want to examine his childhood. What kind of mothering, what kind of fathering, did Henry James and his siblings endure?

THE FAMILY

We don't know much about Mary James. In *A Small Boy and Others,* Henry speaks of his mother in only a few paragraphs. Leon Edel says that when his nephew asked why he hadn't said more, Henry answered, "Oh! my dear boy—that memory is too sacred" (*Henry James: A Life,* p. 14). He idealized her as the "keystone" of the family arch. After her death, he wrote in his journal, "She held us all together, and without her we are scattered reeds" (p. 275).

That she was beloved and central is clear. It is also clear that she ran the family and demanded compliance from husband and children. Compliance was the trade-off for her energetic devotion. Jean Strouse writes, "Mary James, accustomed to managing everyone around her, continued to supervise the emotional lives of her children long after they were grown" (p. 24).

Her children seem to have nursed unconscious resentment of her. Edel points out that although Henry idealized his mother, "she is incarnated in his fiction not as the fragile self-effacing and self-denying woman he pictured in his filial piety. . . . The mothers of Henry James, for all their maternal sweetness, are strong, determined, demanding, grasping women—Mrs. Touchett or Mrs. Gereth, Mrs. Hudson or Mrs. Newsome. They are neither ideal nor ethereal" (*A Life*, p. 276). James Anderson gives us a Mary James who was critical, judgmental, demanding of her children, and a William who felt her pressure strongly and responded to the pressure with hostile humor and psychosomatic illness.[2] Strouse, too, sees Mary as unable to nourish the children emotionally, while their father was "extravagant in his gestures of love" (p. 46). It is as if Mary were in some ways the prescribed Victorian father and Henry Sr., the mother. Strouse quotes Lila Cabot's description of "the James house ruled by Mrs. James where HJ's father used to limp in and out" (p. 44).

Henry James, Sr., was a shaken man. He had not pleased his father, a powerful, wealthy, self-righteous merchant, and only when at thirteen his leg was burned and had to be amputated did he understand how much his father cared for him. (Could it be that the trade-off of illness for understanding in the family began here?) He was oppressed by his father's Calvinist God, felt under His gaze at all times. "To baffle the detective gaze of a suspicious Calvinist Deity, to find a benign and friendly God, this was to be the troubled quest of Henry James Senior" (Edel, *Untried Years*, p. 23).

Living in London as a young man with two young children, he experienced a "great vastation," an invisible shape squatting in the room, "raying out from his fetid personality influences fatal to life" (*Untried Years*, p. 30). "The thing had not lasted ten seconds before I felt myself a wreck; that is, reduced from a state of . . . manhood to one of almost helpless infancy" (p. 30). It is a moment of terror that is repeated in

William's attack of terror at aged twenty-seven, terror that seemed to come at him out of the darkness. And it seems to be echoed in Henry Jr.'s ghost stories, especially "The Jolly Corner." Henry Sr. pulled himself together with the help of the philosophy of Swedenborg—"vastation" is Swedenborg's term for one stage of a process of regeneration. But in a sense he was unmanned by the experience, as he was by the earlier amputation.

Henry Sr. felt uneasy at his lack of a place, a career, and indeed, although he was respected as a man of thought, he was not successful as a writer. And so the children grew up with a father who was crippled, insecure, unsuccessful. A man without a place. Henry Jr. felt as a child that his father's crippled condition and lack of public recognition were one— in his own words, they "melt together." He was faced, Edel writes, with a father "manly, yet weak and feminine . . . and a mother, strong, firm but irrational and contradictory" (*A Life,* p. 15).[3]

A child growing up in Victorian America needed identification with a strong male figure.[4] He needed the father as an ego ideal and as a protection from engulfment by the mother—especially a mother like Mary James.[5] Henry lacked such a father; still, he survived. He was his mother's favorite, and he developed the defensive and compensatory structures we see reflected in his fiction. Most important among these structures is the posture of knowing observer, detached from the flow of experience. This figure stays safe by keeping out of combat, as Henry Sr. was out of combat, a detached intellectual, and as Henry Jr. himself was out of combat during the Civil War, forced out, as he said, by his "obscure hurt." He flees the impinging mother, he flees turbulence and competition much as his father did. Outside the war, outside the economic wars in America, removed from the sexual battlefield, he turns his disability into a position of moral as well as aesthetic authority, then teaches this (unconscious) strategy to his spiritual followers, who need it for much the same reason as James himself. It is a strategy he learned from his father.

Henry James, Sr., in a sense acted out his self-doubt and lack of place by his constant travels with his family. The traveling was purportedly in search of the perfect education for his children, but what the children particularly learned was instability, confusion of direction, absence of anything solid under their feet. To Zurich, to Paris, to London, to New York, to Newport, back to Europe, back to the States. Edel believes that Henry, writing about his childhood, omitted one of the trips to Europe out of embarrassment. They were hotel children, comparable to the dislocated children of military or foreign service families, and yet, unlike such families, not even part of a community of families—they were alone, drifting back and forth. In 1888 Alice writes William, suggesting that he *not* bring his children to Europe: "What enrichment of mind and memory can children have without continuity & if they are torn up by the roots every little while as we were! Of all things don't make the mistake which brought about our rootless and accidental childhood."[6]

It was a childhood of chaos, and the chaos was as much in spirit and intellect as in place. F. O. Matthiessen writes, "Their father sent them to church in much the same spirit that he sent them to the theater. They were to go to all churches in turn, to appreciate and judge for themselves" (p. 82). Freedom or confusion? Howard Feinstein describes the irrational, changing way that Henry James, Sr., dealt with William over his choice of a career:

> In his Fourierest phase, Henry James spoke of the artist in laudatory terms. Yet, when his son wanted to be a painter, he scorned the choice. Then he glorified science, and at first encouraged his son in that direction. But when William became a scientist, his father was full of foreboding about the impact of a scientific career on his moral development. Henry James was devoted to philosophy throughout his adult life and he nurtured his son's philosophical talents. Yet when William turned to philosophy in his mature years, his father vehemently condemned academic philosophers. (P. 90)

I am suggesting that this chaotic, inspiring childhood—with a mother as controlling as Mary James and a father without ground under his feet—this childhood was the basis for the anxiety of emptiness and the tendency toward distancing and regression that Henry James expressed in his art: the figures who are not quite in the world; the detachment and subjectification of perspective; the need to defend the "central ego" and the resulting loneliness; the yearning to reach down into fuller life—and the revulsion built on terror.[7] Deracination and alienation were of great advantage to James; they helped form him into a modernist a generation early. They were also the source of the cross he bore.

ART AND CHAOS

It is not odd that this writer whose self was formed in such an unstable environment should place such weight on the isolated self, should see it—

more than any novelist I can think of before him—as the determinant of reality. It was a *familial* preoccupation.

The core meaning of James's valorization of the artist is that reality in itself is confusion, is "what passes"; experience has no intrinsic meaning, no significance at all until the individual artist lends significance to experience: "Life being all inclusion and confusion, and art being all discrimination and selection."[8] Or again, he writes, "Really, universally, relations stop nowhere, and the exquisite problem of the artist is eternally but to draw, by a geometry of his own, the circle within which they shall happily *appear* to do so."[9] How curiously similar that aesthetic vision is to the philosophy of his brother William! In *Essays in Radical Empiricism*, William James writes, "Our universe is to a large extent chaotic. No one single type of connection runs through all the experiences that compose it";[10] in *Principles of Psychology*, he "marvels at how 'other minds' carve out 'other worlds from the same monotonous and inexpressive chaos.' "[11] And then there is the famous dictum of William's that "the baby, assailed by eyes, ears, nose, skin, and entrails at once, feels it all as one great blooming, buzzing confusion."[12]

There is, we can now see, no inevitability about such a picture of infancy. Daniel Stern, in *The Interpersonal World of the Infant*, gives us the clearest picture of the infant as understood by developmental psychologists today—and it is utterly different: "Can infants also experience nonorganization? No! . . . Only an observer who has enough perspective to know the future course of things can even imagine an undifferentiated state. Infants cannot know *what* they do not know, nor *that* they do not know." Earlier theorists, realizing that infants were in a less organized, differentiated world than older children, attributed to them the experience of undifferentiation.[13] Stern sees the attribution of a state of chaos to infants as the reification of how an adult imagines infancy. I am arguing that the imaginings of Henry and William are very high-level defensive formulations that explain and handle their experience of life as chaos, the self as a fragile constructor of meaning.

Of course, William James is not the only theorist who saw infancy as chaos that gets slowly shaped into order. It is a *period* vision of infancy—indeed, of life. It is the new epistemology. Joyce dramatizes it in *A Portrait of the Artist as a Young Man:* the artist as Everyman, shaping chaos into personal order. But I can feel how compatible a vision it must have been for William James—chaos yielding to creative order—as it was for Henry

James: compatible, I mean, with their experience both of the instability of their family of origin and the instability and moral chaos of their culture.

In response to confusion, chaos, disorganization, the artist at the turn of the century is seen as creating the order of reality. This is the vision of the art novel from Flaubert onward, the vision of modern art. It has become such a familiar vision that we have a hard time seeing it as anything but inevitable. I would argue that the human creation of ordered reality is at the core of the modernist vision.[14] And so, in the study of history, we become historiographers, energized by the insight that history is not "out there" or "back there" but a product created by historians through selection informed by a shaping vision. And in the sciences, we see with Thomas Kuhn (*The Structure of Scientific Revolutions*) that new theory is not a closer approximation of some ultimate model of reality but a means of asking new questions, a heuristic, a piece of human architecture. Knowledge, from Mannheim to Habermas, is not able to be separated from the knower, from human interests.[15] In the novel, this epistemological position is expressed in the exaggerated emphasis on point of view: Who is telling the story? How much does the narrator know? Attribution of omniscience is refused in fiction as in religion; indeterminancy becomes an aesthetic principle. Ultimately, the reader, like the writer, cannot know. Chronology fragments; a story is told backward and forward; it has to be pieced together by a reader, who is forced to imitate the position of the writer. And most important, the novel's *shaping* is what is emphasized, not the life that is shaped, for life without the artist is a "blooming, buzzing confusion."

This is not, as I say, an inevitable vision. I think of Wordsworth's infant, who comes from Heaven, which is his home. For Wordsworth, the growth of human order is the imposition on original reality of an imposed structure. Such structure, though it has compensations, is the betrayal of a truer order. For transcendentalist artists, the world is not chaos but the language of God, the clothes of God. The artist's job is to become a channel for expressing that prior truth. For D. H. Lawrence in our own century, as for Heidegger, though indeed we perceive the world through our interpretive schemas, our foreconceptions, reality is deeply, deeply *there,* and the artist must silence herself, must get beneath its surface and attune herself to it. Ursula, near the end of *Women in Love,* speaks for Lawrence when she condemns Loerke, a prototypical modernist artist who separates art and life: "As for your world of art and your world of reality," she replied, "you have to separate the two, because you can't bear to know what you are. . . . The world of art is only the truth about the real world, that's all— but you are too far gone to see it" (p. 431).

But for Henry James, the separation is primary. And so it is the artist who, stepping back from the world, *makes significance*. It is "the consciousness of the artist," his post of observation at one of the million windows of the house of fiction, that matters.[16]

What a vision of art and life!

The artist is isolated at that window, creating in the act of perceiving. In *The Phenomenology of Henry James*, Paul Armstrong sees James as balanced between epistemologies: "James stands with one foot in the nineteenth century and one foot in the twentieth" (p. 209). While James maintains allegiance to mimesis, he challenges its underpinnings, insisting on the artist's unique world-creation. I agree. But I disagree with Armstrong when he tries to link James to Heidegger. Heidegger insists on a world ready-to-hand, a world not out there to be observed but one in which *Dasein* is immersed. According to Armstrong, in Heidegger, "existence . . . can disclose real possibilities for itself only by resolutely engaging its 'there'" (p. 51). There is no pure, disattached perception. But disattached perception, it seems to me, is just the kind of perception that James's narrators pretend and that James himself needs. Armstrong cites Merleau-Ponty's observation that "the system of experience is not arrayed before me as if I were God, it is lived by me from a certain point of view" (p. 49). Armstrong, going on to speak of James's vision of fiction as a house with many windows, says that it "captures in polyvalent language what I have been trying to clarify systematically with the univocal terms of phenomenology" (p. 51). But in fact the image of artist at window is precisely that of a detached observer; not someone shaping a world in which he or she is immersed but someone standing back like God, separate, absorbing impressions and shaping them into meaning.

It is a privileged position, for from this unique perspective the artist can make something out of the chaos. But chaos—the "misrule and confusion of his father's house" (*Portrait*)—is what the artist has to work with. And then, it is a terribly lonely position. Can the artist communicate what he or she sees? Only to the incredibly sensitive reader; to the reader as soul in affinity—as artist. Such a reader is willing to give up livelihood, as in "The Middle Years"; such a reader can, as in "The Figure in the Carpet," live solely by an understanding of the art. But this is one reader in thousands.

CONTEMPLATIVE SPACE

"Perhaps the greatest breach in nature," William wrote in 1890, is "the breach from one mind to another."[17] Henry James was the Master for Joseph Conrad, and I understand, as have many critics,[18] the congeniality for Conrad in a technique that so emphasized how reality is perceived by a particular self. Conrad's Marlow despairs of being able to bridge the gap between teller and listener: *We live, as we dream, alone.* Whether or not Marlow was derived from the Chinese boxes of narration in *The Turn of the Screw,* it is clear how much affinity Conrad must have felt for a writer like James who emphasized isolated subjectivity. And Ford! "We are all so afraid, we are all so alone." And Woolf: "Here was one room; there another. Did religion solve that, or love?" And Forster, whose "only connect" points, like Conrad's passionate plea for "solidarity," to disconnection, to isolation and separate realities.[19] I don't mean to reduce to simple affinity of anxieties the significance of James as a teacher, but I do want to point out those affinities of isolated subjectivity. If for Conrad the artist is an affirmer of solidarity against the experience of isolated subjectivity, for James solidarity seems almost unattainable; the walls seem almost unbreachable.

As no other writer, James insisted on the dramatic; and yet, as readers have always seen, there is, at least in the late novels, little *external* drama. How can you have both isolation and drama? You can—but at first it seems oxymoronic. In *The Ambassadors* we don't get a rendering of experience—not even of Strether's experience. The story itself is wonderfully dramatic: Strether has been asked by Mrs. Newsome, a rich widow from Woollett, Massachusetts, to go to Paris to save her grown son *from* Paris— to bring him home to take over the family industry; if Strether, a middle-aged widower, succeeds in bringing Chad home, he can marry Mrs. Newsome. But he finds he does not *want* to succeed; he finds in the old world a call to new life. Certainly a dramatic story—and yet, though there are some wonderful moments of overt drama (for instance, the morning Strether calls on Chad's sister and finds Madame de Vionnet there), for the most part the drama we experience is the drama of Strether's contemplation. We don't hear what happened. We don't see, even through Strether's perceptions, events as they occur. We overhear the struggle of his ruminations about the events. "Our friend was to go over it afterwards again and again" (p. 91). What is dramatized is not experience but the interpretation of experience. It is a drama of interpretation.

James's style must dramatize the detached place of contemplation to which the central consciousness—*and the reader*—can withdraw. That isn't simply the *effect* of the style—it is its essential gesture, its essential need. And so we are forced to parse our way through those tortuous sentences, relative clauses tenuously connected to distant abstract nouns.

Here's Strether sitting with Little Bilham and Miss Barrace, intensely *NOT* discussing the undiscussible:

> He wondered what they meant, but there were things he scarce thought they could be supposed to mean, and "Oh no—not *that!*" was at the end of most of his ventures. This was the very beginning with him of a condition as to which, later on, it will be seen, he found cause to pull himself up; and he was to remember the moment duly as the first step in a process. The central fact of the place was neither more nor less, when analyzed—and a pressure superficial sufficed—than the fundamental impropriety of Chad's situation, round about which they thus seemed cynically clustered. Accordingly, since they took it for granted, they took for granted all that was in connection with it taken for granted at Woollett—matters as to which, verily, he had been reduced with Mrs. Newsome to the last intensity of silence. That was the consequence of their being too bad to be talked about, and was the accompaniment, by the same token, of a deep conception of their badness. It befell therefore that when poor Strether put it to himself that their badness was ultimately, or perhaps even insolently, what such a scene as the one before him was, so to speak, built upon, he could scarce shirk the dilemma of reading a roundabout echo of them into almost anything that came up. (Pp. 78–79)

Attended to carefully, this is a very funny passage. The style mimics the reticence, the evasion. The reader and James's narrator are asked to contemplate the comedy of "poor Strether" trying to interpret without even daring to *think* too concretely about the life he was interpreting. Our distance is like Strether's own as he keeps this conversation a "scene"— something to observe, not something to live through.

It *is* dramatic. The narrator is showing us Strether in the initial throes of his changing. And we watch him struggling to interpret and not interpret at the same time. That is the drama of the novel as a whole. Here, in the style, the drama is played out in miniature. And yet the pleasure for James must have been—so much energy goes into it—*the creation in language of the contemplative space.* From this linguistic place of safety, we watch Strether interpret—and *re*interpret. For William James, as much as for Nietzsche, "*theories . . . become instruments, not answers to enigmas, in* *which we may rest*. We don't lie back upon them, we move forward, and, on occasion, make nature over again by their aid."[20] Both William and Henry try to interpret an indeterminate universe—a universe that cannot be finally interpreted. This indeterminacy combined with an obsession to interpret is at the core of the vision underlying Henry James's late fiction.

If James's late style is a masterful instrument, almost like a mantra, for generating a contemplative space from which to observe and interpret, its chief function is to keep James and the reader *at the window*. The quest for knowledge satisfies eros while keeping it at bay, keeping it as I shall show, *precariously* at bay. Know too much and the danger of erotic connection, of erotic engulfment, pulses back. It is a high-wire act, a balancing in a contemplative space between nonbeing and too-full being. This space, created by James's style, is one in which the self will not be dissolved, lost in chaos.

BEING AND NONBEING

The problem for James is that this self is necessarily cut off from full, passional, connected life—life which is, paradoxically, the source, the fountain, from which art springs.

In the late work of Henry James, characters choose limited being because full being is too terrible. "Live all you can; it's a mistake not to," Strether tells Little Bilham (*The Ambassadors*, p. 132). Yet finally Strether himself retreats from new life. First, he runs from one mother, Mrs. Newsome: "It having been but the day before yesterday that he sat at her feet and held on by her garment and was fed by her hand" (p. 196). Then, he runs from two more mothers, Madame de Vionnet, mother to Jeanne and to Chad, and Maria, who replaces Mrs. Newsome as Strether's teacher and nurturer.

Maria is acceptable in the role of reader, of interpreter; but when she tries to be more than that, Strether rejects her. In the preface to *The Ambassadors,* James defines Maria Gostrey's role as purely that of a *ficelle*. He rejects the notion that she is of any importance to Strether; rather, she is there to clarify matters for the reader. I would argue that James is fleeing the implications of Maria's character as much as Strether is fleeing Maria. James defends himself through a focus on technique. Again, he sees life through a window: "The house of fiction has in short not one window, but a million." Always, life is to be seen, seen and examined and interpreted—never touched. If D. H. Lawrence valorizes touch and de-means sight because sight preserves separation, James is the *champion* of sight for the same reason.

Insisting on dramatic objectivity, he shudders at "the *terrible fluidity* of self-revelation" (preface, *The Ambassadors*, p. 11; italics mine). *Terrible fluidity:* this is as much anxious fantasy about immersion in life as it is aesthetic position. I see James posturing as detached observer, acting out in his aesthetics his terror of immersion beneath the surface. In his 1870 letter written after the death of his cousin Minny Temple, James says, "It's the *living* ones that die; the writing ones that survive" (quoted by Strout, p. 52). James *wrote*—and lived, but lived, he feared, by avoiding life.

And yet all James's late fiction is obsessively concerned with getting beneath the surface, with uncovering. In a sense, his stories and novels are detective fiction; the reader and the point-of-view character examine and try to read beneath a surface. Shoshona Felman reads *The Turn of the Screw* as a detective story in which the detective turns out to be the criminal, in which the act of investigation is itself the crime (p. 176 and *passim*). That's true. But it's not true just of *The Turn of the Screw. The Sacred Fount*, "The Jolly Corner," *The Golden Bowl*, and certainly *The Ambassadors* are also stories of detection.

The Ambassadors is a detective story in which the detective does not want to detect too much. Maria, until she learns who Chad's friend is, tries to help Strether learn the truth about Chad's relationship. Maria tells him,

> "You must find out."
> It made him almost turn pale. "Find out any *more?*"
> He had dropped on a sofa for dismay; but she seemed, as she stood over him, to have the last word. "Wasn't what you came out for to find out *all?*"
> (Pp. 117–18)

Apparently not. Little Bilham hints, "You're not a person to whom it's easy to tell things you don't want to know" (p. 123). Why? Because although to know is to keep a distance, to know *all* is to become en-tangled, to touch levels of life that the quest for knowledge is meant to keep remote. "Knowledge, knowledge was a fascination as well as a fear."[21] Jean Strouse points out that while Henry's father believed that man finds God only after confronting evil, yet in the James household he tried to prevent that confrontation. "That basic contradiction" Strouse writes, "fostered in each of the children a preoccupation with morality and a tendency to dichotomize. To be innocent and good meant *not to know* the darker sides of one's own nature. To love and be loved, then, required the renunciation of certain kinds of knowledge and feeling" (p. 18).

James's relationship to knowledge is paradoxical. His emphasis on knowledge is itself a form of detachment from feelings. But go more deeply and knowledge taints the knower, becomes entangling, dangerous. It leads to the fuller feeling that it has tried to keep at a distance. Ruth Yeazell writes, "From the very first moment at which Strether lands at Liverpool . . . *The Ambassadors* becomes one long delaying action" (p. 21). He has, as Yeazell says, "conspired in his own deception" (p. 23). When he enters the French countryside to spend a quiet day, he wants to view the day as a work of art, as a painting by Lambinet. Seeing the lovers in the boat, Strether thinks them "exactly the right thing" (*The Ambassadors*, p. 307). And indeed they are, for, as James hints in the novel, at the taproot of art *is* erotic energy. Strether admires the artist Gloriani but sees in him something "tigerish" (p. 133). When the Lambinet turns into a liaison in which he is implicated, when he discovers that the picture-lovers are Chad and Madame de Vionnet, it seems anything but "exactly the right thing." The pleasure of the Lambinet dissolves into the anxiety of immersion in chaos, the expression of a fluid self that may be lost. At the close of *The Ambassadors*, Strether flees life; he will remain on its surface. His choice is mystified by Strether—and James, too—as a fine unwillingness to have won anything for himself. I see it as flight from full being.

"The Beast in the Jungle," written just before *The Ambassadors*," is of course overtly about the condition of a chosen nonbeing, and in this story, the condition is not valorized as contemplation or aesthetic detachment. May Bartram and John Marcher wait for something that will happen to Marcher, that will mark him. He has "the sense of being kept for something rare and strange" (p. 331). He waits, he never lives. She, who has loved him, has had her experience. But he "has been *the* man, to whom nothing on earth was to have happened" (p. 366). His emptiness is squarely faced, its defensive nature is examined. Strether also wonders whether he wasn't kept by his fate for something that he could not divine; he feels "half ashamed of his impulse to plunge and more than half afraid of his impulse to wait" (*The Ambassadors*, p. 63). Strether is not nearly as cut off from life as John Marcher. But James uses both to express the part of himself which is defended against full libidinal life and active connection with other people, which fears disintegration, chaos in the self, psychic annihilation.[22]

The strain of keeping up his social mask must have been enormous for James. He kept at bay homosexual feelings, only permitting them any sway at all after he met Hendrik Andersen in 1899. A good friend to many women, he ran from entanglements with them. I am thinking especially of Constance Fenimore Woolson, who loved him and, according to Edel, may have served to some extent as a model for the character of May Bartram. (It is likely he felt partial responsibility for her suicide.) His friend Edith Wharton he described as a "firebird" who would catch him up in "her irresistible talons" (Edel, *A Life*, p. 679). Beneath the comedy, he seems to have feared her engulfing energy.

Perhaps what he feared most, however, was his own shadow—the darker nature he sees in the terrifying double in "The Jolly Corner."[23] Written at the same time as *The American Scene* (1906) and just after his return from the United States, "The Jolly Corner" makes more explicit the psychic deal James has cut for himself.

Spencer Brydon, returning in middle age to a New York he fled as a young man, wonders about the person he might have become had he stayed. To Alice Staverton, who loves him and has never married, he confides his fantasy that the ghost of that unlived self still lives in the family house in New York. Surrendering to his obsession, he "hunts" his alter ego. The metaphor is James's—or rather, Brydon's. His "prey" is in the "jungle" of the rear of the house. He "stalks" this "beast of the forest," a "monstrous stealthy cat," through the house until he is himself hunted—and grows terrified. Looking into the face of the ghost, he faints. It is the face of a stranger; he denies to Alice that it could be his double. But she says, "Isn't the whole point that you'd have been different?" ("The Jolly Corner," p. 402).

But, of course, not different enough, for the potentiality to be this monster is there. As in *Dr. Jekyll and Mr. Hyde,* the double is, in James's words, a "brute," a "horror," a "black stranger," but the stranger is the buried self. I remember Virginia Woolf's terrifying dream of looking into a mirror and seeing a beast. Her withdrawal from sensual life and James's are similar.

We can see the meaning for Brydon of life in Europe: Europe represents a monastic withdrawal from the darkness of his own aggressive and erotic life. Brydon's—and America's. For James portrays the America of 1906, the America he had just visited, as monstrous, too. The narrator speaks of the "'swagger' things, the modern, the monstrous, the famous things" (p. 372). And it would be immersion in the national life that would have turned Brydon into the monster: "James highlighted the split in postwar American society between femininity, sickliness, and the appreciation of cultural refinement, on the one hand, and a self-assertive masculine tradition blind to the subtleties of imaginative vision on the other" (Strouse, p. 50). That split is precisely dramatized in "The Jolly Corner."

Brydon feels he might have been a real success had he stayed. But modern America makes him deal daily with a "bristling line of hard unconscious heads" (p. 328). *Bristling* is a word often associated in James's later fiction (especially *The Turn of the Screw* and *The Ambassadors*) with sexuality and aggression. Later in the story, it is Brydon's other self that "bristled there." It is not the potentiality of failure in this world that frightens Brydon; it is "bristling" success. Jean Strouse again: "Henry had withdrawn early from the competitive, masculine fray to a safe inner world, taking the part of the docile, easy 'good' James child" (p. 49). As an adult, he kept this psychic contract, retreating from an America seen as a boiling pot of aggression and sexuality into the life of the detached Master of art.

There are differences. At the end of the story, Brydon is being nursed by Alice Staverton, his head on her lap. Safe in the world of women, Brydon does not make the same psychic deal as James did, nor does he have the same psychic understanding. Brydon is perhaps getting involved in real estate development, and he does take Alice into his arms. He refuses to recognize his double as in any way himself. James, on the other hand, clearly understands the "monster" as a secret sharer, and he ends in no one's arms, withdrawing from the America of aggression and ambition—though, as I shall argue, not withdrawing from a different form of power.

PARADISE

The refuge, the contemplative space James creates, can best be seen in his stories about writers, particularly "The Great Good Place." Here a literary Master, burdened unto death by the personal attentions of his ignorant public, slips away to a kind of restorative clinic while his young friend takes his place in the outside world. Here is James's paradise. It is a refuge, a place of healing, of peace. Here are no abrasive contacts. Minds seem to intuit one another's thoughts. The artist has found a restorative space in himself.

The Great Good Place, the name George Dane gives to the estate/ clinic/monastery, is in fact the creation of the artist, since at the end of the story we discover he has never left his couch. What is the good place, in fact, but a work of imagination, a work of art? Art, then, is the place of refuge and restoration. It is a model of James's own art, not a place in which the self is cast off but rather where "the inner life woke up again" ("The Great Good Place," p. 304). It is an art "all beautified with omissions" (p. 305). It is "more and more a world of reason and order, of sensible visible arrangement" (pp. 302–3). He describes it precisely as James describes high art: "It was high triumphant clearness" (p. 303). It reminds Dane of "some old Italian picture, some Carpaccio or some early Tuscan, the representation of a world without newspapers . . . without the dreadful fatal too much" (p. 305).

But this art, with its "masculine" firmness, is in fact dependent on the female. Its "source" in the story is literally water, the rush of rain that floods his window when he is at his most strained. This flood "seemed the right thing . . . the thing that if it would only last, might clear the ground by floating out to a boundless sea the innumerable objects among which his feet stumbled and strayed" (pp. 288–89). The ordinary personality, the encumbered self, is what needs to be washed away. And it is. When we next find Dane, *in* the Great Good Place, he is in a "broad deep bath of stillness." He and the other "brothers" sit in the bath with "water up to their chins." This water is at once connected to an earlier flood, the terrific rains of the night before: "only a flood of rushing waters in which bumping and gasping were all" (p. 293). If the rushing waters seem like an unconscious allusion to birthing, these "tepid" quiet waters seem a return to a uterine condition. They are, at least, connected to the Mother:

> "The next thing you'll be saying that we're babes at the breast!"
> "Of some great mild invisible mother who stretches away into space and whose lap's the whole valley—?"
> "And her bosom" Dane completed the figure—"the noble eminence of our hill?" (P. 309)

Refuge from the busy, male world to the womb or lap of the mother. The rainwaters that washed Dane's window were seen as the expression of nature, a nature spoken of as "she." If James's story is one of regression to infantile dependence, it is a dependence that can restore the self. It is like a model of therapeutic regression in Winnicott, regression in which the patient can recover his or her true self. Indeed, Winnicott's model is strangely similar to my reading of this story. "The person we are trying to help," he says, needs a new experience in a specialized setting. The experience is one of a non-purposive state" (*Playing and Reality,* p. 55). I am not saying that James has performed his own analysis; only that he has fairly precisely described his need. Dependence when not in the presence of someone who can function as an analyst does not lead magically to the development of a newly restored self. It leads to further dependence, like Alice James's on Katherine Loring. "The Great Good Place" can be read as a psychological fable of James's longing to get rid of the burden of his defensive structures, his "central ego" (in the language of Fairbairn and Guntrip), to sink into regressed levels of the self and be nurtured into new selfhood: "What *was* the general charm? He couldn't . . . easily have phrased it; it was such an abyss of negatives, such an absence of positives and of everything" ("The Great Good Place," p. 293). This regression is in a sense into nada! But it is nada as nirvana. Only in the nothing is something to be found. The world has to stop impinging, has to become the potential space (Winnicott's term) for a person to create the world that is, paradoxically, already there. In "The Capacity to be Alone," Winnicott tells us that "a considerable amount of work has been done on the withdrawn state, a defensive organization implying an expectation of persecution. It would seem to me that a discussion on the *positive* aspects of the capacity to be alone is overdue" (*Maturational Processes,* p. 29). Winnicott connects the capacity to be alone with creative play and notes the need to learn this capacity by first being alone in the presence of the mother. In "The Great Good Place" the artist has imagined what Winnicott would call an "*environment* mother," and when he returns to the ordinary world, he is restored to his creative work.

The story does not, however, deal with the darker aspect of the self found in the emptiness or under the surface. It is as if Marlow were to find the repressed parts of himself by floating down the mother river and out again, never meeting Kurtz, never touching "the horror." So we are left with the hope and sadness of a temporary relief.

But "The Great Good Place" is merely a fable of healing. In the major fiction there is struggle, struggle to contain horror. I have been emphasizing throughout this chapter an unbearably lonely James in a persecutory environment, the James whom Edith Wharton described to Morton Fullerton—needing comfort yet unable to take comfort. In a sense, he is assailed by a ghost similar to the ghost his father experienced in "the great vastation" or the ghost that Spencer Brydon faced in "The Jolly Corner." It may be the ghost of his grandfather, as filtered through his father's fears. The powerful but devout merchant, William: if Henry Sr. looked into the face of the fierce, devout father, perhaps Henry Jr. looked, through his father, into the same face of the fierce grandfather of power. In *The Introductory Lectures,* Freud describes the son developing his superego not from the father but from the father's superego, which was shaped by *his* father. Perhaps the persecutory environment that James struggled to transform is the distillation of his father's experience of persecution at the hands—or, rather, the eyes—of William James of Albany.[24]

In a sense, at the heart of James's dramas is that struggle to transmute the persecutory or chaotic environment into a contemplative space in which the self is restored. He fashions elaborate weavings of language in which to contain the world, to hold it and to shape it. His sentences, especially in his late work, take their objects and weigh them, examine them from all sides, judge and qualify judgment, hold them in the hand like meditative objects. The sentences *contain*—in both senses: they hold and they keep at bay—horror. Maggie in *The Golden Bowl* "kept as tight hold of these reasons and these forms, in her confirmed horror, as the rider of a plunging horse grasps his seat with his knees" (p. 405). At the same time, the sentences contain *the reader*—create a place of safety, under control of the web of language. Meaning makes safety, that is its function. And so the drama, especially in late James, is the struggle of interpretive consciousness to contain horror and chaos.

The sentences weave pockets of safety, but it is the action of interpretation—and interpretation of interpretation—that does the work of containing horror. In *The Golden Bowl* it is the Princess's awareness of Fanny's awareness; it is the play of one mind imagining other minds imagining that transforms the persecutory environment into a contemplative space.

At a crucial moment of *The Golden Bowl,* Maggie happens on a little antique shop and buys a golden bowl. The shopkeeper, uneasy that she hadn't been aware of its secret crack, comes to see her and return some of the money. While he is there, he sees pictures of her husband and Charlotte and recognizes them as an intimate couple who had nearly bought the same bowl four years earlier. Thus, Maggie becomes aware that her husband and Charlotte had secretly known each other intimately before Maggie married him and before Charlotte married her father. This meeting with the shopkeeper who doesn't realize what he is revealing is a wonderful dramatic moment for a novelist—but James refuses it! He has Maggie first tell her *conclusions* to Fanny, who smashes the bowl. Then, quietly, Maggie lets her husband know she knows. Finally, many pages later, James lets us see Maggie ruminating on a follow-up discussion with her husband, a discussion we don't actually see. In her ruminations, we finally hear, in condensed form, the story of the shopkeeper's visit. James's way of giving us the scene of the visit allows us to focus on it as a contemplative object. His narrative strategy is precisely analogous to the way Maggie defuses the love affair between her husband and Charlotte, defuses it without smashing her father's marriage or her own: she contains the explosion in walls of grace and silence and thought.

And just as the silence and the web of awareness constitute Maggie's amazing power, her military strategy, her subtle aggression, her success, so James's style—his creation of contemplative space—is not merely his means of defense and refuge, but his subtle way of asserting power and glory. In *A Small Boy and Others* he describes a dream in which he visits the Galérie d'Apollon in the Louvre. He recalls that the actual visit manifested for him the glory of art and the power of the artist. In the dream he is pursued by a "dimly descried figure," but he turns, victorious, to pursue that figure. As Edel notes, it is a moment associated through the language with Napoleonic power. If so, it is not the power of phallic aggression, of American modernity and manliness, of business, not the power that Spencer Brydon, in "The Jolly Corner," sees in the bristling New York of the turn of the century; rather, it is power expressed in secret—and with aristocratic aloofness. So there is power as well as rest in the contemplative space. James's Great Good Place is the palace of art. It is, after all, a palace—and he is its Master.[25]

I see in James's fiction, as in the fiction of other modernists, gestures of healing, reparative acts that permit him to feel temporarily whole and to make some link, other than alienation, with the world. *Temporarily*— remember that description by Wharton of James's condition in 1910. Further, James, like other modernists, was able to recast flight as heroism: the artist as hero, aristocratic in his self-denial, in his dedication, in his choice of art over life. What starts, then, as defense becomes a position of extraordinary power. It gives someone without a ground of being a place to stand, while it justifies and even valorizes groundlessness. The privacy of the inner life becomes celebrated. James becomes the isolated, wounded artist, the sacred shaper of reality into contemplative space, a space in which I, too, am able to find clarity and rest.

CHAPTER ELEVEN

MOMENTS OF HEALING:

VIRGINIA WOOLF

A LL MODERNIST BRITISH and American fiction reveals the seductive pull of life under a false surface. This regressed life while frightening, while defended against, is itself refuge. At the same time (and this is terribly important and misunderstood) it can be an intimation of authentic, full being.

Here is Mrs. Ramsey, in *To the Lighthouse:*

> When life sank down for a moment, the range of experience seemed limitless. . . . The things you know us by . . . are simply childish. Beneath it is all dark, it is all spreading, it is unfathomably deep; but now and again we rise to the surface and that is what you see us by. . . . This core of darkness could go anywhere, for no one saw it. They could not stop it, she thought, exulting. There was freedom, there was peace, there was, most welcome of all, a summoning together, a resting on a platform of stability. Not as oneself did one find rest ever . . . but as a wedge of darkness. Losing personality, one lost the fret, the hurry, the stir; and there rose to her lips always some exclamation of triumph over life when things came together in this peace, this rest, this eternity. . . . We are in the hands of the Lord. (Pp. 96–97)

The surface, the depth. The personality "you see us by" and the wedge of darkness beneath, that dissolves boundaries between self and other "until she became the thing she looked at." One is alone, separate, but "things came together." Reading modernist texts, I think of "the darkness," of life below the surface, as engendering the anxiety of a loss of orientation. And yet here is darkness as an image of wholeness and peace, a place of true orientation. Here "we are in the hands of the Lord," are in, precisely, a "holding environment."[1] It is a place below, prior to, values, to personality, but that place, far from being nada, is home!

It is this aspect of Mrs. Ramsey's character that Ernest and Ina Wolf don't see in their Kohutian discussion of *To the Lighthouse*.[2] They regard Mrs. Ramsey as a "narcissistically injured person who needs hyperactively to keep the people of her environment enmeshed with her own personality in order to protect her defective self from disintegrating" (p. 46). They ignore the wholeness with which she is in touch. They see the yearning for cohesion as an attempt to repair her inadequate self by merging with others, but fail to see the richness of the place where she gains her power. The place is very rich. But one question I want to ask in this essay is What is the nature of this power? Is it a call to life or to death?

At some moments Woolf's characters reach this place alone, at other moments, in the presence of other people: Clarissa seeing the old woman through the window at the end of *Mrs. Dalloway*, Mrs. Ramsey feeling the coming-together of people at the magnificent dinner party in *To the Lighthouse*. "Things came together" into a unity experienced as ecstasy.

In "A Sketch of the Past" (see *Moments of Being*) Woolf depicts her own moments of ecstasy in childhood. As Ellen Rosenman notes, Woolf describes synesthetically in "a blurred coalescence of sounds and sights" (pp. 8–9) and of touch and smell, so that "sound seems to fall through an elastic, gummy air" (*Moments of Being*, p. 66). The fusion of senses is one of the tropes through which Woolf evokes the unity of experience that composes moments of true being. In the air of the St. Ives of her childhood summers, sound sinks down slowly, she remembers, "as if it were caught in a blue, gummy veil" (p. 66). I think of all the veils, mists, webs in Woolf's fiction. Here is the core, from childhood, of what they express.

This ecstasy in experience-that-is-unified uses imagery that reminds one—perhaps is intended to remind one—of life in the womb: "The impression of the waves and the acorns on the blind; the feeling, as I describe it sometimes to myself, of lying in a grape and seeing through a film of semi-transparent yellow" (p. 65). It is connected life, held being; in other words, the opposite of the disconnected, empty being fundamental to the anxiety underlying modernist fiction.

Her very earliest memory, the first in "A Sketch of the Past," is of her mother's lap. She is literally being "held." The other memories, of "ecstasy" or "rapture," are touched off by this one. Rapturously, she is looking at the gardens: "The buzz, the croon, the smell, all seemed to press voluptuously against some membrane; not to burst it; but to hum round one such a complete rapture of pleasure" (p. 66). It is as if the membrane separating the self from the world were stretched to transparency, almost to nonexistence. The self is in the world, part of the world, held in the body of world-as-mother—this is one way of describing the primary longing in Woolf's fiction. The memories are of light, not darkness, but they express the same fusion of self and world that Mrs. Ramsey longs for and at times experiences in her inner darkness.

It is an eroticized state, this state of ecstatic unity. Here is Clarissa Dalloway remembering moments of sexual feeling for women, when "she did undoubtedly . . . feel what men felt."

> Only for a moment; but it was enough. It was a sudden revelation, a tinge like a blush which one tried to check and then, as it spread, one yielded to its expansion, and rushed to the farthest verge and there quivered and felt the world come closer, swollen with some astonishing significance, some pressure of rapture, which split its thin skin and gushed and poured with an extraordinary alleviation over the cracks and sores. (P. 47)

A *healing*—here the experience of a world swollen with meaning, "some astonishing significance," a world like those early moments of rapture or ecstasy. And if those moments are connected with primal unity with the mother, here, too, is an image of healing connected with love for woman. It is as if the grape burst, as if the alienating, limiting boundary between self and world had disappeared.

Hans Loewald writes: "What the ego defends itself against . . . is not reality but the loss of reality, that is, the loss of an integration with the world such as it exists in the libidinal relationship with the mother."[3] It is as if the many twists and turnings of conscious adult life were ways of coping with the loss of that full reality.

Rosenman compares Woolf's childhood experiences to the "oceanic consciousness" Freud describes in *Civilization and Its Discontents*. Freud suggests that "our present ego-feeling is . . . only a shrunken residue of a much more inclusive . . . feeling which corresponded to a more intimate bond between the ego and the world about it. . . . The ideational contents appropriate to it would be . . . limitlessness and . . . a bond with the universe" (p. 15; see also Rosenman, p. 11). Daniel Stern, in *The Interpersonal World of the Infant*, offers a different model for understanding Woolf's childhood memories. He says that as infants gain language, they do so "at the risk of losing the force and wholeness of original experience" (p. 177). He describes the infant's capacity for "amodal perception"—

experience that crosses sensory modes. Woolf's memories in "A Sketch of the Past" seem a perfect example of the synesthesia of unified sense experience. Here is Woolf's portrayal of her most important memory:

> If life has a base that it stands upon, if it is a bowl that one fills and fills and fills—then my bowl without a doubt stands upon this memory. It is of lying half asleep, half awake, in bed in the nursery at St. Ives. It is of hearing the waves breaking, one, two, one, two, and sending a splash of water over the beach; and then breaking one, two, one, two, behind a yellow blind. It is of hearing the blind draw its little acorn across the floor as the wind blew the blind out. It is of lying and hearing this splash and seeing this light, and feeling, it is almost impossible that I should be here; of feeling the purest ecstasy I can conceive. (*Moments of Being*, pp. 64–65)

I am not suggesting that Woolf's memory is prior to her development of language; simply that it partakes of the quality of global experience that Stern says gets lost as children grow older.[4]

Stern's analysis of global experience is close to what Anton Ehrenzweig calls *undifferentiation*.[5] Opposing it to chaos, he says "the undifferentiated structure of primary-process phantasy corresponds to the primitive still undifferentiated structure of the child's vision of the world" (p. 5). Ehrenzweig is trying to analyze experience that is outside of linguistic orderings, yet holds a "hidden order" (p. 5). This undifferentiated perception is "guided by libido and goes straight for the total individual objects without awareness of their abstract elements" (p. 18). We might see Virginia Woolf's art as an attempt to recover through language this syncretistic, undifferentiated experience.[6]

It is the opposite of Mrs. Dalloway in her narrow bed with the sheets stretched tight, Mrs. Dalloway who lacks "something central which permeated" (p. 46). "Here," Mrs. Dalloway thinks, "was one room; there another. Did religion solve that, or love?" (p. 193). It is this pain of separation, the longing to return, as Freud puts it, to "a more intimate bond between the ego and the world about it" that moves Mrs. Dalloway "to combine, to create." It leads to imagery of the spider's web that hovers invisibly between Richard and Clarissa and to the "myriads of things merged in one thing" of Peter's dream (p. 86). All the longing for connections in *Mrs. Dalloway* and in Woolf's other novels comes from the experience of the isolated self, what Freud calls "a shrunken residue" (*Civilization and Its Discontents*, p. 15) of that fuller self embedded in the world. Underlying Woolf's fiction are the mythologized memories of childhood ecstasy, rapture, unity. The incantation of her fiction may be seen as a way to recover that state—a gesture of healing.

Mythologized memories: not that they are invented but that they take on a fictional shape, like the childhood memories of Wordsworth in *The Prelude*. They express an image of the Good Place, the Lost Place, of embeddedness and unity—an image of the full self that is not permitted expression in the adult world.

The *full self:* it makes a difference whether you believe that Woolf's music simply represents her need for merger, the completion of a narcissistically injured self, or expresses as well intimations of a fuller self. If you begin from an assumption that adult health is found only in the separate, bordered self, then Woolf's yearning to fuse with the larger life around her seems pathological. If you don't start with this assumption, you will see the yearning as evidence of damage—*and*, more important— as healing. D. H. Lawrence very near the end of his life, wrote,

> I am part of the sun as my eye is part of me. That I am part of the earth, my feet know perfectly, and my blood is part of the sea. My soul knows that I am part of the human race, my soul is an organic part of the great human soul, as my spirit is part of my nation. In my very own self I am part of my family. There is nothing of me that is alone and absolute except my mind, and we shall find that the mind has no existence by itself, it is only the glitter of the sun on the surface of the waters.
>
> So that my individualism is really an illusion. I am a part of the great whole, and I can never escape. But I *can* deny my connections, break them, and become a fragment. Then I am wretched. (From the ending of *Apocalypse*, p. 200)

I agree that Woolf expresses the terror of a world without a self, and certainly expresses dependency needs and a fantasy of merger. Later I will suggest that she whispers to us of a state of oneness that is found only in death. But now I am arguing that the music of fusion in Woolf represents the process of (temporarily) evoking the ultimate connectedness of which Lawrence speaks, a kind of prelapsarian wholeness that is real—not pathological.[7]

Why can one not live in that Good Place? One answer, a partial answer, Woolf provides directly after the memories of ecstasy and rapture in the opening pages of "A Sketch of the Past." In an amazingly free flow of associations, Woolf remembers looking at her face in the mirror in the hall at Talland House and feeling shame. She ascribes this to having "inherited a streak of the puritan, of the Clapham sect. At any rate, the looking-glass shame has lasted all my life" (*Moments of Being,* p. 68). She connects this to her father's ascetic, puritanical streak, but then she goes deeper: "I must have been ashamed or afraid of my own body." And immediately she remembers her half-brother Gerald Duckworth exploring her body and her resentment. Then she recalls a dream of looking into a mirror "when a horrible face—the face of an animal—suddenly showed over my shoulder" (p. 69). In other words, ecstasy and rapture approach libidinal impulse too closely. The global self, the oceanic self, threatens the safety of the ordinary self, the central ego.

And so the ordinary self, a barrier to fullness of being, is clung to for safety. Loss of self terrifies. Bernard, in *The Waves,* says, "But how describe the world seen without a self? There are no words" (p. 376). This place beyond words is seen as nothingness. Rhoda (*The Waves*) feels she has no face, imagines herself sinking, dissolving. But if this creates terror, it also creates bliss. At moments, she tells us, when she lets go, "Now my body thaws; I am unsealed, I am incandescent. Now the stream pours in a deep tide fertilizing, opening the shut, forcing the tight-folded, flooding free" (p. 193). It is in loss of self—not in repair of self—that wholeness is found. But it is terrifying. Again, there are two senses of loss of self. As false self, the system of defenses that limit our lives, loss of self is requisite for full being; as coherent structure, loss of self produces "unthinkable anxiety."

A related reason for clutching the security of the limited self is the fear of engulfment by the Mother. I mean Virginia's fear of engulfment by her own mother, Julia, but I also mean the threat that "the membrane" will burst and flood the self, that the ecstasy that she describes, ecstasy of fusion, borders on an experience in which the separate self is dissolved, flooded, lost. The narrow bed, the lack of "something central which permeated," is a *choice*; again, it reduces anxiety at the cost of full life. It is the choice of a separation from, a renunciation of, the mother. If Clarissa Dalloway lacks "something central which permeated," that "something central" is the mother imago. In "A Sketch of the Past" Woolf writes about her mother: "Of course she was central. I suspect the word 'central' gets closest to the general feeling I had of living so completely in her atmosphere that one never gets far enough away from her to see her as a person. . . . She was the whole thing" (*Moments of Being,* p. 83).

The "whole thing" is in a sense exactly what Woolf, like all modern novelists, searches for—coherence, stability, harmony, meaning. The experience I have in reading *Mrs. Dalloway* and *To the Lighthouse* is one of opening my mind to jumble, to fragmentation, to evanescence. These novels acknowledge a radical subjectivity that isolates each of us in space and time, and they mourn for a lost unity. In *To the Lighthouse,* Mrs. Ramsey struggles to cohere the separate souls around the dinner table, "all those scattered about," to unite people through marriage, as Mrs. Dalloway imagined uniting them in her party—"an offering; to combine, to create." Both novels—all of Woolf's novels—struggle to defeat the forces of flux, the effects of time, to find wholeness and permanence.

This lost unity is what the novels strive to recapture. The voice in the novels is *incantation* meant to effect the reunification. I find myself trusting the voice, trusting that somehow, under the jumble, is unity; somehow, beyond the evanescent, is permanence. The constant repetition of imagery, especially imagery of connection (webs, veils, mist) might be compared to the use of magic spells to recapture "that great Cathedral space which was childhood" (*Moments of Being,* p. 81). Woolf risks unity and coherence with her multiplicity of points of view, risks sanity, but there is a secret unity the reader feels under the jumble, for the language slips from consciousness to consciousness, breaching verisimilitude but creating the assurance (for herself, for me) that finally there is unity.[8] The unity occurs in *me.* Woolf uses me as reader to experience the wholeness that the text denies. I am held by the voice; in another sense—the sense of contain and defuse—I "hold" the pain, the dissonance, the losses, all the losses, within my own heart. I become the holding environment. Another way to express this, of course, is to say that Woolf creates a part of herself into someone who can soothe, who can reconcile, who can hold. The text becomes a cathedral, holding her, holding me.

In *Mrs. Dalloway,* Peter Walsh dreams, as he sits on the park bench, of a great female figure, a "spectral presence . . . made of sky and branches" that "he rapidly endows . . . with womanhood" (p. 85). Bouson calls this the "psychocenter of the novel" (p. 141). It is Peter's, not Clarissa Dalloway's, dream, but it might as well be hers. Or, rather, it is the dream of the narrative voice, that voice which haunts us throughout the novel, binding the novel into a poem: "Myriads of things merged in one thing" (p. 86). Peter-dreaming—the novel itself—longs to return from complexity to this figure who will "shower down from her magnificent hands compassion, comprehension, absolution" (p. 86). The longing is finally for merger: "let me walk straight on to this great figure, who will, with a toss of her head, mount me on her streamers and let me blow to nothingness with the rest" (p. 87). Even more clearly, in *To the Lighthouse,* the narrative voice assures us of wholeness as it tells of fragmentation, assures us of something transcending time as it tells of the ravages of time. Mrs. Ramsey has gone but the voice remains, and of course the spirit remains to unify the novel even as it unifies Lily's canvas.

Woolf describes her mother's power in the household: "What a jumble of things I can remember, if I let my mind run, about my mother; but they are all of her in company; of her surrounded; of her generalized; dispersed, omnipresent, of her as the creator of that crowded merry world which spun so gaily in the centre of my childhood" (*Moments of Being,* p. 84). Her mother seems godlike in the "Cathedral space," creating, like Mrs. Ramsey, centrality, a joyful unity. But there is something ominous in that word "dispersed," in the phrase "of her surrounded." She created wholeness, but she was seldom personally available: "Can I remember ever being alone with her for more than a few minutes?" Woolf asks. "Someone was always interrupting" (p. 83). It is this loss—loss of ecstatic unity not only after her mother's death but much earlier—that Virginia Woolf expresses and tries to undo, in her life, especially in her relationships with women, and in her fiction. As Neville says in *The Waves,* "We are in that passive and exhausted frame of mind when we only wish to rejoin the body of our mother from whom we have been severed" (p. 338).

This lost unity is a mixed blessing. To repeat: "One never gets far enough away from her to see her as a person," she writes. One never gets far enough away from her—that's the other side of Woolf's ambivalence. She writes in "A Sketch of the Past" that having written *To the Lighthouse* she "ceased to be obsessed by my mother. I no longer hear her voice; I do not see her" (*Moments of Being,* p. 81). In a sense she imagined that the writing of that novel exorcised her mother's too-powerful spirit, exorcised her own hunger for the absent mother. The exorcism did not really occur—I think we can see that in her later work and diaries and in her suicide—but it is ambivalently longed for. If she longs for merger, then at the same time, fearing engulfment, she longs for separation as does Lily Briscoe in *To the Lighthouse.* But then, like Lily, she longs, too, for some ghost of the mother to fill the void—as in Lily's canvas, so in Woolf's life: Madge Vaughan, Violet Dickinson, Vita Sackville-West, Ethel Smyth, Vanessa.[9] More: she fantasizes merger, the loss of individuation and of separation, merger, through imagination, with sacred wholeness, with the great female figure the weary traveler sees at the end of the road.

The order, the wholeness, that Julia Stephen creates and Woolf longs for is seen as a circle around a center, a web—the "circle of life" that Mr. Ramsey needs to hold him. It is a female order. There is another kind of order available to Woolf, and this she utterly rejects. We see it in her criticism, we see it in her fiction. In "Modern Fiction" (1919) she speaks of the traditional exigencies of the "realistic" novel as "some powerful and unscrupulous tyrant" who has the writer in thrall. This tyrant kills the living spirit—"embalming the whole"; yet "the tyrant is obeyed." Woolf plans to rebel on behalf of life, life seen in the figure of a woman—Mary Carmichael, Mrs. Brown.

This attack on the tyrant in aesthetics is analogous to Woolf's attack on the same tyrannical male spirit in the novels. Dr. Bradshaw, who swooped down and "shut people up," is the antagonist to the spirit of evanescent connections, of nets and webs and mists, "the unseen part of us, which spreads wide" (*Mrs. Dalloway,* p. 232). He was "capable of some indescribable outrage," Clarissa considers—"forcing your soul, that was it" (p. 281). He has destroyed his wife. "There had been no scene, no snap; only the slow sinking, water-logged, of her will into his" (p. 152). He wants "dominion." So, too, does the very masculine Lady Bruton, who should have been a "general of dragoons"; so, too, does the proselytizing Miss Killman. Clarissa, for all her faults, loves life as it is. "Had she ever tried to convert any one herself? Did she not wish everybody merely to be themselves?" (p. 191). These tyrants want to confine it, to kill it. The Goddess Proportion, whom Bradshaw worships, "has a sister, less smiling, more formidable. . . . Conversion is her name and she feasts on the wills of the weakly, loving to impress, to impose" (p. 151). This spirit in the novel, essentially masculine although its devotees may be women, is the same as the aesthetic of the traditional novel. It is rigid, it imposes its view of reality, it kills life. In *To the Lighthouse* its image is more complicated, for Mr. Ramsey, helpless and insecure, is so much more complex a character than Dr. Bradshaw. But like Bradshaw, he bullies, he is a petty tyrant. And like Woolf's version of the aesthetics of the traditional novel, his thought is rigid, stultified. Even his thinking about his progress as a philosopher—he has gotten to Q, now if he could only get to R—is a parody of the linearity of masculine thought. It marches as he, militarylike, marches and recites "The Charge of the Light Brigade."

The source of these figures is, of course, Leslie Stephen, or rather the figure of Leslie Stephen internalized by his daughter. For the full Leslie Stephen was not only a tyrant, a bully of the spirit, whose ranting masked his sense of failure; he was also a loving grandfather as much as a father (she describes him as being the age of a grandfather), a tender, generous father-grandfather, the guide of his daughter's study, encourager of her writing.[10] But the introjected father was the demanding tyrant. She writes in her diary in 1928: "Father's birthday. He would have been . . . 96, yes, today; & could have been 96, like other people one has known; but mercifully was not. His life would have entirely ended mine. What would have happened? No writing, no books;—inconceivable."[11] She often turns to her father's critical writing, she says in "A Sketch of the Past," "to stiffen my fluid vision" (*Moments of Being*, p. 115). Fluid is female, like web, like circle. Fluid must be resisted, fluid can engulf. It is fluid she turns to to find her final peace. If the artist must be "woman-manly or man-womanly," if she praises Proust for his "combination of the utmost sensibility with the utmost tenacity," then she needs her father's stiffening. She needs his "very simply constructed view of the world" (p. 115). But . . . Then there is the other father, the father who if he had lived would have destroyed her life. He is not the literary critic but the tyrant: "It was the tyrant father—the exacting, the violent, the histrionic, the demonstrative, the self-centered, the self-pitying, the deaf, the appealing, the alternately loved and hated father—that dominated me then" (p. 116). The tyrant who dominated her is the spirit of the traditional novel, the rigidity of masculine thought, the force behind wars—responsible for the marching boys with their "marble stare" that Peter Walsh observes, "as if one will worked legs and arms uniformly, and life, with its varieties, its irreticences, had been laid under a pavement of monuments and wreaths and drugged into a stiff yet staring corpse by discipline" (*Mrs. Dalloway*, pp. 76–77). It is in flight from this tyrant that the spirit wants rest in merger with the great female figure, wants to be "blown to nothingness."

And yet—and this seems particularly important—the tyrant is, finally, pitifully weak. Particularly I mean Leslie Stephen, who, especially after his wife's death, beat his chest, wept, went through bizarre histrionics to gain pity. A distinguished man of letters, a Victorian patriarch in the eyes of the world, he was in his own eyes a failure and an object of his own pity. But I mean also the masculine spirit generally, and in aesthetics, the tyranny of the realistic novel. For, according to Woolf, the realistic novel, trying to cram life into its rigid structure, its "two and thirty chapters," utterly fails.

I am arguing that the dynamics of Virginia Stephen's family of origin have been translated into her fiction and into her aesthetics. Further, they have been the material for her way of perceiving reality—her mother central and centering, yet absent, her father, beneath the pretense of authority, a man to be rescued from falling apart. Most important, they have been the source of her longing for cohesion, for wholeness. This longing is expressed and partly satisfied in her art.

"But how describe the world seen without a self?" Bernard asks (*The Waves*, p. 376). The question echoes throughout modernist literature, which is full of the anxiety of a world separated from self, engendering anxiety that the self, reflecting an empty world, is empty or unreal or that it will dissolve. The question of the relation of self and world is central to Woolf's fiction. In *To the Lighthouse* it is echoed, oddly enough, in the philosophy of Mr. Ramsey—oddly, because he is the least sensitive, most pragmatic character. His son Andrew tells Lily that his father's work is about " 'subject and object and the nature of reality.' " Andrew adds, " 'think of a kitchen table . . . when you're not there' " (p. 38). Mr. Ramsey's problem is that he asks the question in premodernist fashion. That is, he asks assuming that subject is separated from object, that the object can be examined and shaped by the rational subject. The question that he struggles with from P to Q to R answers itself when the separation is understood as illusory. The world seen without a self. What is it to be without a self? For Woolf, it is—though frightening—not disappearance, but loss of artificial boundaries. It is fusion: Mrs. Ramsey "became the thing she looked at" (p. 97).

The failure of the realistic novel is the failure of Mr. Ramsey's assumption, the Victorian assumption of a separation of subject and object, self and world. For Woolf, reality properly understood is never separate, a social object to be examined. The world is not without self; it is full of self, drenched in self. World and self are aspects of one phenomenon. And so the terrible modern isolation and fragmentation are not final. World-as-self is the self healed—healed for the moment, until the apprehension dissolves. "We are in the hands of the Lord."

Woolf's aesthetics manifest the healed self, the self suffusing the world and suffused by the world: in her fiction the healing fusion is symbolized and enacted, giving us an aesthetics of healing.

Or is it an aesthetics of madness?

When self is so intermingled with world, the unsettling question is Am I reading the world or reading *into* the world, making it up out of my self? In the brief story "An Unwritten Novel," the narrator imagines that she knows an old woman riding on a train—knows, as if from the inside. But at the end, her imaginings about the woman's story are confounded. The story she has imagined as the woman's life is just that, a story. Subject and object are irredeemably separate, and "life's bare as bone." In the final lines, she recovers: "If I fall on my knees, if I go through the ritual, the ancient antics, it's you I embrace, you I draw to me—adorable world!" (*CSF*, p. 115). In *Mrs. Dalloway*, Septimus and Clarissa are both in a world suffused with self. Metaphors of webs, nets, tree branches—interconnections: "The leaves being connected by millions of fibres with his own body" (Septimus, p. 32); "being laid out like a mist between the people she knew best, who lifted her on their branches as she had seen the trees lift the mist, but it spread ever so far, her life, herself" (Clarissa, p. 12). For Clarissa the connections are metaphor; for Septimus they are literal. Septimus and Clarissa sing a duet without listening to each other. The simple fact of that duet—music echoed back and forth between them—creates a sense of the interfusion of self and world. While each of us aches at his, at her, isolation ("I am alone; I am alone!"), the form of the novel denies isolation: we are all one.

Like the narrator in "An Unwritten Novel," Clarissa sees life going on finally unknowable and loves it for . . . itself. Septimus, however, needs to control it with paranoid vision, as if the narrator of "An Unwritten Novel" were to insist that the woman on the train remain true to the narrator's story. For Clarissa, the world intimates meanings, and she sees herself "making it up . . . creating it every moment afresh" (p. 5). Septimus is not aware that the world is his doing. He insists he knows what it is telling him, and it is telling him one specific thing. His paranoia forces the world to dramatize and symbolize the story of his pain. Clarissa, who loves life, lets it be: "She would not say of any one in the world now that they were this or were that" (p. 11). And this is the difference between sanity and madness. The mad Septimus, while he has glimmerings of truth, is finally, as much as Dr. Bradshaw, as much as Doris Kilman, as much as the traditional novelist, as much as the rational philosopher Ramsey, someone who imposes himself on the world.

Septimus and Clarissa are splittings of one original character, who was to have killed herself. But in the novel, although they echo each other, they are no longer one. Clarissa carries Septimus's madness in her and Septimus, intimations of her sanity, but they represent essentially different natures and define between them the sane and the mad way of apprehending the interconnection of self and world.

SANE	MAD
One loves things in themselves. There's no denial of their unknowability, their thing-ness.	One "knows" what things mean. One imposes an idea, a sense of proportion, one is a devotee to the goddess Conversion, one demands a single meaning. Literal reading of interpenetration of self and world.
One apprehends a web, a pattern, connectedness, an intimation of oneness. Metaphoric reading of interpenetration of self and world.	One experiences no supporting environment, no connections. One is alone, isolated, closed off.

Clarissa loves life. I am permitted a sane, healing way of experiencing the interpenetration of subject and object. It is wholeness. But what if wholeness is so tied to fusion and fusion (by definition) to loss of boundaries and of self, finally to dissolution and death, that the longing expressed in the novels is ultimately, secretly, a longing for death?[12] In his essay on Poe, Lawrence speaks about the limit of closeness: "The central law of all organic life is that each organism is intrinsically isolate and single in itself. . . . The moment its isolation breaks down, and there comes an actual mixing and confusion, death sets in (*Studies in Classic American Literature*, p. 66). Lawrence's pseudoscience (for he sees it as more than metaphor) is a way of expressing the danger of the seductive pull toward fusion. To return to Mrs. Ramsey's haunting words from *To the Lighthouse:* "Not as oneself did one find rest ever . . . but as a wedge of darkness" (p. 96). Rest, peace, is found only in the loss of self; one is not apart but a part. And what I am a part of is, in Mrs. Ramsey's words, "unfathomably deep." Woolf's prediction of, her yearning for, death by drowning, seems transparent. Is this beautiful passage a disguised expression of schizoid regression?

As I showed in Chapter 5, Harry Guntrip (cohering insights of Fairbairn, Winnicott, and Balint) explores the ultimate yearning of the schizoid personality to withdraw into a deeply regressed state: "The barrier between the conscious and the unconscious may be very thin in a deeply schizoid person and the world of internal objects and relationships may flood into and dominate consciousness very easily. Deeper down . . . lies the ultimate 'return to the womb' state of the introverted regressed schizoid" (p. 42). And he tells us (italics his), "*The wish to return to the womb can also be felt as a wish to die*" (p. 54).

I feel that this impulse, along with the love of life, does vibrate throughout Woolf's fiction. It vibrates in me when I read her. My own secret, regressive longings find a seductive but safe form of expression in my reading. In all my absorbed reading of fiction, as in my concentrated watching of plays, films, or operas, as in my deep attentiveness to music, I regress in that my separate ego, especially its "reflexive self-representation" (Roy Schafer's term)[13] is temporarily put aside. In Ernst Kris's view, my ego regulates the regression, and the regression is temporary and "in the service of the ego" (see especially pp. 177, 312). I become one with the work, so much so that if I read and then sleep, I dream in the rhythm of the work, in its inner music. But when I speak of my "secret, regressive longings" satisfied by reading Woolf, I am describing something more: it is often closer to the satisfaction of the *Liebestod*, a verbal music that holds me in a place of comfort, griefs assuaged, conflicts reconciled, fragmentation healed. Healed in unlife. It is the music of infantile regression, a return to a time—though such a time, a time of pure fusion, is an adult myth more than a childhood experience—prior to individuation. Shades of the prison house have not closed, paradise has not been lost. I am immersed in the flood.

If the music of the prose—its web of imagery floating from mind to mind, its lyrical cadences—if the music holds me in this place of fusion-in-death, then in the *narrative* I need—Woolf needed—a Septimus Smith to die for us. "Death was an attempt to communicate; people feeling the impossibility of reaching the centre which, mystically, evaded them; . . . rapture faded, one was alone. There was an embrace in death" (pp. 280–81). Mrs. Dalloway longs to "plunge," as she once did, through the open doors at Bourton, to break through the glass that seems to separate her from life—the window of her isolated room. It is Septimus who takes the plunge—to his death.[14] Clarissa can temporarily lose herself in his loss of self, can temporarily "die." And Virginia Woolf—this is the real point—can experience giving it all up and feeling, in the self that remains, more alive, more whole.

As Brooks Bouson notes, critics tend to sentimentalize Septimus's madness and death; she argues that Woolf urges "reader after reader to deemphasize the novel's manifest negativity and poeticize its embedded themes: disintegration anxiety, madness, and suicide."[15] And it is true that readers want her fiction to affirm only life, to affirm wholeness not in the womb but *in our own world*, for we are, in fiction so haunting as hers, deeply complicitous with its secret fantasies.

But then I have to ask, are we complicitous with simply a yearning for ultimate rest, for womb, for unlife? What are we talking about, fullness of undifferentiated unity or death wish? Can wholeness be experienced in our ordinary world? Do we get there in Woolf's fiction?

I find myself filled with contradictory answers. But my most deeply felt answer is that *Woolf's text itself* provides a place for experiencing not just wholeness but fullness of being. It is a place of holding, of healing, and it is very much in this world. And when I leave the text, I take with me not just assurances of wholeness but improved sensory equipment to feel such wholeness in my ordinary life.

J. Hillis Miller is simply wrong when he argues that "only by throwing it away can life be preserved" (p. 197). For there is Clarissa, there is Mrs. Ramsey, there is Miss La Trobe, all operating in their daytime lives, in their narratives, to create wholeness and fullness. Each is flawed, each is needy. Each disbelieves: "How's this wall, the great wall, which we call . . . civilization, to be built by . . . orts, scraps, end fragments like ourselves" (*Between the Acts*, p. 131). *Still*, "still, for one moment she held them together" (p. 72). Miss La Trobe, artist of theater, Clarissa Dalloway, artist of parties, Mrs. Ramsey, artist of family—they create and intuit the creation of moments of coherence. They combine, they create. It is not death, not Septimus's suicide, in which wholeness is found, but in the coming together, at Mrs. Dalloway's party, of the disparate elements of life. Septimus's suicide, if sentimentalized by readers, is not sentimentalized by Woolf. His suicide is not the secret pulse of Mrs. Dalloway, but her release into life. Clarissa goes back to find Sally and Peter; then come the astonishing final pages in which past becomes present, time and distance (for a moment) cease to matter, and (in an amazing sleight of hand) we are made to forget about Clarissa. Then Peter asks himself:

> What is this terror? what is this ecstasy? . . . What is it that fills me with extraordinary excitement?
>
> It is Clarissa, he said.
>
> For there she was. (P. 296)

I can hardly read this passage without tears welling and my chest working hard to keep feeling down. There she *is*, as if back from the darkness, but *not* into fragmentation, dissonance, evanescence; rather, she is gathered into wholeness, the past living in the present, the separate characters brought together, Clarissa completing the circle or defining the center of the circle. Wholeness in life, not in regression.

I began this chapter with a passage in which Mrs. Ramsey experiences unity under the self. At the dinner party, she experiences it again:

> It partook, she felt, carefully helping Mr. Bankes to a specially tender piece, of eternity; . . . there is a coherence in things, a stability; something, she meant, is immune from change, and shines out . . . in the face of the flowing, the fleeting, the spectral, like a ruby; so that again tonight she had the feeling she had had once today, already, of peace, of rest. Of such moments, she thought, the thing is made that endures.
>
> "Yes," she assured William Bankes, "there is plenty for everybody" (p. 158)

A tender piece [,] of eternity. Wholeness is found with eyes open in this numinous, candlelit room; it is immanent in a piece of the shared Boeuf en Daube, as if Mrs. Ramsey is a priestess and this ordinary room a temple.

The coming-together, the healing, is of course temporary. And the writing of her fiction, in which the healing is accomplished, did not finally heal Virginia Woolf. Each time, she collapsed under the strain and, perhaps, under the loss of that moment of wholeness she could sustain only at the moment of writing. But the fiction remains, and in the fiction there *is* plenty for everybody.

CHAPTER TWELVE

D. H. LAWRENCE AS HEALER

O F ALL MODERNIST writers, D. H. Lawrence is most the healer. Nearly everything he wrote was a gesture of healing, an enactment of healing.[1] He was conscious of this role; sometimes he derided it, sometimes he saw the attempt to heal as impossible and self-destructive. Keith Sagar writes, "The artist is a healer, but what is the healer to do when confronted with a body wholly diseased" (p. 119). It is an agony for Lawrence to feel people denying their own potentiality for vivid life, for true being; for Lawrence, life is immersion, not detached perception, so there is no way to be healed in an utterly sick world. He has to be *in touch*.[2] If Being is One and is embodied, then part of his own being could easily develop gangrene. During the war he wrote to Cynthia Asquith, "I am infinitely hurt by being broken off from the body of my fellow creatures" (Nehls, 1:312). In this magnificent concluding passage from *Apocalypse*, written just before he died, Lawrence expresses most richly his immersion in life:

> I am part of the sun as my eye is part of me. That I am part of the earth my feet know perfectly, and my blood is part of the sea. My soul knows that I am part of the human race. . . . In my own very self, I am part of my family. There is nothing of me that is alone and absolute except my mind, and we shall find that the mind has no existence by itself, it is only the glitter of the sun on the surface of the water.

He never gave up. At his worst he tries to heal by preaching to the sick, telling them to take up their crutches and walk. At his best, Lawrence seeks to change the world by rendering the phenomenology of sickness, drawing from his own sickness to create images of sickness in England, projecting characters out of split-off aspects of himself—cancers, wounds.

I think it is because I intuit his need to heal himself that I can bear his overbearing demand that I change *my* life. The controlling intellectual in "The Blind Man" is named Bertie, Lawrence's own childhood nickname. Birkin the soul-doctor is infected with the disease he diagnoses; indeed, Birkin, like Lawrence, is able to diagnose in the first place because it is his disease, too. He is Hermione, he is Gerald. Gerald, Clifford, Cathcart, and the speakers in many of the poems—they all express a sickness in Lawrence himself as well as in the modern world.

The root of the sickness is the false self, the mask of ego that separates itself from embodied being. Lawrence's analysis looks back to William Blake's vision of our cosmic self, the self that we limit, imprison, falsify in "single vision and Newton's sleep." Like Blake, Lawrence is a religious psychologist, asserting the possibility of a deeper and truer life under the false self. In essays, poetry, and fiction, he preached the courage to break through the mask to a full being that could outsing the "voices of my accursed human education" ("Snake").

In "Song of a Man Who Has Come Through" he longs to open himself to life: "Not I, not I, but the wind that blows through me!" The speaker asks for openness to some force beyond or beneath the self. The openness will bring him—bring us—new life: "we shall find the Hesperides." But to open is frightening:

> What is the knocking?
> What is the knocking at the door in the night?
> It is somebody wants to do us harm.

The speaker reassures himself:

> No, no, it is the three strange angels.
> Admit them, admit them.

The imagery is passive while it is active: he asks to be a "wedge/Driven by invisible blows"—male force, but passive to a force beyond the self. The imagery is androgynous: the (female) house, the male force entering. While Lawrence's fiction and poetry and essays always want to open the door to the three strange angels, voices beg to keep the door closed, to live in the ego. Lawrence's characters fear flooding, they fear engulfment. Yet it is only from beyond the ego, in the darkness, in the blood, that new life can spring forth. The essential religious drama in Lawrence is this encounter of ego and life.

This drama is similar to the analysis by object-relations psychologists of schizoid character structure.[3] According to W. R. D. Fairbairn and Harry Guntrip, schizoids fear the collapse of the self, and so they remove themselves from contact; or to say it in another way, they are split—schizoid: the self that remains in contact is a facade that protects the full self from impingement, from engulfment, from disintegration.

Now, that surface self, too, needs to be protected, protected from the judgment of other people, from emptiness, and from one's own deeper life—authentic being, including libidinal life. Life below the surface terrifies. And yet, Guntrip writes, "the deeper and more secret, withdrawn self . . . appears to be endowed with a great capacity to attract and draw down more and more of the rest of the personality into itself" (p. 64), until the surface personality is a thin, unreal mask—with everything real just below, cut off, seductive, explosive. Like the dead Michael Furey (in Joyce's "The Dead"), the repressed returns, requiring more and more repression: dynamics of anxiety and defense leading to a deadening (the paralysis that Joyce attributes to Dublin, for example) and hence to increased seduction of the repressed parts of the psyche.

D. H. Lawrence, better than anyone I can think of, understood this dynamic of mask and subterranean energies. Gerald in Lawrence's *Women in Love* is a perfect example of the schizoid character: so cool and self-contained yet afraid that he has no true self of his own, and under conditions of threat needing to dissolve and "sink to rest in the bath of [Gudrun's] living strength" (p. 337). He fears the implosion of his surface—like his father, who "would die, as an insect when its shell is cracked" (p. 207). Another character with a shell, the Scottish intellectual Bertie, in "The Blind Man," is shattered by the touch of the blind, passionately male, dark Maurice; having been touched, Bertie "was like a mollusc whose shell is broken" (*Stories,* 2:365).

Lawrence often imagines a woman about to be opened up to deeper life. Women are as much a part of an androgynous Lawrence as are his male characters. When he expresses the process of transformation in a poem, his imagery erotically conjoins male and female elements. When he turns to fiction, these elements are manifested as men and women, and the women are as much Lawrence as are the men. Connie and Ursula may be usefully seen not as women captivated by Lawrentian men, but as representatives of the self that needs to be broken down, to be entered and changed by a force Lawrence always imagines as male.

As reader, I am, like these figures, to be entered, opened, transformed. I am induced to open myself to terrible power. It is sacred power, it is my own power. Lawrence is a religious healer, taking me through the process of rebirth.[4] I undergo an opening and a glimpse at a fuller state of being, "the self I had," as Yeats puts it, "before the world was made." Lawrence uses me as that aspect of himself which is resistant to change but which *can* be opened. As he speaks to me as reader, he is, I think, able to make *himself*, temporarily, into the healed, fuller being. As he opens me to my transformation, his writing permits him to enact his own.

He exorcizes the sickness and suggests the possibility of healed life partly by incantation. The repetitions in his prose are not mistakes, because they are not intended as descriptions or explanations—I didn't say it right the first time; I'll try it again. Rather, they are what they are in Whitman, the repetitions of a faith-healer inducing a hypnagogic state, a state in which one can undergo imaginatively religious transformation: the discarding of dead life and the opening to true being.

> I often think one ought to be able to pray, before one works—and then leave it to the Lord. Isn't it hard, hard work to come to grips with one's imagination—throw everything overboard. I always feel as if I stood naked for the fire of Almighty God to go through me—and it's rather an awful feeling. One has to be so terribly religious, to be an artist. (*Letters*, 1:519)

It is as difficult to speak of the nature of the true self as it would be for a Christian to say what it is to "live in Christ." "New Heaven and Earth," that long, wonderful, mysterious poem which describes the transformation, uses Christian imagery to describe Lawrentian "resurrection." But the speaker says, "Ah no, I cannot tell you what it is, the new world." Like any religious psychologist, Lawrence can only suggest through metaphor and paradox its darkness and otherness, its mystery, not to be explicated. It is not reached through the conscious mind, it is the enemy of personality; it is not self at all but loss of self, yet it is singleness rather than blurred or fused being.

LAWRENCE AND PARADISE

"New Heaven and Earth" is about the process of transforming oneself so one can live in the world-as-paradise:

> . . . here, in the other world, still terrestrial
> myself, the same as before, yet unaccountably new.

Paradise is the condition of the resurrected self, the self reborn. Lawrence tries to take us there, to take himself there, by creating an incantatory, burning prose, and by rendering moments of wonder, rendering the ecstasy of being alive, with "living organic connections" restored, the "bliss" of a "paradisal unit," whether the unit is Birkin and Ursula or Mellors and Connie. But he has great difficulty taking us there; he can more successfully dramatize the longing for paradise and take us to *false* paradises.

And that's precisely what he does in "The Man Who Loved Islands." In this late story he shows us a fool's paradise, how the retreat to paradise destroys paradise and the regressed self, looking for peace, finds monsters.

The story is simple. A man who always wanted an island of his own acquires a succession of three islands, each one smaller, more isolated, less populated: the first, a "world" with families, the second a "refuge" with just a lover, the third a "few acres of rock." Leaving his lover and their daughter, he goes off alone to his bare rock, where, in winter in a fierce snowstorm, he feels the breath of the snow upon him.

I agree with David Willbern that the reader is encouraged to both identify with and stay separate from the protagonist.[5] Lawrence must have seen in himself the same yearnings and seen, too, where they lead. He was also a man who loved islands. If Cathcart let himself be called "the Master," Lawrence at times saw himself as the Christ—an aristocratic, Nietzschean Christ (the oxymoron expresses the contradiction in Lawrence). I am thinking not only about his story "The Man Who Died," but in his real life, about his preaching, his relationship to disciples, and his replaying of the Last Supper, with John Middleton Murry in the role of Judas (see Nehls 2:295–303). Lawrence is also aware of his own proud, hostile isolation, his need for a clean separateness. In this need he not only resembles the character in "The Man Who Loved Islands," but he is similar to Mellors in *Lady Chatterley's Lover* (written partly in the same year). Nor is Cathcart only a negative character (unlike, say, Clifford Chatterley): Cathcart apprehends beauty in the world, he begins with sensuous awareness, he finds sexual desire rising in himself. The difference is that Lawrence, unlike Cathcart, was aware of the rage he felt toward most people he met, toward the surface life that wasn't true life, aware, too, of his own need to play the savior: he makes this quite clear in his criticism of Birkin in *Women in Love*.

Lacking the same awareness, Cathcart resembles many of Lawrence's control-ridden characters who attempt to turn the world into a human machine: again Gerald Crich and Clifford Chatterley come to mind. Lawrence sees as obscene the attempt to withdraw from sensual contact with life and to create a paradise, willing nature into submission. This is what Gerald does—and he dies in a projection of his own inner frozenness. In fact, both Gerald and Cathcart die in snow. Cathcart, in "The Man Who Loved Islands," "felt its breath on him" (*Stones*, 3:746). In *Women in Love,* Gerald meets his end in a cul-de-sac, a "cradle of snow." His death is connected to Gerald's mother, who is described as a "snow flower" and to the mother-surrogate Gudrun, whose home seems to be in the "navel" of snow. Interpreting "The Man Who Loved Islands," Willbern speaks, correctly I believe, of "the devouring embrace of a maternal snow-creature" ("Malice in Paradise," p. 238), and that description also fits perfectly Gerald's end in *Women in Love*. In both fictions, Lawrence examines schizoid withdrawal and longing for regression that ends in annihilation of real contact with the world and therefore in annihilation of the self.

His depiction of a false paradise gives us a way of intuiting this religious psychologist's sense of a real paradise. Paradise in Lawrence is real when it is the unconscious expression of a whole relationship, especially a sensual relationship, of two separate people, a man and a woman: Mellors and Connie, Birkin and Ursula. It is found in darkness, in the mystery underlying selfhood. Paradise is false when it is created by the will. I am thinking of the relationship of Gerald or Clifford to his mining community, of Skrebensky (*The Rainbow*) to society, of Hermione to sensuality. And so when Cathcart thinks, "Why should it not be the Happy Isle at last? Why not the last small isle of the Hesperides, the perfect place, all filled with his own gracious, blossom-like spirit? A minute world of pure perfection, made by man himself" (p. 725), then in the light of the rest of Lawrence's work we have to read the wish as hateful (if seductive) to Lawrence. Why not "the last small isle of the Hesperides"? *Because* that isn't the way to find the Hesperides! In "Song of a Man Who Has Come Through," Lawrence offers the way: it is only by yielding oneself, opening oneself to "the wind that blows through me," that "we shall come at the wonder, *we shall find the Hesperides*" (italics mine). Cathcart will find only his repressed self, projected, like Ahab's, murderously out onto the world.

The sickness—and its cure—is explored brilliantly in "New Heaven and Earth."

I was so weary of the world,
I was so sick of it,
everything was tainted with myself.

Lawrence was not free of Cathcart's sickness, but he saw it as sickness. The world as emanating from the self, so that

> I was a lover, I kissed the woman I loved,
> And God of horror, I was kissing also myself.
> I was a father and a begetter of children,
> And oh, oh horror, I was begetting and conceiving
> > in my own body.

The world as projection, so that there is no *thou;* no *other.* The self is trapped in narcissistic merger or narcissistic isolation. Many critics have seen in Lawrence the conflict between the desire for separateness and the yearning for merger.[6] But finally, *the need to stay absolutely separate and the need to merge are poles of the same condition of psychic illness.*[7] Both needs end in the deathly, mothering snow or in the smothering womb. Health, on the other hand, is both a "proud singleness" *and* the ability to touch.

The poem offers a kind of religious prescription, but to say "prescription" falsifies, because it is rather the falling away of prescriptions and proscriptions. The transformation happens through the death—or at least the quietude—of the ego.

> God, but it is good to have died and been trodden out,
> trodden to nought in sour, dead earth,
> quite to nought
> absolutely to nothing
> nothing
> nothing
> nothing.

> For when it is quite, quite nothing, then it is everything.
> When I am trodden quite out, quite, quite out,
> every vestige gone, then I am here
> risen, and setting my foot on another world
> risen, accomplishing a resurrection.

Again, I hear the word that echoes throughout modernist literature, "nothing." But how differently Lawrence says it from Hemingway. It is only when the ego is broken, when the old "I" is "nothing," that it is "everything," that new life can enter. It is only in the darkness, in the not-self, in the world that the self doesn't want to gobble up (as Kurtz in *Heart of Darkness* wanted to devour it) that the world isn't *turned into* the self: it is only in the world-as-otherness that the new life can come into being.

For Lawrence, the image of that new life is in touch—the touch of the not-me:

> . . . I put out my hand in the night, and my hand
> touched that which was verily not me.

He has touched the flank of his wife. Before this, when he touched her, "it was I who touched and I who was touched." The speaker discovers a real Other, and in doing so, truly finds the Hesperides

> . . . a new earth, a new I, a new knowledge, a new
>   world of time.

The character in "The Man who Loved Islands" plays out the alternative, deathly process. Like Gerald, he cuts himself off from people and things, tries to solipsize them. In his retreat, he tries to block out everything but the beautiful, comfortable aspects of the island. But his retreat is also regression, and in this regression to darker, more sensuous life, the world takes on the qualities of aggression that the man denies in himself.[8] The attempt to create paradise through the will leads finally to the perception of hell.

For Lawrence the only way to paradise is through the void, into the darkness under the self. All modernist novelists deal in some way with the experience of the void. That pun again: they write about nothing.[9] Most use darkness, too, as a metaphor of unconscious life, the life of impulse, the life under the ego. But none, not even Woolf, trusts the void or the darkness as Lawrence trusts: he completely trusts himself to them.

The *darkness* is not the same as *the void* or *nothingness*. *The darkness* refers to the regressive, impulse-laden aspects of the individual psyche and the social and natural world. It refers to the unknown place beneath received values, beneath whatever we have agreed to call reality. It evokes the place to which one wants to regress, in which the authentic self—I might say the reborn self—hides; it also evokes the savagery and wish for death in that place. *Nothingness* or *the void* refers to a discovery: the discovery that what we think of as the real is only a set of agreements; that when you look under official reality you find no ground upon which to stand, that is, no source of meaning or of what we call reality. What you find are human beings making up the world and its meanings and hiding that fact from themselves. How can you be held? It is like trying to pick yourself up off the ground. Lawrence can accept the void because he knows another world exists beyond it, in the darkness, where we *can* be held.

What Lawrence is doing, then, is relocating the place in which we have our real being, relocating paradise. Lawrence accepts the condition of the world as empty and the self, mirrored there, as unreal. He accepts the condition of the conventional world as *not* a holding environment.[10] But, as a religious writer, he offers the experience of another world that is not empty, another self that is charged, holy. This alternative reality *is* a holding environment. *We can be held in the darkness!* We don't want to trust it because we can't know it with our minds. But it is, finally, the mind that is the obstacle finally where the void resides: "The old, dark religions understood. 'God enters from below,' said the Egyptians, and that's right. Why can't you darken your minds and know that the great gods pulse in the dark, and enter you as darkness through the lower gates" (*Letters,* 2:725). Lawrence believes in what is to be found in the darkness. I hear Faulkner struggling to believe but only able to chant the "old verities." Lawrence finds restorative energy in the darkness, in the silence.

MINING FOR CARBON

This trust in a paradise to be found in the darkness, found when we are silent, is his basic psychological faith and the basis of his aesthetics. And these are really the same! In his much-quoted letter to Edward Garnett, he writes:

> You mustn't look in my novel for the old stable ego of the character. There is another ego, according to whose activity the individual is unrecognizable, and passes through, as it were, allotropic states which . . . are states of the same radically unchanged element. (Like as diamond and coal are the same pure single element of carbon. The ordinary novel would trace the history of the diamond—but I say, "Diamond, what! This is carbon! and my diamond might be coal or soot, and my theme is carbon). (*Letters,* 1:281–82)

He is defending his focus on the unconscious state of characters, the state of their essential being rather than their personalities. It is as if he is tuning into psychic signals from the underworld that the characters themselves, broadcasting them, can't possibly know. He is not, like a traditional nineteenth-century British novelist, exploring motives. Rather, he is concerned with experience taking place within the unseen core of his characters.

Here is Lawrence apparently digging for the carbon beneath Gudrun's surface:

The world was finished for her. There was only the inner, individual darkness, sensation within the ego, the obscene religious mystery of ultimate reduction, the mystic frictional activities of diabolic reducing down, disintegrating the vital organic body of life.

All this Gudrun knew in her subconsciousness, not in her mind. (*Women in Love*, p. 443)

This feels fake; it's Lawrence using Gudrun as a puppet for expressing his ideas—an essay in the *guise* of a mining operation on a character. It's simply a traditional omniscient author posing as an untraditional explorer of soul. It's Lawrence as Cathcart. On the other hand, in this passage on Gerald Lawrence seems to me to achieve something closer to his promise:

He went on more or less mechanically with his business, but this activity was all extraneous. The real activity was this ghastly wrestling for death in his own soul.

But as the fight went on, and all that he had been and was continued to be destroyed, so that life was a hollow shell all round him, roaring and clattering like the sound of the sea, a noise in which he participated externally, and inside this hollow shell was all the darkness and fearful space of death, he knew he would have to find reinforcements, otherwise he would collapse inwards upon the great dark void which circled at the centre of his soul. (P. 314)

Here Lawrence seems to be interpreting what Gerald couldn't possibly say for himself, would never agree with, and yet fundamentally lives.

But I find Lawrence even closer to his promise when he doesn't actively interpret the "carbon": the passage in which Mrs. Morel, locked out by her husband, feels the presence of the fragrant white lilies under the moon; or when Ursula in *The Rainbow* apprehends the horses; or when Ursula and Birkin come back together in love after a ferocious fight never explicitly resolved. In each case I feel I am realizing something essential about a character, something that the character can't explain, that even Lawrence can't explain. It is then that he enacts true being, enacts rather than espouses life beneath the old, dead lie. He enacts it in *me*. Just as Birkin asks Ursula to teach her pupils the essential facts about catkins— their sexual outline—rather than their accidental properties, Lawrence at his best allows me to feel the essential mystery living in the darkness beneath surfaces.

The darkness beneath surfaces.

In a late essay, "Nottingham and the English Mining Countryside," Lawrence speaks about the men of his father's day:

> Under the butty system, the miners worked underground as a sort of intimate
> community, they knew each other practically naked, and with curious close
> intimacy, and the darkness and the underground remoteness of the pit "stall,"
> and the continual presence of danger, made the physical, instinctive, and
> intuitional contact between men very highly developed. . . . They brought with
> them above ground the curious dark intimacy of the mine, the naked sort of
> contact, and if I think of my childhood, it is as if there was a lustrous sort of
> inner darkness, like the gloss of coal, in which we moved and had our real
> being. (*Phoenix*, pp. 135–36)

I can't help but think of the metaphor of "carbon" when I read this
description of mining. Lawrence, in a sense, identifies with his father the
miner when he goes down under the surface, down into the darkness.
"Real being" is found in the darkness, is associated (and mythologically,
this is extremely unusual) with the male; the source of renewal is male.
Lawrence the writer shapes his writing to be a kind of *mining* in the
darkness—an identification with his father.

Lawrence's attitude (at first unconscious, then very conscious) toward
his father, toward The Father, is a good part of what separates him from
other modernist novelists. Although grounded in this dark power associated with his father, Lawrence still has to tap it, to remythologize his
father from the drunk, wrecked cripple of his mother's household to the
secret source of power.[11]

LAWRENCE AND THE MOTHER IMAGO

There is no turning to the father for Lawrence at the time of his mother's
death. He regarded Arthur Lawrence, like the fictional Walter Morel, as a
gruff, insensitive bully. Only gradually over the years does Lawrence grow
to appreciate his father—appreciate consciously. Yet even in *Sons and
Lovers,* as critics have seen and far more than Lawrence himself realized,
the father (for all his crudeness) is a more attractive figure than the frozen,
impinging, guilt-producing mother, who is the "voice of my education,"
the voice of the cultural surface beneath which the artist needs to mine.

We think of Lawrence as the child of a loving mother—perhaps overly
loving, substituting, as did Paul Morel's mother, son for husband. And we
think of Lawrence as a loving son, caught in an oedipal fixation.[12] But
there is a considerably darker side to Lawrence's relation to mothering.
Again and again in *Fantasia of the Unconscious,* Lawrence bitterly attacks

parents (by which he always means mothers) who arouse in their children a "dynamic response" to their "own insatiable love-will."

> You have done what it is vicious for any parent to do: you have established between your child and yourself the bond of adult love . . . I do not speak of sex. I speak of pure sympathy, sacred love. And this is fatal. It is a sort of incest. It is a dynamic, *spiritual* incest. (P. 153)

Lawrence is furious at mothers who throw the child's system out of balance. Thus, Lawrence places blame for his own emotional sickness and even his physical debilities on his mother. The magnificent poems on her death, wholly tender, which turn mother into child, himself into mother ("if but I could have wrapped you in myself") or lover ("My love looks like a girl tonight") contain no anger. But in "The Virgin Mother," in which the speaker *does* speak in the role of a son, a son born twice—once from her womb, once from her soul—the anger comes through as irony: the son born of this mother is to be

> Free of all hearts, my darling.
> Of each heart's entrance free.

Strange praise!

> And so my love, my mother,
> I shall always be true to you,
> Twice I am born my dearest:
> to life and to death, in you
> And this is the life hereafter
> Wherein I am true.

What sort of praise is this? The poem ends, ". . . my soul lies helpless / Beside your bed." It is bitter, lacerating praise of his own crippling and of his crippler.

Lawrence's childhood devotion was complicated by unacknowledged rage. His rage seems to be grounded in pre-oedipal fury at the split-off "bad" mother, the devouring, engulfing, rejecting, all-powerful mother of infancy. What seems clear is not mother love but fierce ambivalence rooted in infancy—a separation anxiety that flowered ambivalently into yearning for regression to a symbiotic or fused attachment while raging against engulfment. In Frieda, Lawrence reenacts the relationship and struggles inside it most of his brief life. If he longs for attachment to the mother, he also has to kill her to escape.

Lawrence's autobiographical Paul Morel is, after all, a boy who *literally kills his mother.* To prevent her constant suffering from cancer, he and his sister give her an overdose of laudanum. They love her, but "they laughed together like two conspiring children" (*Sons and Lovers,* p. 394). It is a mercy killing, and yet it is not without darker meaning. For though the boy in the novel loves her, it is clear that unless he can prevent his mother from impinging on his life, he can never be a free man; even after her death, her regressive pull is terrific, a pull toward union with her in death. Like most of the mothers of modernist writers (Eliot, James, Fitzgerald, Hemingway, Faulkner), she controls, demands, impinges, and her child internalizes her demands and cannot break free. Without a fierce mother like Lydia Law-rence, there would most likely have been no art at all. If she made him crooked, at least she made him! But through all of Lawrence's fiction, the mother-figure destroys the independence and sucks the life of her son.[13] She is the Magna Mater, strangling the male as Diana Crich strangles the young doctor who tries to save her. The Lovely Lady (of the story "The Lovely Lady") kills one son and nearly destroys the life of her remaining son. The mother in "The Rocking-Horse Winner" creates demands that destroy her son's integral relation to life, that turn him into an industrialist of the nursery, producing money for his mother until he dies.

And this figure of worship is not just a strangler, a devourer; she is not even loving—she is a goddess of the snow. Paul's mother in "The Rocking-Horse Winner" was thought " 'such a good mother. She adores her children.' Only she herself, and her children themselves, knew it was not so." In the fairy-tale tone we see Paul's mother as wicked stepmother, posses-sion-hungry, narcissistic. Margaret Mahler tells of two-year-old children who feel ambivalent anger toward an absent mother. One sought "auto-erotic and narcissistic gratifications such as violent rocking on the rocking horse" (p. 116). Paul's rocking, then, is not only oedipal activity in the mother's service but an autistic ritual to regain wholeness, enacted by a child whose mother is *not there.* We know very little about the real Lydia Lawrence. What I think we do know is a mother imago projected by an enraged son caught in the ambivalence of separation anxiety—wanting merger, wanting separation.

THE POWER OF THE FATHER

Gradually Lawrence sees his father as the source of health and strength; or rather, he is able to imaginatively recreate his father into an image of male power with which he can then identify and from which he can take sustenance.

In the past several years psychoanalysts have emphasized the early relationship between infant and mother. And that was a necessary corrective for a model of development that seemed to place all its weight on oedipal struggle. But is is also necessary to insist on the importance of the dyadic bond between child and father—the pre-oedipal father, the father not of superego struggle but, in the words of Peter Blos, of "quasi-maternal bonding by substitution."[14] But the father is not merely a "replication of the mother" (Blos, p. 26). He is also a support against maternal reengulfment; he is an ally in the process of individuation—of becoming a separate person. He shapes the ego ideal (pp. 38ff) and is crucial in the development of male sexual identity (p. 22 and *passim*). Blos recognizes the boy's deep need for his father's blessing. *Lawrence is the only modernist who can take blessing from his father.* It is what permitted him to identify with the center rather than long for the center, to assert knowledge rather than uncertainty. It permits him his arrogance and his rage, because this affirmation of the dark power of the father is, after all, a created orientation. Lawrence is perhaps as self-imagined as is Ford or Conrad or Fitzgerald. But the shape of his imagining is of power and attunement. Lawrence *knows*—knows so assuredly that it is sometimes hard to place him with the modernists, for whom epistemological doubt seems so crucial. But modernist anxiety exists in Lawrence, anxiety of emptiness and of engulfment, of loss of self. He keeps that anxiety at bay by identifying with a mythologized father.

THE AESTHETICS OF BEING

James Joyce, like Lawrence, also struggles to reinvent the Father. But the father Joyce needs is not the phallic father of darkness, an identification to tie the artist to the earth. Quite the opposite. In the persona of Stephen Dedalus Joyce replaces the bullying failure imagined as Simon Dedalus with another Daedalus, the "fabulous artificer." And then (in perhaps the most-quoted passage on aesthetics in modern literature), he identifies, as artist, with the artist-god, who, "like the God of the creation, remains within or behind or beyond or above his handiwork, invisible, refined out of existence, indifferent, paring his fingernails" (*Portrait*, p. 215). As I argue in Chapter 6, this is Joyce's defense against his own anxiety, as Eliot's "escape from personality" is his. It is defense, offering distance from life and control over life—defense reified into an aesthetic. For Lawrence, this aesthetic of the artist-god is an abomination, everything in modernism and modernity he loathes.

Joyce's artist-god bears a relation to natural reality similar to that of Lawrence's schizoid industrialist. It is an image not of salvation but of what we need salvation from. Stephen imagines himself a "priest of eternal imagination, transmuting the daily bread of experience into the radiant body of everliving life" (*Portrait*, p. 221); Lawrence's empty industrialist sees himself as "godlike," creating a perfect system out of "the resistant Matter of the earth" (*Women in Love*, p. 220). Of course, neither the product nor the motive force are the same for Stephen and Gerald. Joyce's Stephen hopes to create art through the force of imagination; Gerald Crich creates only an industrial machine and the forces are will and intellect. And yet the similarity is striking. Neither the artist nor the industrialist is present in his work. And both have disdained *touch*.

The relation of Joyce's artist-god to his creation is like the relation of Gerald Crich to his mines. Rather than knowing the life in the mines, rather than submitting to the darkness, Gerald turns "upon the inanimate matter of the underground and reduce[s] it to his will." Like Stephen's artist-god, "Gerald was the God of the machine, Deus ex Machina" (p. 220). "Gerald was hardly necessary anymore. . . . What he was doing seemed supreme, he was almost like a divinity" (p. 224).

The similarity is no accident, for Joyce's view of the priest-artist is Lawrence's view of the industrialist-artist. In Clifford Chatterley he describes someone who is industrialist and literary artist, and in both capacities Chatterley is out of touch. Indeed, he uses both capacities to keep out of touch with life, to keep in distant control, like Joyce's artist-god.

Again, in Loerke, the gnomelike artist who takes Gudrun from Gerald, Lawrence makes the connection between modern art and modern industry quite explicit: it isn't just that Loerke's art *serves* industry and is *suggested by* industry, but also, like the industrialist, his ideology masks a relationship of narcissistic isolation and sadistic control. It is because he accepts his own nothing, because he has forsaken his soul, that he takes the arrogant stance of the artist entitled to stand above creation.[15] Just as Gerald beats his mare to keep her still in her terror or nearly snaps the neck of Winifred's rabbit to make it pose, so Loerke beats his model, a child, his mistress, to keep her still. Both are contemptuous of ordinary life and the natural world and insist, as does Joyce, on the separation of the work and the world.

Near the end of *Women in Love,* Ursula speaks for Lawrence when she condemns Loerke, who separates art and life: " 'As for your world of art and your world of reality,' she replied, 'you have to separate the two, because you can't bear to know what you are. . . . The world of art is only the truth about the real world, that's all—but you are too far gone to see it' " (p. 422). This passage is a critique of modernist aesthetics and the tradition of the art-novel. If Flaubert wished that he could write a novel "about nothing at all," Lawrence wants to tell the truth about the life and death of civilization. In this he is deeply opposed to most modernist writers, for whom the reality that matters is the reality created by the artist.

For Lawrence (as for Heidegger) reality is deeply, deeply *there,* and the artist must burrow beneath its surface and attune himself to it. That is his religious function. The modernist split between the work of art and the real world is another manifestation of the basic soul-sickness that Lawrence wants to cure.

For Lawrence, since reality is *there,* the artist cannot make it, but instead must be open to it. "Not I, not I, but the wind that blows through me." If reality is to be found in the darkness, the artist must act as the miner's tool:

> "If only I am keen and hard like the sheer tip of a wedge driven by invisible
> blows,
> "The rock will split, we shall come at the wonder, we shall find the
> Hesperides."

Paradise, like truth, like the new, whole self, cannot be made; it must be found—and found in inner darkness, in stillness.[16] If Lawrence is the miner, then he is as much the mine itself, the source of truth. As artist, then, he is male and female, acting as agent of the father in the body of the mother, which is also himself.

That's one skein of metaphors. In another, of course, it is in the active encounter with the Other that the self is remade; the wonder of that encounter is Lawrence's paradigm for art, in contrast to the Jamesian and Joycean control of chaos by the artist.

Wonder. Lawrence leads us into a world which hums and burns with its own life. With Being. Here's a simple example, this descriptive passage from *Women in Love:* "By the road the blackthorn was in blossom, white and wet, its tiny amber grains burning faintly in the white smoke of blossom. Purple twigs were darkly luminous in the grey air, high hedges glowed like living shadows, hovering nearer, coming into creation. The morning was full of a new creation" (p. 39). This can hardly even be called description; that is, we don't actually see outline. We don't know diamond from coal. But we are brought inside the life of things, the life that cannot be created by the imposition of self on matter.

To assert truth is narcissistic, mechanical, false; as Birkin says to Ursula, "While ever either of us insists to the other, we are all wrong" (p. 243). The healing attitude is to open oneself to truth, to approach the world in *wonder*. "The unknown, the new world!" Lawrence's attitude toward Being is very close to Heidegger's. George Steiner, in his *Martin Heidegger,* says, "Man's 'thrownness into the clearing of Being' . . . renders equally fatuous the Cartesian centrality of the *ego* and the Sartrean scenario of individual existence as the source of freely chosen essence. Man only *is* to the extent that he stands open to Being in what Wordsworth would have called a 'wise passiveness'" (p. 129).

And yet Lawrence, better able than any modern writer to make me experience the world in wonder, *cannot stop* insisting. Too often in his life and in his work he manifests the sickness he diagnoses; he is Cathcart, the Master. In fiction and poetry as well as essay he becomes his own enemy, a truth-machine. In *The Odyssey,* when Menelaeus wrestles with Proteus, he is warned not to let him go no matter how he changes shape. The ego is as much a trickster as Proteus, the battle as difficult. The wonder is that Lawrence was, at times, able to hold Proteus down and explore, not espouse, new being. He is able to bring me into moments of healed life, into Being-there with him.

NOTES

PREFACE

1. Richard Poirier is also aware of the paradox of the self happily declaring the end of selfhood: "The voice we hear in the more eloquent passages in Foucault is often narcissistically determined that it be admired for the operatic extremity of the cultural role proposed for its author" ("Writing Off the Self," p. 219).

CHAPTER 1. UNTHINKABLE ANXIETY

1. The group of writers I'm considering could be described partly as writers who modeled their work and aesthetics on Flaubert's. I have avoided Wharton, Dos Passos, Dreiser, Steinbeck, Galsworthy, and Bennett because they are not modernist in sensibility and Gertrude Stein and Wyndham Lewis because, although they were influential as teachers, they never became part of the canon. I've limited this study to a few major writers of fiction, rather than exploring European modernism as a whole. For a recent study of European modernist fiction and of modernist art and literature more generally, see Frederick R. Karl, *Modern and Modernism: The Sovereignty of the Artist 1885–1925*. See also Modris Eksteins's *Rites of Spring: The Great War and the Birth of the Modern Age*. A wonderful discussion of the development of British modernist theory is found in Michael Levenson's *A Genealogy of Modernism*. I still greatly admire Irving Howe's *The Idea of the Modern*, especially the essays by Trilling and by Howe himself; and see also Lawrence B. Gamache's "Towards a Definition of Modernism" and Stanley Sultan's *Eliot, Joyce and Company*, especially his chapter, "Our Modern Experiment," with its extensive bibliography of recent studies on modernism.

2. Loëwenberg, "The Psychohistorical Origins of the Nazi Youth Cohort," in *Decoding the Past: A Psychohistorical Approach*, p. 242.

3. See especially Eksteins, *Rites of Spring, passim;* see also Malcolm Bradbury, *The Social Context of English Literature*, especially p. 66, and Marshall Berman's introduction to *All That Is Solid Melts into Air: The Experience of Modernity*.

4. D. W. Winnicott, in *The Maturational Processes and the Facilitating Environment* and throughout his work, posits a condition of literal and figurative "holding" that fosters psychic continuity. He also sees the world itself when it is in harmonious relation to the individual, and therapy in particular, as a "holding environment." See also Masud Khan, "Vicissitudes of Being, Knowing and Experiencing in the Therapeutic Situation" in *The Privacy of the Self*. I am applying the term more generally to a relationship with the environment in which the individual is sufficiently supported to enable him or her to be a fully alive person.

5. John Henry Newman, "The Aboriginal Calamity," pp. 79–81. Newman's God is God-the-*Father*, of course, but I would argue that the Victorian sense of an absent God reflects the absence of both male and female asepects of the ground of being.

6. *The Diary of Virginia Woolf,* 5:63.

7. As I shall show in a later chapter, the new patients are largely the result of the development of new families and a changed relation to community. The Freudian model became inadequate because the Freudian family and relation to the community had changed.

8. Heinz Kohut, *The Restoration of the Self,* especially p. 73. By 1977, Kohut had broken explicitly with drive theory as a way of explaining defects in the self. His patients were those with narcissistic personality disorders or narcissistic behavior disorders (p. 193). Of course, Kohut is using *narcissistic* neither in the popular sense of self-centered and selfish, nor even in Freud's sense that refers to an infantile stage in which the world exists as part of the self (primary narcissism) or a later regression to this relationship (secondary narcissism). For Kohut, narcissistic refers simply to issues of the constructed self. His patients demonstrated failures in the structure of the self, due to failures in the development of empathy or of an idealized self-object.

9. Winnicott does not discuss the schizoid character per se, but his discussion of the false self is similar.

10. See R. D. Laing's diagram in *The Divided Self,* p. 85.

11. W. Ronald D. Fairbairn explores the oral nature of schizoid feelings in *Psychoanalytic Studies of the Personality;* see also Bernard C. Meyer, *Joseph Conrad: A Psychoanalytic Biography.*

12. Winnicott, *Playing and Reality,* p. 116.

13. See Louis Sass, "Introspection, Schizophrenia, and the Fragmentation of Self"; see also his "Time, Space, and Symbol: A Study of Narrative Form and Representational Structure in Madness and Modernism."

14. See Ellen Bayuk Rosenman, *The Invisible Presence: Virginia Woolf and the Mother-Daughter Relationship.*

15. See David Willbern's discussion of Shakespeare's use of images of nothing and their relation to identity in "Shakespeare's Nothing."

16. The novel whose subject is the struggle to know the world and to create a

coherent self: better than any other, this describes Joyce's *Portrait*. Joyce's anxiety is different in some ways from that of other modernists. The world is paralyzing and confusing but not empty; the inner theater is full of conflict but not emptiness. The self needs to be created; ultimately, the self is an assemblage of voices, dissolving into the voices of the culture. But Joyce is not terrified of the void; the deadness of Dublin is the deadness of repression, not emptiness. Joyce's family, his need to shape a self and a world, and his epistemology fit well the terms of my discussion in this book. But I must admit the quality of anxiety in Joyce is different. If I were to imagine Joyce looking into the mirror, what he would see might be a cubist portrait—but not *nothing*.

17. Armstrong, in *The Challenge of Bewilderment: Understanding and Representation in James, Conrad, and Ford,* is interested in the representation of a world open to interpretation. I am not concerned with epistemological investigation in itself as much as in the psychological meaning of such investigations.

18. See, for example, Sondra J. Stang, "A Reading of Ford's *The Good Soldier*"; Mark Schorer, *Introduction to the Good Soldier;* Eugene Goodheart, "What Dowell Knew: A Reading of *The Good Soldier*"; and Arthur Mizener, *The Saddest Story: A Biography of Ford Madox Ford.*

19. Theodore Dreiser, " 'The Saddest Story': Theodore Dreiser on *The Good Soldier,*" pp. 48–49.

20. See Shoshona Felman's brilliant "Turning the Screw of Interpretation." Earlier critics, like Edmund Wilson, have argued either for or against the reliability of the governess; Felman shows how this critical debate is embedded in the text itself.

21. See "Projective Identification and Imaginative Empathy," Cowan's introduction to *D. H. Lawrence and the Trembling Balance,* which deals subtly and at some length with these issues:

If I did not see parts of myself in Lawrence, I would not have stayed with him for so long. My recognition of parts of my own life and being in him has enriched my response to his work. On an immediate level, such reader response may begin in primary identification marked by a state of "primary confusion" of boundaries between self and object. But I try to avoid merely transferring my needs and responses to Lawrence and then presenting in criticism those parts of myself as if they were his. While I have often used what I know from my own human existence, which necessarily includes the introjected objects of my inner world, I have tried to avoid confusing myself with Lawrence or my objects and experience with his. I have tried, in other words, to move beyond the "primary confusion" of boundaries toward secondary identification as empathic connection. My attempt has been, however imperfectly, to understand Lawrence's own ideas and feelings, to approach his writings openly, without too many preconceptions of my own, to see *him*. (P. 13)

22. It is only Heidegger who, especially in his later work, is able to let being speak for itself, not to fear being that is not imposed on by human meaning-making.

23. See Daniel Stern, *The Interpersonal World of the Infant,* pp. 10, 46, and *passim.*

24. See Winnicott, *Playing and Reality,* p. 97; see also his posthumously published "Fear of Breakdown."

25. Kohut, *How Does Analysis Cure,* p. 16.

26. Conrad's preface to *The Nigger of the "Narcissus,"* pp. 145, 147.

27. D. H. Lawrence, *Phoenix,* p. 366.

28. See Harry Guntrip, *Schizoid Phenomena, Object Relations and the Self,* p. 97. In his examination of schizoid withdrawal, schizoid regression, and schizoid anxieties, Guntrip elaborates on the explorations of Fairbairn and Winnicott.

29. See Erik Erikson's *Childhood and Society* for a discussion of the role of grandfathers in the development of American identity.

30. He sees it as a willful act, a breaking away.

PART 2. NO GROUND TO STAND ON

1. See Daniel Schneider, *D. H. Lawrence: The Artist as Psychologist.*

2. See Jean Paul Sartre, *Search for a Method.* Sartre, while not denying the usefulness of class analysis, insists on considering "real men who live and make history" rather than abstract classes (p. 50). He emphasizes the family as the primary instrument of mediation. "It is . . . inside the particularity of a history, through the peculiar contradictions of *this* family, that Gustave Flaubert unwittingly served his class apprenticeship" (p. 58). "The family," Sartre writes, "is constituted by and in the general movement of History, but is experienced, on the other hand, as an absolute in the depth and opaqueness of childhood" (p. 62).

3. See Charles Newman, *The Post-Modern Aura,* pp. 23–26. Newman quotes a letter by Flaubert from 1852 and argues that already all the "basic assumptions and contradictions of Modernism are . . . in place" (p. 23); See also Karl, *Modern and Modernism,* pp. 40–79.

CHAPTER 2. FAMILY GHOSTS

1. Eli Zaretsky, in *Capitalism, the Family, and Personal Life,* writes, "Increasingly cut off from production, the contemporary family threatens to become a well of subjectivity divorced from any social meaning" (p. 55).

2. Zaretsky, p. 33.

3. This is the title of Christopher Lasch's book on the modern family. See also the chapter, "Love," in Walter Houghton's brilliant *The Victorian Frame of Mind, 1830–1870.*

4. Steven Mintz, *A Prison of Expectations: The Family in Victorian Culture,* p. 13.

5. Stephen Kern, "Explosive Intimacy: Psychodynamics of the Victorian Family," p. 438.

6. In Max Horkheimer's "Authority and the Family," p. 126.

7. Alexander Mitscherlich, *Society without the Father,* p. 145. Jean Strouse, in her *Alice James,* quotes George Fredrickson in a footnote:

> Social historians have shown that the traditional ideal of unquestioning obedience to patriarchal authority began to be displaced in the early nineteenth century by the more egalitarian image of the family as held together primarily by mutual affection. It is at least arguable that the Christian view of the relationship between man and God had always been closely correlated with prevailing conceptions of parenthood and that what was new was . . . a transformed notion of parental authority that made the remote and severe patriarch of earlier times an inappropriate symbol for divinity in an age that exalted a more affectionate and consensual style of family life. (P. 16)

8. Steven Mintz, *A Prison of Expectations,* writes: "The authority of the father was increasingly cut off from the support of the broader culture. Market values and the values of political liberalism, which rewarded self-reliance and independence and personal responsibility, penetrated into the home and threw into question traditional assumptions about paternal authority" (pp. 61–62).

9. See Bruce Mazlich's *James and John Stuart Mill,* in which he argues for a *historicized* reading of the oedipus complex:

> Somewhere between the late eighteenth and early nineteenth centuries, sons began to adopt a different posture towards their fathers. . . . The Oedipus complex was handled at first in a slightly different, and eventually in a totally new way. A relationship, formerly patterned and secure, became problematic. Filial rebellions became more intense, and their fizzling out into submission less common and complete. The psychic price, in anxiety and guilt, became acute, and its prevalence increasingly epidemic. (P. 18)

10. See Judith Hughes, *Emotion and High Politics: Personal Relations at the Summit in Late Nineteenth-Century Britain and Germany,* chapters 2 and 3, in which she contrasts the training of Bismarck and Gladstone.

11. See Peter Ackroyd, *T. S. Eliot: A Life;* James E. Miller, Jr., *T. S. Eliot's Personal Waste Land;* George Whitehead, "T. S. Eliot: The Psychobiographical Approach."

12. Bruce Bawer, in *The Middle Generation,* writes: "None of them grew up in anything even remotely resembling a stable, solid home. Each was estranged from his father, and three of the four had destructively close ties to overly possessive mothers. All developed an early sense of rootlessness and alienation. Guilt over feelings of resentment towards the parents plagued each of them well into adult-

hood." Bawer sees the self-pathologies of these writers in relation to their shaky childhoods: "In each of them, the problem of the absent father was compounded by the omnipresent mother. . . . We find the mothers encouraging narcissism in their sons, while at the same time damaging the young men's self-images" (p. 5).

13. It is, indeed, as I explained in the first chapter, the pattern of my own upbringing. When I began this study, I wasn't aware that my vision of these writers was shaped partly by my experience of the dynamics in my own family of origin. That doesn't make my observation false; it means I have been sensitized to this family pattern and its effects on a child who becomes a writer.

14. I will deal with the James, Stephen, and Lawrence families at greater length in the chapters devoted to James, Woolf, and Lawrence.

15. Quoted by Douglas Goldring in *Trained for Genius: The Life and Writings of Ford Madox Ford*, p. 21.

16. Quoted by Peter Loëwenberg, "The Psychohistorical Origins of the Nazi Youth Cohort," p. 269.

17. Ernest Wolf and Ina Wolf, " 'We Perished Each Alone': A Psychoanalytic Commentary on Virginia Woolf's *To the Lighthouse*," p. 39. While I feel the Wolfs miss, in their discussion of Mrs. Ramsey, her strength and power, and the degree to which she is in touch with life below its surface, I am persuaded by their analysis and that of Ellen Rosenman that Julia Stephen was an *invisible* presence for Virginia.

18. Virginia Woolf, "Reminiscences," in *Moments of Being*, p. 40.

19. See the caustic, brilliant demolition of DeSalvo by Quentin Bell, "Who's Afraid for Virginia Woolf?" Bell attacks, with great wit, DeSalvo's "reckless treatment of the evidence," her hobbyhorse interpretations. I want to point out, in addition, DeSalvo's constant fall into the fallacy of the undistributed middle (monkeys are animals, people are animals, therefore people are monkeys). In DeSalvo's paradigm, abused children have symptoms X and Y, Virginia had symptoms X and Y, therefore Virginia was an abused child. This argument is unfortunate, for some of DeSalvo's readings are illuminating and useful.

20. The Canadian novelist John Peter liked to tell a story he had heard from Siegfried Sassoon. On a walk one day with Forster, Sassoon noticed that Forster was upset. "It's Mother," Forster said. "I asked her for a key to the house this morning, and she's sulking." At the time, Forster was hardly an adolescent; he was about sixty years old (personal communication).

21. See Peter Hultberg, "The Faithless Mother: An Aspect of the Novels of E. M. Forster." Oddly, Hultberg doesn't deal with *Where Angels Fear to Tread*, though this novel powerfully supports his position.

22. See Millicent Bell, "A Farewell to Arms: Pseudoautobiography and Personal Metaphor." Bell tells us that already on the opening page of *A Farewell to Arms*, not after the wound is incurred, the deadened spirit appears. And she points to the longing for fusion between the lovers, the longing for regression.

23. See Stern, *The Interpersonal World*, pp. 203–22 for a discussion of selective attunement, failures in attunement, etc. See also Winnicott, who, in "Mirror-role of Mother and Family in Child Development" and in many other essays, discusses the failure of the mother to reflect the baby to the baby. If instead she reflects "her own mood or, worse still, the rigidity of her own defenses" the baby does not develop a sense of its own existence, and it may withdraw or develop a false self in response (p. 27); see also "Psychoses and ChildCare" from *Collected Papers: Through Paediatrics to Psychoanalysis*, in which Winnicott clarifies the development of the false self under conditions of impingement (pp. 223–28).

CHAPTER 3. CHAOS

1. Karl, *Joseph Conrad: The Three Lives*, p. 20.
2. Thomas Moser, *The Life in the Fiction of Ford Madox Ford*, p. 138.
3. See Chapter 1 for a discussion of "holding environment."
4. Kohut, *The Restoration of the Self*, pp. 28–33, "considers the structural and functional deficiencies of the patient's self as the primary disorder" in agoraphobia and considers panic at oedipal wishes a *secondary* process. He points to failure of the mother to calm, failure of the father to respond (pp. 29–30). We don't need Kohut, however, to understand that Ford's agoraphobia expressed terror of disintegration, terror that he would be engulfed or would dissolve in emptiness.
5. Quoted by Mizener, *The Saddest Story*, p. 7.
6. See Terry Eagleton's introduction to *Exiles and Emigrés*, for example. He seems to regard literary changes in terms of battles, referring to a literature "dominated . . . by foreigners and expatriates," who defeat the "unchallenged sway of non-English poets and novelists" (p. 3). Twenty years later, in a recent lecture given at the University of Massachusetts, Amherst, Eagleton used the same metaphors of struggle between the center and the periphery.

PART 3. LIVING WITH CHAOS

1. See Leon Edel, *Henry James: A Life*, on the relationship with Andersen.
2. See Emile Delavenay's *D. H. Lawrence and Edward Carpenter: A Study in Edwardian Transition*.
3. See Paul Delany, *D. H. Lawrence's Nightmare: The Writer and His Circle in the Years of the Great War*, pp. 88–91.
4. See Delany, pp. 309–15. The evidence is slight, only inference from a letter by Frieda to John Middleton Murry. Delany suggests that even the relationship with Hocking was likely to have been idealized, involving little more than kissing or embraces.
5. See my essay "D. H. Lawrence: Psychic Wholeness through Rebirth"; see

also James Cowan's "Lawrence and Touch" for a balanced perspective on homo-erotic impulses.

CHAPTER 4. THE IMPOSTOR

1. See Erikson, "The Problem of Ego Identity," in *Identity and the Life Cycle,* p. 109. Erikson uses the terms to denote *"individual identity . . . continuity of personal character . . . ego synthesis . . .* inner *solidarity* with a group's ideals and identity."

2. See Roy Schafer, "The Construction of Multiple Histories," "Narration in the Psychoanalytic Dialogue," and "The Imprisoned Analysand" in *The Analytic Attitude.* See also Donald Spence, *Narrative Truth and Historical Truth: Meaning and Interpretation in Psychoanalysis,* and Berger and Luckmann, *The Social Construction of Reality.*

3. See Phyllis Greenacre, *Emotional Growth: Psychoanalytic Studies of the Gifted and a Great Variety of Other Individuals,* especially 2:538; see also Louise Kaplan, *Adolescence: The Farewell to Childhood,* especially her chapter, "The Impostor: A Masculine Pursuit of Perfection."

4. Kaplan continues: "The point is not that there is such a thing as a bona fide ideal of masculinity and that it can be conveyed only by a father. Rather, when the mother has a problematic sense of masculinity the absence of a father becomes a complication to the boy's acquisition of a sense of gender difference" (*Adolescence,* p. 303).

5. Moser continues, "By 1913 he had experienced much of the history of the typical, gifted, middle-aged, middle-class male suicide: early evidence of instability and disregard for the truth; rejection by father; early death of father; multiple marriages; heavy drinking; fluctuations in income; physical disability, especially involving shortness of breath; talk of self-destruction; a competitive or self-absorbed spouse. But by writing *The Good Soldier* Ford had conquered the worst symptom of all: disappointment in the use of one's potential" (*The Life in the Fiction of Ford Madox Ford,* p. 196).

6. Cited by Bernard Meyer, *Joseph Conrad: A Psychoanalytic Biography,* pp. 133–34.

7. Quoted by Max Saunders, "A Life in Writing: Ford Madox Ford's Dispersed Autobiographies," p. 47.

8. Ford tells this bizarre anecdote in *Memories and Impressions,* pp. 78–80.

9. I am using Kohutian vocabulary in this description of self pathology. In the next paragraph I cite Masud Khan, an object-relations theorist. I don't feel any significant incompatibility between a Kohutian formulation of the development of and damage to the self and descriptions by object-relations theorists. Both are suggestive and are not, at least for my purposes, contradictory.

10. The version of Ford's *Ladies Whose Bright Eyes* now read was published in 1935, but the original version was published in 1911.

CHAPTER 5. JOURNEY INTO CHAOS

1. I use *merger* to describe the wish for losing individuation, becoming one with an internalized figure, especially the mother; I prefer *fusion* to name the state of union.

2. Mario A. Jacoby, *Longing for Paradise: Psychological Perspectives on an Archetype*, p. 7.

3. Kohut would see evidence of failure of both poles of the structure of the self: a lack of maternal empathy and a failure of the father in offering ideals.

4. See Karl, *Joseph Conrad: The Three Lives*, pp. 478–79. Included in the album is the copy of a poem by the Polish novelist Jóseph Korzeniowski, "whose very name," Karl points out, "recalled Conrad to his true name before his alleged 'desertion' of Poland. . . . He could . . . have afforded to purchase writing paper for a few pages of notes on a new story; but he chose to use a historical document with its handwritten Polish as the basis of his own story of a 'desertion.' "

5. See Ian Watt's convincing discussion of the source of confusion in the passage (*Conrad in the Nineteenth Century*, pp. 325–31).

6. See Meyer, *Joseph Conrad*, p. 53; see also pp. 61, 63.

7. See Chapter 4 for a discussion of Forster's fantasies about women; see also Hultberg, "The Faithless Mother."

8. Far more than his male characters, Joyce is able to fully imagine a woman, a magnificent woman, in fact, in Molly. I find Molly truer, wiser, and fuller than any of Forster's women or Lawrence's women or certainly the women in Conrad and Hemingway. Joyce and James, in spite of their anxieties, are able to imagine wonderful women characters. But of course, I am a man speaking; speaking, I admit, uneasily.

CHAPTER 6. THE AESTHETICS OF ORDER

1. What is the danger of going under the surface? For purposes of this study, it doesn't matter whether the dangers under the surface represent (1) regression, as traditional psychoanalysis would claim, to primal process thought, to unconscious fantasy bubbling out of a libidinous life that the ego needs to repress; (2) a siren's call to return to an original unity that threatens the self with engulfment or dissolution; or (3) disintegration by-products, as both Kohut and British object-relations theorists put it. Kohut argues that when the self is defectively structured, that is, not shaped by a "mirroring self-object" or an "idealized self-object," children exhibit castration fears, incestuous desires, and explosions of aggression.

They are not primal or "natural," but disintegration by-products. Object-relations theorists argue that neurotic symptoms are defenses against ultimate schizoid regression or the ultimate annihilation of the true self. For all these theorists, symptoms do not arise from an insoluble conflict between orginal impulse and civilized control. For my purposes what really matters is that life beneath the surface is understand as both seductive and dangerous.

2. See Paul Delany's wonderful book *D. H. Lawrence's Nightmare: The Writer and His Circle in the Years of the Great War.*

3. James E. Miller, Jr., *T. S. Eliot's Personal Waste Land.*

4. T. S. Eliot, "Tradition and the Individual Talent," in *The English Modernist Reader, 1910–1930,* ed. Peter Faulkner, pp. 87, 89, 90.

5. Sigmund Freud, *Civilization and Its Discontents,* p. 40; see also Freud's *Totem and Taboo* for a discussion of compulsion neurosis and its relationship to magic and the omnipotence of thought.

6. Quoted by Peter Faulkner in *The English Modernist Reader,* p. 19.

7. From James's preface to *The Ambassadors,* p. 11.

CHAPTER 7. THE AESTHETICS OF CHAOS

1. This has become a truism in modernism. Beckett is the master of the irony that he is falsifying by using language, yet in saying so, he is using language. See, for example, Ihab Hassan, *The Dismemberment of Orpheus: Toward a Postmodern Literature,* pp. 3–23.

2. Winnicott, "Fear of Breakdown," p. 104; Winnicott's italics.

3. See James Gleick, *Chaos: Making a New Science.* Contemporary chaos theory in the sciences finds order hidden in the apparently disorderly, random processes of organic life.

4. Winnicott refers to the "impingement of the environment so that the individual must become a reactor to this impingement. The sense of self is lost in this situation and is only regained by a return to isolation" ("Paediatrics and Psychiatry," *Collected Papers,* p. 222).

5. I discuss darkness as the place of new life in Chapter 12.

6. Jonathan Rose, in *The Edwardian Temperament: 1895–1919,* shows that the yearning for connection, for unity, is a common theme in the period before World War I; see especially pp. 27–40.

7. J. Hillis Miller treats the word *see* almost literally and contrasts it with the world assimilable to language. My discussion is in affinity with his, but along with Ian Watt I would argue that *see* is not meant in an impressionist but a symbolic sense. Conrad is after an underlying truth beneath appearances.

8. Virginia Woolf, "Mr. Bennett and Mrs. Brown," p. 128.

9. See Richard Poirier's brilliant essay, "Writing Off the Self," in which he sees in Emerson and Stevens a joy in the transparent eyeball, in selfless experience. In

my book, *Saul Bellow: In Defense of Man*, I examine Bellow's longing, underneath his defense of the self, for selflessness. "When striving stops," Augie March says, "the truth comes as a gift."

10. See Armstrong's *Challenge*, in which he writes, "Bewilderment throws into question the interpretative constructs we ordinarily take for granted as our ways of knowing the world" (p. 2).

CHAPTER 8. GESTURES OF HEALING

1. By internal objects I mean the figures, originally from childhood, who populate our internal dramas—split-off selves, ego ideals, rejected presences through which we dramatize and experience reality.

2. I am thinking here of the tyranny of her father and the loss of her mother, but still more of the incestuous sexual abuse she had to undergo in silence, especially painful after she had lost her mother. But that she was not protected by her mother from sexual abuse by her half brother must have been painful from the start; Louise DeSalvo, who presses her thesis too far, is surely right about this. We don't know the extent of the abuse. It may be that she needed to hold onto the memory of abuse as a way of naming her experience of helplessness. What's more important to me than the fact of abuse is its psychological impact and meaning in her childhood and after.

3. I do so at some length in Chapter 11.

4. Melanie Klein is the important precursor of play therapy. But she emphasized the interpretation of content in play, both in the language and in the symbolic language of play, rather than the *effect* of play and a child's working-out in the drama of play itself; See Klein's "The Psycho-Analytic Play Technique: Its History and Significance."

5. Greenacre, "Play in Relation to Creative Imagination," in *Emotional Growth*, 2:562.

6. Winnicott, "On Communication," in *The Maturational Processes and the Facilitating Environment*, p. 184.

7. I have borrowed this Winnicottian formulation from Prof. Murray Schwartz.

8. This idea was suggested to me by Dr. Joel Rosen.

9. See Greenberg and Mitchell's formulation of Fairbairn:

It is the experience of these internal objects and the projection of them onto the outside world that produces pathological suffering. . . . Love objects are selected for or made into withholders or deprivers so as to personify the exciting object, promising but never fulfilling. . . . Defeat is orchestrated again and again to perpetuate the longing and need of the libidinal ego for the fulfillment of the promise of the exciting object. Success is equated with a betrayal of that promise . . . and hence threatens to rupture those internal ties. . . . Psycho-

pathology persists, old pain returns, destructive patterns of integrating relations with others and experienced life are perpetuated—because beneath the
pain and the self-defeating relations and organizations of experience lie ancient
internal attachments and allegiances. . . . The re-creation of the sorrow, suffering and defeat are forms of renewal and devotion to these ties. (*Object Relations in Psychoanalytic Theory*, pp. 173–74)

10. See Christopher Bollas's *The Shadow of the Object: Psychoanalysis of the
Unthought Known.*

11. See Meredith Skura, *The Literary Use of the Psychoanalytic Process,*
especially chapter 5, "Literature as Transference: Rhetorical Function," and chapter 6, "Literature as Psychoanalytic Process."

12. Bollas writes, "In order to find the patient we must look for him within
ourselves" (*The Shadow of the Object*, p. 202).

13. See Schafer's "The Sense of an Answer," especially pp. 203–04.

14. Kohut would speak of my role as that of a mirroring self-object.

15. Berger and Luckmann, *The Social Construction of Reality*, p. 151.

16. See Brooks Bouson's *The Empathic Reader* in which she argues that texts
like *Heart of Darkness* engender rescue fantasies in their readers.

17. See Gail Reed's fine article "Toward a Methodology for Applying Psychoanalysis to Literature" (especially pp. 36, 38); see also the essay by Felman,
"Turning the Screw of Interpretation" (to which I have often referred in this book),
a brilliant examination of critical debate reenacting the struggle in the text itself.

18. Perhaps it is this dangerous constellation of uses to which the reader is put
by Lawrence that accounts for the resistance and even anger many of Lawrence's
readers have felt.

CHAPTER 9. HEALING THE CULTURE

1. Cited by Bruce Robbins, "Modernism in History, Modernism in Power,"
p. 243.

2. Lionel Trilling, "On the Modern Element in Modern Literature," in Howe,
The Idea of the Modern, p. 60; see also Modris Eksteins, *Rites of Spring*. Eksteins
sees modernism essentially as liberation, political even when it eschews politics.

3. Cary Nelson, *Repression and Recovery: Modern American Poetry and the
Politics of Cultural Memory, 1910–1945*, p. 241.

4. See, for example, Jackson Lears, *No Place of Grace: Antimodernism and the
Transformation of American Culture, 1880–1920*, especially pp. 5–42; see also
Houghton, *The Victorian Frame of Mind*, especially pp. 1–27 and pp. 54–92.

5. Houghton, *The Victorian Frame of Mind*, p. 66; see also Lears, *No Place of
Grace:* "In both Europe and America the anti-modern impulse was rooted in what
might aptly be called a crisis of cultural authority" (p. 5).

6. See Jan Dizard and Howard Gadlin's *The Minimal Family*, pp. 119, 135–36; see also Mintz, *A Prison of Expectations*.

7. Paul Fussell, *The Great War and Modern Memory*, especially chapter 1.

8. See Eksteins, *Rites of Spring*; see also Rose, *The Edwardian Temperament*; Eric Hobsbawm, *The Age of Empire: 1875–1914*; Barbara Tuchman, *The Proud Tower: A Portrait of the World before the War: 1890–1914*; and Martin Green, *The Von Richthofen Sisters*.

9. Loëwenberg, *Decoding the Past*.

10. Trilling, "The Two Environments."

11. The best study I know that deals directly with these contradictions is Levenson's *A Genealogy of Modernism*.

12. See John Clayton, *Saul Bellow: In Defense of Man, passim*.

CHAPTER 10. THE PSYCHOLOGICAL STRATEGY OF HENRY JAMES

1. See *The Letters of Edith Wharton*, ed. R. W. B. Lewis and Nancy Lewis, p. 202. We don't know how accurate Wharton's report may be. I feel I hear Wharton's own romantic shaping of the scene. Still, if her report is at all reliable, James was deeply in need of a "Great Good Place" of restoration.

2. James Anderson, in his "In Search of Mary James," squeezes his evidence too hard, taking as evidence of maternal failure William's praise that his wife's conduct "made me for the first time *fully* understand what the word 'mother' means" (p. 64). Still, Anderson's case for seeing Mary as a self-sacrificing but often unempathic, anxious, and controlling mother is strong.

3. See Ann Douglas, *The Feminization of American Culture*. While not a minister, Henry James, Sr., as philosopher and public speaker, arguably fits her description of the feminized clerics in America.

4. Such identification was especially important in Victorian America, with its exaggerated, ideal conceptions of manhood.

5. See Peter Blos, *Son and Father: Before and beyond the Oedipus Complex*, p. 2; and *passim*. See also Kohut's work, especially *The Restoration of the Self*, pp. 171–72. In Kohut's terms, Henry James was brought up by a mother who loved him but failed in empathy, failed in acting as a mirroring self-object, and by a father who could not be the idealized self-object the son needed to support his own developing self.

6. Quoted by Jean Strouse, *Alice James*, p. xvii.

7. See Guntrip, *Schizoid Phenomena*, especially p. 64.

8. Henry James's preface to *The Spoils of Poynton*, in *The Novel and Tales of Henry James*, 10:v.

9. Henry James's preface to *Roderick Hudson*, in Henry James, *The Art of Criticism*, pp. 260–61.

10. Bruce W. Wilshire, ed., *William James: The Essential Writings*, p. 180.

11. Paul B. Armstrong, *The Phenomenology of Henry James*, p. 109. William James's quotation is from his *Principles of Psychology*, 2:289.

12. William James, "Discrimination and Comparison," *The Principles of Psychology*, p. 462.

13. Stern, *The Interpersonal World*, p. 46.

14. Postmodernism can be partly seen as a further doubting that there is any unified subject to be the knower, the shaper. The subject is actually what is "spoken," not the speaker.

15. See Jürgen Habermas, *Knowledge and Human Interests;* see also Berger and Luckmann, *The Social Construction of Reality.* Edward Said, "Representing the Colonized: Anthropology's Interlocutors," asks whether the whole field of cultural anthropology is so tainted by its western-centered lens as to be unsaveable as a discipline.

16. Henry James's preface to *The Portrait of a Lady*, in *Art of Criticism*, pp. 290–91.

17. Quoted by Strouse, *Alice James*, p. xii.

18. See, for example, Watt, *Conrad in the Nineteenth Century*, pp. 200–214.

19. See Rose, *The Edwardian Temperament*, especially pp. 27–40. Rose sees the yearning after connection, synthesis, coherence, solidarity as an Edwardian preoccupation.

20. William James, *Pragmatism*, in *The Modern Tradition*, eds. Richard Ellmann and Charles Feidelson, Jr., p. 438 (James's italics).

21. Ruth Yeazell uses this quotation from *The Golden Bowl* as the epigraph to her brilliant *Language and Knowledge in the Late Novels of Henry James.*

22. Guntrip, in *Schizoid Phenomena*, describes James as schizoid and emphasizes his noninvolvement, loneliness, withdrawal (pp. 98–100). I think Guntrip oversimplifies. James had deep friendships, passionate feelings for art and literature. He was, in his own way, intensely in the world. But schizoid tendencies surely exist and are both defenses and what is defended against in the fiction. Guntrip's description of schizoid retreat is at least suggestive:

> The part of the self that struggles to keep in touch with life feels intense fear of the deeper and more secret, withdrawn self, which appears to be endowed with a great capacity to attract and draw down more and more of the rest of the personality into itself. Hence extensive defenses are operated against it. If those defenses fail, the ego of everyday consciousness experiences a progressively terrifying loss of interest, energy, zest, verging towards exhaustion, apathy, derealization of the environment, and depersonalization of the conscious ego. It becomes like an empty shell out of which the living individual has departed to some safer retreat." (P. 64)

23. Cushing Strout, in "Henry James's Dream of the Louvre, 'The Jolly Corner,' and Psychological Interpretation," warns against simple biographical readings of

"The Jolly Corner" that "do not try hard enough to comprehend the story as a drama of irony before they situate it biographically" (p. 50). He accurately points out differences between James and the character of Brydon.

24. I am grateful for this suggestion to Dr. Edward Emery.

25. See Strout, "Henry James's Dream of the Louvre, 'The Jolly Corner,' and Psychological Interpretation"; see also *Autobiography,* p. 196, and Leon Edel, *Henry James: The Master,* pp. 442–47.

CHAPTER 11. MOMENTS OF HEALING: VIRGINIA WOOLF

1. See Chapter 1 for a discussion of Winnicott's concept.

2. Ernest Wolf and Ina Wolf, " 'We Perished Each Alone': A Psychoanalytic Commentary on Virginia Woolf's *To the Lighthouse.*" See also Brooks Bouson's illuminating discussion of Mrs. Dalloway in her *The Empathic Reader.* Like the Wolfs, and applying the same Kohutian position, Bouson emphasizes the narcissistic injuries of Woolf and her characters. She sees them as empty, incomplete, needing merger.

3. Hans Loewald, "Ego and Reality," p. 12.

4. See Louise DeSalvo's discussion of the same passage of memory. It is an instance of DeSalvo's tendency to misread in order to push her interpretation. She says,

> What makes this early memory poignant is that Virginia is calling into question her very right to exist—'it is almost impossible that I should be here' is another way of saying 'my existence is threatened; that I should cease to exist is a very real possibility.' From as early as she could remember, from her first significant memory, she did not take her right to exist for granted; she considered it almost a miracle that she continued to survive. The fact of her own simple survival is what she remembers as having given her the purest ecstasy that she has known as a child. (*Virginia Woolf: The Impact of Childhood Sexual Abuse on Her Life and Work,* p. 102)

What a bizarre, distorted reading of a sentence that, in context, obviously implies wonder at the glory of Being—not thanks for survival.

5. Anton Ehrenzweig, *The Hidden Order of Art: A Study in the Psychology of the Artistic Imagination.*

6. James Narremore, in *The World without a Self: Virginia Woolf and the Novel:* "Throughout Mrs. Woolf's work, the chief problem for her and for her characters is to overcome the space between things, to attain an absolute unity with the world, as if everything in the environment were turned to water" (p. 242). He enlarges on this unity in a wonderfully precise passage:

> On the one hand is the world of the self, the time-bound, landlocked, everyday world of the masculine ego, of intellect and routine, where people live in fear of

death, and where separations imposed by time and space result in agony. On the other hand is a world without a self—watery, emotional, erotic, generally associated with the feminine sensibility—where all of life seems blended together in a kind of "halo," where the individual personality is continually being dissolved by intimations of eternity, and where death reminds us of a sexual union. (P. 245)

7. Brooks Bouson would say that I have been taken in by Woolf's strategy. She argues that "Woolf entices her reader to affirm her central character" (*The Empathic Reader*, p. 152).

8. J. Hillis Miller makes a similar observation in *Fiction and Repetition*, p. 181; he also points out that "the narrator is that 'something central . . .' a power of union and penetration which Clarissa Dalloway lacks" (p. 178).

9. See, for example, Betty Kushen, *Virginia Woolf and the Nature of Communion*.

10. See Alex Zwerdling, *Virginia Woolf and the Real World*, p. 183.

11. *Diary*, 3:208.

12. James Narremore discusses the question in *The World without a Self*: "Her barely concealed eroticism is . . . related to the wish to find some permanent, all embracing union: in effect, to the death-wish" (pp. 242–43).

13. Schafer, *Aspects of Internalization*, especially chapter 5. Schafer sees the temporary, controllable putting aside of the "reflexive self-representation" as that which enables a daydream to take place.

14. J. Hillis Miller and other critics also note that the metaphor of plunging connects Clarissa and Septimus. See Miller's *Fiction and Repetition*, p. 185.

15. Bouson, *The Empathic Reader*, p. 152. Bouson emphasizes the way Woolf manipulates the critic, who becomes a "critic-rescuer," completing Clarissa. She offers many examples of critical readings that try to "rescue" both Septimus and his suicide. I don't accept Bouson's implication of unconscious manipulation of the reader. I would argue that Woolf creates a world that can hold her and make her whole. We live in that world and are afraid to reveal to ourselves its secrets.

CHAPTER 12. D. H. LAWRENCE AS HEALER

1. Daniel Schneider has written a fine book (*D. H. Lawrence: The Artist as Psychologist*) in which he traces Lawrence's ideas back to Schopenhauer and Nietzsche and examines psychological constructs in Lawrence's *Psychology of the Unconscious, Fantasia of the Unconscious*, and novels. I am not interested in analyzing Lawrence's theory but rather in attuning myself to his essential gesture of healing.

2. See Cowan's essay, "Lawrence and Touch."

3. See Chapter 1, "Unthinkable Anxiety."

4. Many critics have discussed rebirth as central to Lawrence, including Donald Gutierrez's *Lapsing Out: Embodiments of Death and Rebirth in the Last Writings of D. H. Lawrence.*

5. David Willbern, "Malice in Paradise: Isolation and Projection in 'The Man Who Loved Islands,'" p. 239.

6. See, for example, Murray Schwartz's "D. H. Lawrence and Psychoanalysis: An Introduction."

7. See Mark Karpel, "Individuation: From Fusion to Dialogue." Karpel, developing the insights of Fairbairn and other object-relations theorists, demonstrates that impulses toward fusion and toward isolation actually form part of the same syndrome and are absolutely different from the dialogic relationship of individuals, who can be both close and separate.

8. In an analysis similar to mine, Willbern describes brilliantly what he calls "Lawrencian regression": "Nostalgia for past sensual loveliness (appropriately oral: 'a scent of honeysuckle') arouses yearning for a time 'when the blood had a different throb.' The arousal of desire for such a primal past brings with it the emergence of 'strange floods of passion' which turn into 'violent lusts and imaginations of cruelty' and which are projectively located in the external environment, where they are then feared." ("Malice in Paradise," p. 233).

9. See Willbern, "Shakespeare's Nothing," for a discussion of the puns and paradoxes of "nothing" in Shakespeare.

10. See Chapter 1 for a discussion of Winnicott's term, "holding environment."

11. Arthur Lawrence was not actually a drunk, though he drank; nor a wreck, for he continued to work and support his family; nor emotionally crippled, though he was an outcast within his own family. But drunk and wreck and cripple he *was* in the family mythology.

12. The standard book on Lawrence as oedipal son is Daniel Weiss's *Oedipus in Nottingham.*

13. See Judith Ruderman's *D. H. Lawrence and the Devouring Mother: The Search for a Patriarchal Ideal of Leadership.* Ruderman explores Lawrence's conflict between desire for merger with and fear of engulfment by an all-consuming mother (see especially, pp. 173ff).

14. See Blos, *Son and Father.* Blos discusses the boy's need for bonding with his father and with the development and resolution of what he calls the "isogender" (negative) complex in adolescence. He shows the importance of the dyadic bond with the father in the formation of male sexual identity (seen for example, p. 22).

15. It pains me that Loerke is "probably Jewish, or half-Jewish," that Lawrence uses the Jew, as he uses self-assertive women, as images of degeneration. I also find myself embarrassed that Lawrence, to whose work I feel so close, has such a naive

understanding of African arts and cultures. I try to remember that Lawrence's Jew, worker, African, woman, have metaphorical significance within his system and that although the system can tell us a great deal about life, the parts can tell us very little.

16. See Leo Bersani's fine essay, "Lawrentian Stillness."

BIBLIOGRAPHY

Ackroyd, Peter. *T. S. Eliot: A Life.* New York: Simon and Schuster, 1984.

Anderson, James. "In Search of Mary James." *The Psychohistory Review* 8 (1979): 63–70.

Armstrong, Paul B. *The Challenge of Bewilderment: Understanding and Representation in James, Conrad, and Ford.* Ithaca: Cornell University Press, 1987.

———. *The Phenomenology of Henry James.* Chapel Hill: University of North Carolina Press, 1983.

Axline, Virginia. *Play Therapy.* New York: Ballantine, 1969.

Bawer, Bruce. *The Middle Generation.* Hamden, Conn.: Shoestring Press, 1986.

Bell, Millicent. "A Farewell to Arms: Pseudoautobiography and Personal Metaphor." In *Ernest Hemingway: The Writer in Context,* edited by James Nagel, pp. 107–28. Madison: University of Wisconsin Press, 1984.

Bell, Quentin. *Virginia Woolf: A Biography.* New York: Harcourt Brace Jovanovich, 1972.

———. "Who's Afraid for Virginia Woolf?" *New York Review of Books,* 15 March 1990, pp. 3–6.

Berger, Peter L., and Thomas Luckmann. *The Social Construction of Reality: A Treatise in the Sociology of Knowledge.* Garden City, N.Y.: Anchor, 1967.

Berman, Marshall. *All That Is Solid Melts into Air: The Experience of Modernity.* New York: Simon and Schuster, 1982.

Bersani, Leo. "Lawrentian Stillness." In *D. H. Lawrence: Modern Critical Views,* edited by Harold Bloom, pp. 179–200. New York: Chelsea, 1986.

Blos, Peter. *Son and Father: Before and Beyond the Oedipus Complex.* New York: Free Press, 1985.

Blotner, Joseph. *Faulkner: A Biography.* New York: Random House, 1984.

Bollas, Christopher. *The Shadow of the Object: Psychoanalysis of the Unthought Known.* New York: Columbia University Press, 1987.

Bouson, J. Brooks. *The Emphatic Reader.* Amherst: University of Massachusetts Press, 1989.

Bradbury, Malcolm. *The Social Context of English Literature.* New York: Schocken, 1971.

Bruccoli, Matthew. *Some Sort of Epic Grandeur.* New York: Harcourt Brace Jovanovich, 1981.

Clayton, John. "D. H. Lawrence: Psychic Wholeness through Rebirth." *Massachusetts Review* 25 (Summer 1984): 200–21.

———. *Saul Bellow: In Defense of Man.* 2d ed. Bloomington: Indiana University Press, 1979.

Clifford, James. *The Predicament of Culture.* Cambridge: Harvard University Press, 1988.

Conrad, Joseph. *Almayer's Folly* (1895). New York: Penguin, 1947.

———. *Heart of Darkness* (1901). Edited by Robert Kimbrough. Norton Critical Edition. New York: Norton, 1971.

———. *Lord Jim* (1900). Boston: Houghton Mifflin, 1958.

———. *A Personal Record.* New York: Doubleday, 1912.

———. Preface to *The Nigger of the "Narcissus,"* by Joseph Conrad, pp. 145–47. Norton Critical Edition. New York: Norton, 1979.

Cowan, James. *D. H. Lawrence and the Trembling Balance.* University Park: Pennsylvania State University Press, 1990.

———. "Lawrence and Touch." *D. H. Lawrence Review* 18 (Summer–Fall 1985–86): 121–37.

Delany, Paul. *D. H. Lawrence's Nightmare: The Writer and His Circle in the Years of the Great War.* New York: Basic, 1978.

Delavenay, Emile. *D. H. Lawrence and Edward Carpenter: A Study in Edwardian Transition.* New York: Taplinger, 1971.

Demos, John. *Past, Present, and Personal: The Family and the Life Course in American History.* New York: Oxford University Press, 1986.

DeSalvo, Louise. *Virginia Woolf: The Impact of Childhood Sexual Abuse on Her Life and Work.* Boston: Beacon, 1989.

Deutsch, Helene. "The Imposter." *Psychoanalytic Quarterly* 24 (1955): 483–505.

Dicks, Henry V. *Marital Tensions.* London: Routledge, 1967.

Dinnerstein, Dorothy. *The Mermaid and the Minotaur.* New York: Harper and Row, 1976.

Dizard, Jan, and Howard Gadlin. *The Minimal Family.* Amherst: University of Massachusetts Press, 1990.

Douglas, Ann. *The Feminization of American Culture.* New York: Knopf, 1977.

Dreiser, Theodore. " 'The Saddest Story': Theodore Dreiser on *The Good Soldier.*" In *Ford Madox Ford: The Critical Heritage,* pp. 47–51. London: Routledge, 1972.

Eagleton, Terry. *Exiles and Emigrés: Studies in Modern Literature.* New York: Schocken, 1970.

————. *Marxism and Literary Criticism*. Berkeley: University of California Press, 1976.

Edel, Leon. *Henry James: A Life*. Rev. ed. New York: Harper and Row, 1985. 1-volume, condensed edition of original 5 volumes. *Henry James: The Untried Years: 1843–1870; Henry James: The Conquest of London: 1870–1881; Henry James: The Middle Years: 1882–1895; Henry James: The Treacherous Years: 1895–1901; Henry James: The Master: 1901–1916* (1953–72).

Ehrenzweig, Anton. *The Hidden Order of Art: A Study in the Psychology of the Artistic Imagination*. London: Weidenfeld and Nicolson, 1967.

Eksteins, Modris. *Rites of Spring: The Great War and the Birth of the Modern Age*. Boston: Houghton Mifflin, 1989.

Ellmann, Richard, and Charles Feidelson, Jr., eds. *The Modern Tradition: Backgrounds of Modern Literature*. New York: Oxford University Press, 1965.

Erikson, Erik H. *Childhood and Society*. New York: Norton, 1963.

————. *Identity and the Life Cycle*. New York: Norton, 1980.

Fairbairn, W. Ronald D. *Psychoanalytic Studies of the Personality*. London: Routledge, 1952.

Faulkner, Peter, ed. *The English Modernist Reader, 1910–1930*. Iowa City: University of Iowa Press, 1986.

Faulkner, William. *As I Lay Dying* (1930). New York: Vintage, 1987.

————. *The Sound and the Fury* (1929). New York: Vintage, 1954.

Feinstein, Howard M. *Becoming William James*. Ithaca: Cornell University Press, 1984.

Felman, Shoshona. "Turning the Screw of Interpretation." *Yale French Studies* 55/56 (1977): 94–207.

Fitzgerald, F. Scott. *The Crack-Up*. Edited by Edmund Wilson. New York: New Directions, 1945.

————. *The Great Gatsby* (1925). New York: Scribner's, 1953.

————. *Tender Is the Night* (1933). New York: Schribner's, 1961.

Ford, Ford Madox. *The Good Soldier*. New York: Vintage, 1983.

————. *Memories and Impressions*. New York: Ecco, 1985.

Forster, E. M. *A Passage to India* (1924). New York: Harcourt Brace Jovanovich, 1984.

Foucault, Michel. *The Foucault Reader*, ed. Paul Rabinow. New York, 1984.

Freud, Sigmund. *Civilization and Its Discontents*. Edited by James Strachey. New York: Norton, 1961.

Furbank, P. N. *E. M. Forster: A Life*. London: Secker and Warburg, 1979.

Fussell, Paul. *The Great War and Modern Memory*. New York: Oxford University Press, 1975.

Gamache, Lawrence B. "Towards a Definition of Modernism." In *The Modernists: Studies in a Literary Phenomenon*, edited by Lawrence B. Gamache and Ian S.

MacNiven, pp. 32–45. Rutherford, N.J.: Fairleigh Dickinson University Press, 1987.

Gilbert, Sandra, and Susan Gubar. *No Man's Land: The Place of the Woman Writer in the Twentieth Century.* 2 vols. New Haven: Yale University Press, 1988.

Gleick, James. *Chaos: Making a New Science.* New York: Penguin, 1987.

Goldring, Douglas. *Trained for Genius: The Life and Writings of Ford Madox Ford.* New York: Dutton, 1949.

Goodheart, Eugene. "What Dowell Knew: A Reading of *The Good Soldier.*" *Antaeus* 56 (Spring 1986): 70–80.

Gordon, Mary. "A Man Who Loved Women, a Womanly Man." *Antaeus* 56 (Spring 1986): 206–14.

Green, Martin. *The Von Richthofen Sisters: The Triumphant and Tragic Modes of Love: Else and Frieda von Richthofen, Otto Gross, Max Weber, and D. H. Lawrence.* New York: Basic, 1971.

Greenacre, Phyllis. *Emotional Growth: Psychoanalytic Studies of the Gifted and a Great Variety of Other Individuals.* 2 vols. New York: International Universities Press, 1971.

Greenberg, Jay R., and Stephen A. Mitchell. *Object Relations in Psychoanalytic Theory.* Cambridge: Harvard University Press, 1983.

Guntrip, Harry. *Schizoid Phenomena, Object Relations and the Self.* New York: International Universities Press, 1969.

Gutierrez, Donald. *Lapsing Out: Embodiments of Death and Rebirth in the Last Writings of D. H. Lawrence.* Rutherford, N.J.: Farleigh Dickinson University Press, 1980.

Habermas, Jürgen. *Knowledge and Human Interests.* Boston: Beacon, 1971.

Hassan, Ihab. *The Dismemberment of Orpheus: Toward a Postmodern Literature.* 2d ed. Madison: University of Wisconsin Press, 1982.

Hemingway, Ernest. *Farewell to Arms* (1929). New York: Scribner's, 1986.

———. *For Whom the Bell Tolls.* New York: Scribner's, 1940.

———. *The Short Stories of Ernest Hemingway.* New York: Scribner's, 1966.

Hobsbawm, Eric. *The Age of Empire: 1875–1914.* New York: Pantheon, 1987.

Horkheimer, Max. "Authority and the Family." In *Critical Theory.* New York: Herder and Herder, 1972.

Houghton, Walter. *The Victorian Frame of Mind, 1830–1870.* New Haven: Yale University Press, 1985.

Howe, Irving, ed. *The Idea of the Modern.* New York: Horizon, 1967.

Hughes, Judith. *Emotion and High Politics: Personal Relations at the Summit in Late Nineteenth-Century Britain and Germany.* Berkeley: University of California Press, 1983.

———. *Reshaping the Psychoanalytic Domain: The Work of Melanie Klein,*

W. R. D. Fairbairn, and D. W. Winnicott. Berkeley: University of California Press, 1989.

Hultberg, Peter. "The Faithless Mother: An Aspect of the Novels of E. M. Forster." In *Narcissism and the Text: Studies in Literature and the Psychology of Self*, edited by Lynn Layton and Barbara Ann Shapiro, pp. 233–54. New York: New York University Press, 1986.

Jacoby, Mario A. *Longing for Paradise: Psychological Perspectives on an Archetype*. Boston: Sigo, 1985.

James, Henry. *The Ambassadors*. Norton Critical Edition. New York: Norton, 1964.

————. *The Art of Criticism*. Edited by William Veeder and Susan Griffin. Chicago: University of Chicago Press, 1986.

————. "The Beast in the Jungle." In *The Turn of the Screw and Other Stories*, pp. 323–66. New York: Bantam, 1981.

————. *The Golden Bowl*. New York: Meridian, 1972.

————. "The Great Good Place." In *Eight Tales from the Major Phase*, edited by Morton Zabel, pp. 287–313. New York: Norton, 1969.

————. "The Jolly Corner." In *The Turn of the Screw and Other Stories*, pp. 367–403. New York: Bantam, 1981.

————. *The Novels and Tales of Henry James*. New York Edition. Vol. 10. New York: Scribner, 1908.

————. *Shorter Masterpieces*. 2 vols. Totowa, N.J.: Barnes and Noble, 1984.

James, William. *The Principles of Psychology*. 2 vols. New York: Dover, 1950.

Joyce, James. *A Portrait of the Artist as a Young Man* (1916). Edited by Chester Anderson. Norton Critical Edition. New York: Viking, 1968.

————. *Ulysses*. New York: Vintage, 1986.

Joyce, Stanislaus. *My Brother's Keeper: James Joyce's Early Years*. New York: Viking, 1958.

Kaplan, Louise. *Adolescence: The Farewell to Childhood*. New York: Simon and Schuster, 1984.

Karl, Frederick R. *Joseph Conrad: The Three Lives*. New York: Farrar, Straus and Giroux, 1979.

————. *Modern and Modernism: The Sovereignty of the Artist 1885–1925*. New York: Atheneum, 1988.

————. *William Faulkner: American Writer*. New York: Weidenfeld and Nicolson, 1989.

Karpel, Mark. "Individuation: From Fusion to Dialogue." *Family Process* 15 (1976): 65–82.

Kern, Stephen. "Explosive Intimacy: Psychodynamics of the Victorian Family." *History of Childhood Quarterly* 1 (1974): 438–61.

Khan, Masud. *The Privacy of the Self*. New York: International Universities Press, 1974.

Kiely, Robert. *Beyond Egotism: The Fiction of James Joyce, Virginia Woolf, and D. H. Lawrence.* Cambridge: Harvard University Press, 1980.

Klein, Melanie. "Infantile Anxiety Situations." In *Love, Guilt, and Reparation.* London: Hogarth, 1975.

———. "The Psycho-Analytic Play Technique: Its History and Significance." In *New Directions in Psychoanalysis: The Significance of Infant Conflict in the Pattern of Adult Behaviour,* edited by Melanie Klein et al. London: Maresfield Reprints, 1977.

Kohut, Heinz. *How Does Analysis Cure.* Chicago: University of Chicago Press, 1985.

———. *The Restoration of the Self.* New York International Universities Press, 1977.

Kris, Ernst. *Psychoanalytic Explorations in Art.* New York: International Universities Press, 1952.

Kushen, Betty. *Virginia Woolf and the Nature of Communion.* West Orange, N.J.: Raynor, 1983.

Laing, R. D. *The Divided Self.* New York: Pantheon, 1969.

Lasch, Christopher. *Haven in a Heartless World.* New York: Basic, 1977.

Lawrence, D. H. *Apocalypse.* New York: Viking, 1966.

———. *The Collected Letters of D. H. Lawrence.* Edited by Richard Aldington. 2 vols. New York: Viking, 1962.

———. *The Complete Poems of D. H. Lawrence.* New York: Viking, 1971.

———. *The Complete Poems of D. H. Lawrence.* Edited by Vivian de Sola Pinto and Warren Roberts. 2 vols. London: Heinemann, 1964.

———. *The Complete Short Stories.* 3 vols. New York: Viking, 1961.

———. *Phoenix: The Posthumous Papers of D. H. Lawrence.* New York: Viking, 1972.

———. *Psychoanalysis of the Unconscious* and *Fantasia of the Unconscious.* New York: Viking, 1960.

———. *The Rainbow.* New York: Viking, 1961.

———. *Selected Poems.* New York: Viking, 1959.

———. *Studies in Classic American Literature.* New York: Viking, 1961.

———. *Women in Love* (1920). New York: Viking, 1960.

Lears, Jackson. *No Place of Grace: Antimodernism and the Transformation of American Culture, 1880–1920.* New York: Pantheon, 1981.

Levenson, Michael H. *A Genealogy of Modernism.* Cambridge: Cambridge University Press, 1984.

Loewald, Hans W. "Ego and Reality." *International Journal of Psychoanalysis* 32 (1951): 10–18.

Loëwenberg, Peter. *Decoding the Past: A Psychohistorical Approach.* New York: Knopf, 1982.

Lynn, Kenneth. *Hemingway.* New York: Simon and Schuster, 1987.

McDougall, Joyce. "On Psychic Deprivation." In *Theaters of the Body: A Psycho-analytic Approach to Psychosomatic Phenomena*. New York: Basic, 1989. Forthcoming.

Matthiessen, F. O. *The James Family*. New York: Knopf, 1961.

Mazlich, Bruce. *James and John Stuart Mill*. New York: Basic, 1975.

Meyer, Bernard C. *Joseph Conrad: A Psychoanalytic Biography*. Princeton: Princeton University Press, 1967.

Meyers, Jeffrey. *Hemingway: A Biography*. New York: Harper and Row, 1985.

Miller, J. Hillis. *Fiction and Repetition*. Cambridge: Harvard University Press, 1982.

Miller, James E., Jr. *T. S. Eliot's Personal Waste Land*. University Park: Pennsylvania State University Press, 1977.

Milner, Marion. *The Hands of the Living God*. New York: International University sities Press, 1969.

———. "The Role of Illusion in Symbol Formation." In *New Directions in Psychoanalysis: The Significance of Infant Conflict in the Pattern of Adult Behaviour*, edited by Melanie Klein et al. London: Maresfield Reprints, 1977.

Minter, David L. *William Faulkner: His Life and Work*. Baltimore: Johns Hopkins University Press, 1980.

Mintz, Steven. *A Prison of Expectations: The Family in Victorian Culture*. New York: New York University Press, 1983.

Mintz, Steven, and Susan Kellogg. *Domestic Revolutions: A Social History of American Family Life*. New York: Free Press, 1988.

Mitscherlich Alexander. *Society without the Father*. London: Tavistock, 1969.

Mizener, Arthur. *The Saddest Story: A Biography of Ford Madox Ford*. New York: World, 1971.

Moser, Thomas C. *The Life in the Fiction of Ford Madox Ford*. Princeton: Princeton University Press, 1980.

Narremore, James. *The World without a Self: Virginia Woolf and the Novel*. New Haven: Yale University Press, 1973.

Nehls, Edward, ed. *D. H. Lawrence: A Composite Biography*. 3 vols. Madison: University of Wisconsin Press, 1958.

Nelson, Cary. *Repression and Recovery: Modern American Poetry and the Politics of Cultural Memory, 1910–1945*. Madison: University of Wisconsin Press, 1989.

Newman, Charles. *The Post-Modern Aura*. Evanston, Ill.: Northwestern University Press, 1985.

Newman, John Henry. "The Aboriginal Calamity." In *Victorian Prose*, edited by Kenneth Allott and Miriam Allott, pp. 79–81. Harmondsworth: Penguin, 1956.

Noland, Richard. "Narcissism and Adulthood in the Novels of F. Scott Fitzgerald." In manuscript.

Poirier, Richard. "Writing Off the Self." In *Visions of Apocalypse,* edited by Saul Friedländer et al., pp. 216–41. New York: Holmes and Meier, 1985.

Reed, Gail. "Toward a Methodology for Applying Psychoanalysis to Literature." *Psychoanalytic Quarterly* 51 (1982): 19–42.

Robbins, Bruce. "Modernism in History, Modernism in Power." In *Modernism Reconsidered,* edited by Robert Kiely. Cambridge: Harvard University Press, 1983.

Rose, Jonathan. *The Edwardian Temperament: 1895–1919.* Athens: Ohio University Press, 1986.

Rosenman, Ellen Bayuk. *The Invisible Presence: Virginia Woolf and the Mother-Daughter Relationship.* Baton Rouge: Louisiana State University Press, 1986.

Ruderman, Judith. *D. H. Lawrence and the Devouring Mother: The Search for a Patriarchal Ideal of Leadership.* Durham, N.C.: Duke University Press, 1984.

Sagar, Keith. *D. H. Lawrence: Life into Art.* Athens: University of Georgia Press, 1985.

———. "D. H. Lawrence: The Man and the Artist." In *The Modernists: Studies in a Literary Phenomenon,* edited by Lawrence B. Gamache and Ian S. MacNiven, pp. 114–25. Rutherford, N.J.: Fairleigh Dickinson University Press, 1987.

Sale, Roger. "Ford's Coming of Age: *The Good Soldier* and *Parade's End.*" In *The Presence of Ford Madox Ford,* edited by Sondra J. Stang, pp. 109–14. Philadelphia: University of Pennsylvania Press, 1981.

Sartre, Jean-Paul. *Search for a Method.* New York: Vintage, 1968.

———. *The Words.* New York: Fawcett, 1964.

Sass, Louis. "Introspection, Schizophrenia, and the Fragmentation of Self." *Representations* 19 (Summer 1987): 1–34.

———. "Time, Space, and Symbol: A Study of Narrative Form and Representational Structure in Madness and Modernism." *Psychoanalysis and Contemporary Thought* 8 (1985): 45–85.

Saunders, Max. "A Life in Writing: Ford Madox Ford's Dispersed Autobiographies." *Antaeus* 56 (Spring 1986): 47–69.

Schafer, Roy. *The Analytic Attitude.* New York: Basic, 1983.

———. *Aspects of Internalization.* New York: International Universities Press, 1968.

———. "The Sense of an Answer: Ambiguities of Interpretation in Clinical and Applied Psychoanalysis." In *The Future of Literary Theory,* edited by Ralph Cohen, pp. 188–207. New York: Routledge, 1989.

Schneider, Daniel J. *D. H. Lawrence: The Artist as Psychologist.* Lawrence: University Press of Kansas, 1984.

Schorer, Mark. Introduction to *The Good Soldier,* by Ford Madox Ford. New York: Vintage, 1983.

Schwartz, Murray. "D. H. Lawrence and Psychoanalysis: An Introduction. *D. H. Lawrence Review* 10 (1977): 251–69.

Schwartz, Murray M., and Coppélia Kahn, eds. *Representing Shakespeare: New Psychoanalytic Essays*. Baltimore: Johns Hopkins University Press, 1980.

Skura, Meredith Anne. *The Literary Use of the Psychoanalytic Process*. New Haven: Yale University Press, 1981.

Solotaroff, Theodore. "Silence, Exile, and Cunning." *New American Review* 8 (1970): 201–19.

Spence, Donald P. *Narrative Truth and Historical Truth: Meaning and Interpretation in Psychoanalysis*. New York: Norton, 1982.

Stang, Sondra J. "A Reading of Ford's *The Good Soldier*." *Modern Language Quarterly* 30 (1969): 545–63.

Steiner, George. *Martin Heidegger*. New York: Viking, 1979.

Stern, Daniel. *The Interpersonal World of the Infant*. New York: Basic, 1984.

Strouse, Jean. *Alice James*. Boston: Houghton Mifflin, 1980.

Strout, Cushing. "Henry James's Dream of the Louvre, 'The Jolly Corner,' and Psychological Interpretation." *The Psychohistory Review* 7 (Summer–Fall 1979): 47–52.

Sultan, Stanley. *The Argument of* Ulysses. Middletown: Wesleyan University Press, 1964.

———. *Eliot, Joyce and Company*. New York: Oxford University Press, 1987.

Trilling, Lionel. "The Two Environments," *Encounter* 25 (July 1965).

Tuchman, Barbara. *The Proud Tower: A Portrait of the World before the War: 1890–1914*. New York: Bantam, 1967.

Wälder, Robert. "The Psychoanalytic Theory of Play." *Psychoanalytic Quarterly* 2 (1933): 208–24.

Watt, Ian. *Conrad in the Nineteenth Century*. Berkeley: University of California Press, 1979.

Watts, Eileen H. "Beckett's Unnamable: Schizophrenia, Rationalism, and the Novel." *American Imago* 45 (Spring 1988): 85–106.

Weinstein, Philip M. *The Semantics of Desire: Changing Models of Identity from Dickens to Joyce*. Princeton: Princeton University Press, 1984.

Weiss, Daniel. *Oedipus in Nottingham*. Seattle: University of Washington Press, 1962.

Wharton, Edith. *The Letters of Edith Wharton*. Edited by R. W. B. Lewis and Nancy Lewis. New York: Scribner, 1988.

Whitehead, George. "T. S. Eliot: The Psychobiographical Approach." *Southern Review* (Adelaide) 73 (1977): 3–26.

Willbern, David. "Malice in Paradise: Isolation and Projection in 'The Man Who Loved Islands.'" *D. H. Lawrence Review* 10 (1977): 223–39.

———. "Shakespeare's Nothing." In *Representing Shakespeare: New Psychoana-*

lytic Essays, edited by Murray M. Schwartz and Coppélia Kahn, pp. 244–63. Baltimore: Johns Hopkins University Press, 1980.

Wilshire, Bruce W., ed. *William James: The Essential Writings.* Albany: State University of New York Press, 1984.

Winnicott, D. W. *Collected Papers: Through Paediatrics to Psychoanalysis.* London: Hogarth, 1975.

———. "Fear of Breakdown." *International Review of Psycho-Analysis* 1 (1974): 103–7.

———. *The Maturational Processes and the Facilitating Environment.* New York: International Universities Press, 1965.

———. "Mirror-role of Mother and Family in Child Development." In *The Predicament of the Family,* edited by Peter Lomas. New York: International Universities Press, 1967.

———. *Playing and Reality.* London: Tavistock, 1971. (Paperback, 1982).

Wolf, Ernest S., and Ina Wolf. "'We Perished Each Alone': A Psychoanalytic Commentary on Virginia Woolf's *To the Lighthouse.*" *International Review of Psychoanalysis* 6 (1979): 37–47.

Woolf, Virginia. *Between the Acts.* Harmondsworth: Penguin, 1972.

———. *Collected Essays of Virginia Woolf.* Edited by Anne Olivier Bell. 4 vols. London: Hogarth, 1966.

———. *The Complete Shorter Fiction of Virginia Woolf.* Edited by Susan Dick. New York: Harcourt Brace Jovanovich, 1985.

———. *The Diary of Virginia Woolf.* Edited by Quentin Bell and Anne Olivier Bell. 5 vols. New York: Harcourt Brace Jovanovich, 1975–80.

———. *The Essays of Virginia Woolf.* Edited by Andrew McNeillie. San Diego: Harcourt Brace Jovanovich, 1986.

———. *A Haunted House and Other Short Stories.* New York: Harcourt Brace Jovanovich, 1972.

———. *The Letters of Virginia Woolf.* Edited by Nigel Nicolson and Joanne Trautman. 6 vols. New York: Harcourt Brace Jovanovich, 1975–80.

———. *Moments of Being.* Edited by Jeanne Schulkind. 2d ed. New York: Harcourt Brace Jovanovich, 1985.

———. *Mrs. Dalloway* (1925). New York: Harcourt Brace Jovanovich, 1953.

———. *To the Lighthouse* (1927). New York: Harcourt Brace Jovanovich, 1955.

———. *The Waves* (1931). In *Jacob's Room & The Waves.* New York: Harcourt, Brace, n.d.

Yeazell, Ruth. *Language and Knowledge in the Late Novels of Henry James.* Chicago: University of Chicago Press, 1980.

Zaretsky, Eli. *Capitalism, the Family, and Personal Life.* New York: Harper and Row, 1986.

Zwerdling, Alex. *Virginia Woolf and the Real World.* Berkeley: University of California Press, 1986.

Index

anxiety: of inner chaos, 15–16, 18, 26, 101; modernist, contrasted to other kinds, 3–13, 17–22; nothingness, emptiness, hollowness, and, 4, 6, 7–12, 18–22, 101; as source of modernist art, 5–22; "unthinkable anxiety," 18, 22, 79, 103, 171. *See also* chaos; individual authors; modernism
aristocratic individualism and posturing, 43, 65, 67, 68, 93
Armstrong, Paul, 13, 15, 154
Axline, Virginia, 119

Baldwin, James, 140–41
Bawer, Bruce, 33, 203 n.12
Bell, Millicent, 204 n.22
Bell, Quentin, 204 n.19
Bellow, Saul, x, 93, 124, 142
Blos, Peter, 37–38, 195
Bollas, Christopher, 123–24
Bouson, J. Brooks, 127, 213 n.2, 214 n.7

canon formation, 5
chaos: different sense of, in Lawrence, 106; as energy basic to modernist aesthetic, 100–114; exploration of, search for healing within, 74–83, 100–114, 140–42; fear and control of, in art, 26, 62, 91–99. *See also* anxiety; holding environment; self
childhood, 25–55. *See also* individual authors
Conrad, Joseph: aesthetic aims, 5, 18, 112; childhood of, 35–36, 48; gesture of healing in, 127–28; heroic posture of, 5, 106; as impostor, 68–69; longing for

paradise, infantile regression in, 75, 80; misogyny of, 83–85; psychic struggle and pathology of, 18–19, 25–26, 35–36, 49, 68–69, 75–80, 83–85, 106, 123, 126–28; traditional values in, 94, 127, 142. Works: *Almayer's Folly*, 18; *Chance*, 69, 83–84, 127; *Heart of Darkness*, 11–12, 18, 75–76, 78–79, 84–85, 112, 127; letter to Edward Garnett, 76–77, 126–27; *Lord Jim*, 18, 75–79, 127; *Nostromo*, 18; *A Personal Record*, 79; Preface to *Nigger of the "Narcissus,"* 5, 21, 142; *Victory*, 83
Cowan, James, 201 n.21

defamiliarization. *See* modernism: defamiliarization in
Demos, John, 31
DeSalvo, Louise, 40, 204 n.19, 209 n.2, 213 n.4
Dizard, Jan, and Howard Gadlin, 30

Eagleton, Terry, 205 n.6
Edel, Leon, 147, 149, 150–51, 165
Ehrenzweig, Anton, 169
Ekstein, Modris, 102, 138–39
Eliot, T. S., 33, 95–96
emptiness. *See* anxiety
Erikson, Erik, 62, 67
exile, 32, 47–55

Fairbairn, W. R. D., 8, 184, 209 n.9
family: myth of decline from past glory, 43 (*see also* aristocratic posturing); in relation to modernism, 25–46. *See also* childhood; individual authors

Kaplan, Louise, 63–66
Karl, Frederick R., 16, 207 n.4
Khan, Masud, 68
King Lear, 11
Kohut, Heinz, 8, 18, 40, 205 n.4
Kris, Ernst, 119

Lawrence, D. H.: aesthetics of, 96–98,
107, 195–98; childhood of, 25, 36–37,
49; darkness in, 189–92; emptiness, loss
of self in, 10, 22; as healer, 182–83,
198; versus Joyce, 195–96; mother and
father in, 37, 192–95; nonmodernist
epistemology of, 153–54; paradise in,
185–90; psychic struggle and pathology
of, 60, 122, 183–84; rebirth in, 10,
106–9, 184–85, 187–90; response of,
to Hemingway, 19. Works: *Apocalypse*,
170, 182; "The Blind Man," 184; letter
to Edward Garnett, 190; "The Man
Who Loved Islands," 185–90; "New
Heaven and Earth," 138, 187–89;
"Nottingham and the English Mining
Countryside," 191–92; "Rocking-Horse
Winner," 194; "Song of a Man Who
Has Come Through," 183; *Sons and
Lovers*, 108, 122; *Women in Love*, 10,
196–97
Lears, Jackson, 137
Leavis, F. R., 134
Levenson, Michael, 102, 133
Loewenberg, Peter, 4, 138
Lowell, Robert, 134–35

Mazlich, Bruce, 203 n.9
merger, 74, 80, 207 n.1
Meyer, Bernard, 78, 79, 80
Miller, James F., Jr., 95–96
Milner, Marion, 22
Mintz, Stephen, 30, 203 n.8; and Susan
Kellogg, 30–31
mirroring, 8–10, 205 n.23
misogyny, 83–87
Mitscherlich, Alexander, 30
modernism: aesthetic of chaos in, 100–114
(*see also* anxiety; chaos; family; postmodern); aesthetic of separate reality
rather than imitation in, 96–97; anxiety
(*see* anxiety); capitalism and, 26, 132;
creation of protective orders in, 91–99;
cultural acceptance of, 132–44; de-

familiarization in, 103–4, 111; epistemological questioning and doubt, 13–
18, 154; healing in, 3–4, 117–31, 143
(*see also* individual authors); heroic
position in, 5, 105–6, 140–44; traditional values in, 94, 127, 142–43
mother, maternal imago, 37, 74–76. *See
also* childhood; individual authors
Musil, Robert, 103–4

Narremore, James, 213 n.6
Nelson, Cary, 133, 134
New Criticism, 133, 135
Newman, Charles, 94, 202 n.3
Newman, John Henry, 6, 11
Nietzsche, Friedrich, 13, 25
nothingness or nada. *See* anxiety

object-relations school of psychoanalysis,
7–8

paradise, longing for, 74–76, 80–83
pathology. *See* self, pathology of
patriarchy, 33
play, healing through, 119–23
Poirier, Richard, 9, 199 n.1, 208 n.9
postmodern, contrasted to modern, x, 5,
140
psychoanalysis as model of reading, 124–
26

readers and reading, 124–31
Reed, Gail, 130
regression, infantile, 18, 19–20, 74–75,
80, 82
Rose, Jonathan, 138, 208 n.6

Sartre, Jean Paul, 17, 202 n.2
Sass, Louis, 9
Schafer, Roy, 63, 125
schizoid pathology. *See* self, pathology of
self: defensive orders, 91–99 (*see also* anxiety); false and authentic, 8; longing for
selflessness, 10; loss, disintegration of, 6,
7, 11, 18, 19
self, pathology of: confusion over identity,
62–73; schizoid, 8, 22, 68; sex role confusion, 60–61; suicide, 19, 20–21. *See
also* anxiety; holding environment
self-fictionalization, self-creation, 32, 62–
73